THREE
MIDWESTERN
PLAYWRIGHTS

THREE MIDWESTERN PLAYWRIGHTS

Indiana University Press

HOW FLOYD DELL,
GEORGE CRAM COOK,
AND SUSAN GLASPELL
TRANSFORMED
AMERICAN THEATRE

MARCIA NOE

This book is a publication of

Indiana University Press
Office of Scholarly Publishing
Herman B Wells Library 350
1320 East 10th Street
Bloomington, Indiana 47405 USA

iupress.org

Manufactured in the United States of America

First printing 2022

Cataloging information is available from the Library of Congress.

ISBN 978-0-253-06182-9 (hardback)
ISBN 978-0-253-06183-6 (paperback)
ISBN 978-0-253-06184-3 (ebook)

TO MY HUSBAND,

Robert Lloyd Marlowe,

AND TO THE MEMORIES OF

Loren Logsdon and David D. Anderson,
cherished scholar-mentors

CONTENTS

THREE
MIDWESTERN
PLAYWRIGHTS

Introduction

Three Midwestern Playwrights and the Provincetown Players

TWO LOVE TRIANGLES ANIMATE this book, one driven by free love and the other by true love. When Floyd Dell fell in love with his best friend's wife, Mollie Price Cook, their affair was brief but blissful. When George Cram Cook fell in love with Susan Glaspell and left Mollie and his two children to marry her, their ten-year union endured until his death, continually tested by infidelity and alcoholism.

These love stories run parallel to the larger story that this book relates, a part of the Provincetown Players' story that has not yet been told. This larger story focuses on the ways in which three Midwestern playwrights' involvement in progressive activities in early twentieth-century Davenport, Iowa, helped shape the trajectory and theatre practice of the company. Established in 1915 by twenty-nine charter members (among them Dell, Cook, and Glaspell), the Provincetown Players was one of sixty-three amateur theatres that were formed in the United States during that decade. By 1926, there were five thousand.[1]

Today, the Provincetown Players is best known for discovering Nobel laureate Eugene O'Neill and producing sixteen of his plays.[2] But by 1922, when the group produced its last play, it had made several equally significant contributions to American theatre. In just eight years, the company had developed an alternative to the commercial Broadway stage, establishing a laboratory for new playwrights to experiment and

1

introducing new forms of theatre and new staging techniques to the American public.[3] Dorothy Chansky points out that beyond these innovations, little theatres like the Provincetown Players accomplished the essential mission of building an educated and appreciative audience for the New Drama in America. Dell, Cook, Glaspell, and, of course, O'Neill, as well as the other Provincetown playwrights, played a key role in this effort.

This book argues that the Provincetown Players would not have become the theatre company that it did without Dell, Cook, and Glaspell's early involvement in socially progressive movements in Davenport, Iowa, during the first decade of the twentieth century. In Davenport, Dell became a feminist and a leader in the city's Socialist Party. In Davenport, Cook ran for public office as a Socialist and, along with Glaspell, led a movement for free speech and religious freedom. In Davenport, Cook and Dell founded the Monist Society, a group of free thinkers that included Glaspell. This activism shaped not only their own plays but also the aesthetic and theatre practice of the company itself.

When they came together in Davenport in 1903, Glaspell was a former journalist and promising short-story writer, Cook was an author and former college English professor, and Dell was a high school junior who would soon be publishing poems in national magazines. Twelve years later they would found the Provincetown Players and produce their plays there, plays that were shaped in large part by their authors' early radicalism. These plays would spoof the craze for Freudian psychology and modern art, protest against World War I, explore changing gender dynamics, and enact the importance of free speech in a democracy. A middle-aged Cook would die in Greece in 1924, but Dell and Thomas Mitchell of *Gone with the Wind* fame would collaborate on a Broadway hit in 1928, and Glaspell would win the Pulitzer Prize for drama in 1931.

The fuse of this transformative stick of dynamite was lit when Dell, Cook, and Glaspell discovered something called the New.

Three came together in 1903 in Davenport

12 years later helped found Provincetown Players

1

Three Midwestern Playwrights Discover the New

Bliss was it in that dawn to be alive
But to be young was very Heaven!

—WILLIAM WORDSWORTH

something in the or n first decade of 20th C

"IN THE YEAR 1911 there were signs that the world was on the verge of something," wrote Floyd Dell. "Something was in the air. Something was happening, about to happen—in politics, in literature, in art. The atmosphere became electric with it."[1] Six years earlier, Albert Einstein had developed his theory of special relativity; three years earlier, Sigmund Freud had brought his theories of the mind to Clark University. Nine years later, National Women's Party leader Alice Paul would see the fruits of over one hundred years of feminist activism when American women won their constitutional right to vote, and eleven years later, Noble Sissle and Eubie Blake would kick off the Harlem Renaissance with their musical, *Shuffle Along.* Just two years after Dell's landmark year, George Gershwin would sit down at his brother's piano and begin a career in musical innovation that would give the world some of the greatest compositions of the Jazz Age, and visitors to the postimpressionist art exhibited at New York City's Sixty-Ninth Regiment Armory would react with shock, anger, and ridicule to Marcel Duchamp's *Nude Descending a Staircase* because they could find neither a nude nor a staircase in the painting.

3

Dell and his contemporaries—the writers, painters, and activists who wintered in Greenwich Village and summered in Provincetown, Massachusetts—believed that the "something" that was on the way was nothing less than a new social order. Indeed, the word *new* was on the lips of many as they wrote about and discussed the revolutions in thinking, painting, writing, composing, and organizing society that were changing minds and changing America. Adam Hochschild describes the period that Dell found so transformative: "It was a remarkable moment that saw a flood tide of new immigrants, a flourishing of new forms of art, a zenith of crusading journalism, and dramatic strikes and demonstrations as working people and women demanded their rights. It was also a moment when many believed that on the horizon was a revolutionary upheaval that would wipe away forever the barriers of class, race, and inequality that so marred America's promise."[2]

Susan C. Kemper situates the founding of the Provincetown Players within the cultural moment that Hochschild delineates above: "That transitional period in American history which Henry F. May has identified as 'the end of American innocence.'"[3] In this 1959 study, May traces the beginnings of the New to the early twentieth-century demise of commonly held beliefs in the inevitability of progress and the inviolability of Victorian values and aesthetic standards.[4] John Galsworthy's Victorian throwback Soames Forsyte, bumbling through the modern world, epitomizes the conflict between the Old and the New that characterized the early twentieth century. An entire worldview that posited a God-created-and-ordered universe with clearly defined conventions and values gave way under the influence of thinkers such as Karl Marx, Albert Einstein, Charles Darwin, and Sigmund Freud, whose theories had the cumulative effect of displacing the human person from the center of the moral and cultural universe. Dell portrays this seismic cultural shift in his third novel, *Janet March* (1923), in the words of theatre impresario Vincent Blatch:

> The nineteenth century, Janet dear, was a time when everybody believed in law and order. That's why it seems such a queer time to us now—and why we can't read its books or admire its great men, they seem so foolish. They saw law and order everywhere—in the movements of the stars and in the colors on a butterfly's wing. They had discovered the laws of progress. . . . There were to be no more wars. Machinery was to do away with human labor. Everyone was to be happy and virtuous. There was a solution to every problem.[5]

This intellectual revolution profoundly impacted Dell and his colleagues. "The old world was finished, they believed—the world of Victorian America, with its stodgy bourgeois art, its sexual prudery and smothering patriarchal families, its crass moneymaking and deadly class exploitation," writes Christine Stansell. "The new world, the germ of a truly modern America, would be created by those willing to repudiate the cumbersome past and experiment with form, not just in painting and literature, the touchstones of European modernism, but also in politics and love, friendship and sexual passion."[6]

Stansell also points out that "in part, the association of art and life came from anarchist beliefs in a self whose creative powers were unleashed by revolutionary ferment."[7] This book takes Stansell's assessment as its premise in relating the experiences of three proponents of the New—Floyd Dell, George Cram (Jig) Cook, and Susan Glaspell—and argues that their involvement in cultural and political activities spawned by the New in early twentieth-century Davenport, Iowa, significantly informed not only the plays that they would later write for the Provincetown Players but also the aesthetic and theatre practice of the company itself. Their commitment to leftist ideals such as free speech, feminism, Socialism, and pacifism, expressed through their writing and also through their life choices, would become a force for change in early twentieth-century America. Dell, Cook, Glaspell, and their friends lived their politics through their art, professing a belief in a seamless joining of art and life. As Veronica Makowsky notes, "Glaspell and her fellow artists operated under the premise that art and life were inextricably linked."[8]

Immersed as they were in the New, Dell, Cook, and Glaspell were not blind to the extremes to which it could be taken or to the ways in which the New could be embraced by those more interested in performing radical chic than in authentically committing themselves to progressive ideas and causes. Over time they became cognizant of the complexities and ambiguities inherent in their subjects, and their plays reflect this awareness. Dell's Provincetown comedy *King Arthur's Socks* (1916) juxtaposes the early twentieth-century Greenwich Village present with medieval times to create a sense of universality as it enacts the complexities of gendered power dynamics. Glaspell and Cook's one-act comedies *Suppressed Desires* (1915) and *Tickless Time* (1918), as well as Cook's one-act comedy *Change Your Style* (1915), turn on a series of reversals to poke fun at proponents of the New who have taken their enthusiasms to extremes. Glaspell's *Close the Book* (1917), *The People* (1917), and *Chains of Dew* (1922) are comedies in which characters who regard themselves as progressive are confronted with the limitations of their enlightened minds. The New Woman, the New Art, the New Psychology, the New Politics, and the New Science inspired and informed the plays of Dell, Cook, and Glaspell, which reflect the cultural milieu in which they lived and wrote and enact a critique of that culture.[9]

In 1894, the New Woman came striding out of Sarah Grand's essay in the *North American Review* to contend with the pious, pure, domestic, and submissive True Woman who reigned in the American cultural imaginary.[10] Often pictured wearing a divided skirt, smoking a cigarette, or riding a bicycle, the New Woman was educated, athletic, independent, socially conscious, and professionally active. Although some were fearful that the New Woman would become mannish and crude, her image was more commonly evoked by Charles Dana Gibson's lovely Girl, who reflected an early twentieth-century reality that saw an exponential growth in female matriculation in colleges and universities, numerous jobs and professions newly opened to women, and social movements for women's suffrage and birth control legalization led by fierce female champions.

In this early twentieth-century reality, the New Woman manifested as Rose Pastor Stokes lending her oratorical gift to the birth control movement; Elizabeth Gurley Flynn waving the red flag to rally striking silk workers in Paterson, New Jersey; Henrietta Rodman fighting for the rights of female teachers in New York City; and Ida B. Wells crusading against lynching across America and throughout the world. In the fiction of this period, the New Woman appeared as Willa Cather's Thea Kronborg singing grand opera, Frances E. W. Harper's Iola Leroy working for social uplift, Elia W. Peattie's Kate Barrington hauling abusive husbands into family court, and Edna Ferber's Emma McChesney breaking feminist ground in the business world—first as a traveling saleswoman and later as a corporate executive.[11]

The Greenwich Village and Provincetown that Dell, Cook, and Glaspell inhabited were replete with New Women who sought to free society from its bourgeois shackles, thus reflecting the New Woman's role in bringing about, in the words of Martha H. Patterson, "the synthesis of the personal and the political for a transformation politics."[12] Glaspell was a charter member of the Lucy Stone League and of Heterodoxy, a feminist lecture and discussion club for "unorthodox women who did things and did them openly" that met for lunch biweekly.[13] She was pro-suffrage, as were Dell and his coeditor on *The Masses*, Max Eastman, who co-founded the Men's League for Woman Suffrage of New York State in 1909. In 1913, Dell published *Women as World Builders: Studies in Modern Feminism*, a book that profiled ten New Women, among them Charlotte Perkins Gilman and Emma Goldman. Modernist New Women in Greenwich Village included Eastman's sister, Crystal, and his wife, Ida Rauh, both lawyers; poet Edna St. Vincent Millay; and Mabel Dodge, whose salon welcomed proponents and practitioners of every variation of the New. As Ellen Kay Trimberger concludes, "The New Woman in the early twentieth-century United States was a central player in a modernist movement stressing the opening of the self to levels of experience that could be fused into a new and original whole."[14]

Among the New Woman characters in the plays of Dell, Cook, and Glaspell are a birth control activist, a free speech advocate, an experimental botanist, a proponent of free love, a Freudian acolyte, and a pacifist. Of the three playwrights, Dell was the most enthusiastic about feminism; through his Socialist lens, he saw gender equality primarily as a way to fight capitalism. However, the feminist Holy Trinity of that day—free love, legal birth control, and companionate marriage—was anything but a deal breaker for Dell, who cut quite a swath through the lovely ladies of Davenport, Chicago, and Greenwich Village before marrying the love of his life in 1919. He remained a lifelong feminist, and New Women can be seen in much of his oeuvre, ranging from the bohemian Egeria in *Love in Greenwich Village* (1926) to the eponymous protagonist of his tenth novel, *Diana Stair* (1932).

The New Art gained a strong foothold in Provincetown, Massachusetts, a finger of land curving three miles into the Atlantic Ocean that beckoned to pirate and pilgrim, to playwright and boatwright, and, most especially, to artists because of the quality of its light. As Leona Rust Egan explains, "Following the arrival of the railroad in 1873, Provincetown became a motherlode for palette and pen." In the early twentieth century, Provincetown had become well known for its art schools; by 1916 there were five such institutes enrolling a total of six hundred students. Chief among them was Charles Webster Hawthorne's Cape Cod School of Art, founded in 1899, an academic art school that enrolled 110 students who painted on the beach. Among Hawthorne's opposite number were Charles Demuth, B. J. O. (Bror) Nordfeldt, and Marguerite and William Zorach, avant-garde artists who also became charter members of the Provincetown Players.[15]

The academic and avant-garde art schools embraced competing aesthetics. The former, endorsed by the National Academy of Design, emphasized composition and the human figure, prioritized drawing over color, and venerated past models. The latter eschewed the traditions that academic artists revered, abandoning realism for a more presentational style that challenged the status quo in art and culture: "This was a guerilla war waged against the bourgeois class and its domination," contends Martin Green, "its representatives in the ateliers, its Renaissance traditions, and its Greek and Roman heritage."[16] It was this aesthetic conflict that inspired Jig Cook's one-act comedy *Change Your Style*.

Although a similarly rebellious group of realists, the Ashcan school, was also dominant at this time, the representational aesthetic of its artists—George Bellows, Robert Henri, John Sloan, and their colleagues—failed to spark the excitement of the truly radical practitioners of modern art and their admirers that was first engendered by the exhibitions of artists such as Rodin and Matisse and later by the display of thirteen hundred postimpressionist works in the Armory Show. The politics of the New also supported avant-garde art: "One of the reasons the New Art attracted so much attention around 1915 was that aesthetic radicalism then seemed allied to political radicalism," argues Green.[17]

Alfred Stieglitz, who called himself a revolutionary, saw art as a tool for social change. Like the Greenwich Village radicals who were immersed in the New and aimed to integrate their art and their politics with their daily lives to remake the world, Stieglitz believed in the liberating power of art, arguing that "only competing art forms, diverse means of expression, alternative life-styles, a reintroduction of the sacred into the modern life, and new relationships between men and women could lead to meaningful change."[18] Perhaps the best example of the marriage between art and politics was the 1913 Paterson Pageant, organized by John (Jack) Reed and Mabel Dodge to raise funds for the striking silk workers in Paterson, New Jersey. To dramatize the strike and its effect on workers' lives, hundreds of silk workers marched down Fifth Avenue to Madison Square Garden, where they enacted scenes from the strike.

As John C. Burnham observes, "In 1915, a New Psychology meant mostly the teachings of Sigmund Freud and what he called psychoanalysis."[19] In 1909, Freud himself came to the United States to give a series of lectures at Clark University, and in 1913 his book *The Interpretation of Dreams* was translated into English and published in the United States. Also at that time, Mabel Dodge was psychoanalyzed, first by Smith Ely Jelliffe and later by Dr. A. A. Brill, the chief advocate of Freudian theory in the United States, who spoke at Dodge's salon during the winter of 1913. Freudianism soon became all the rage among Greenwich Villagers. "You could not go out to buy a bun without hearing of some one's complex," Glaspell famously wrote.[20] Floyd Dell embraced psychoanalysis as eagerly as he had embraced feminism. "Everybody in the Village had been talking the jargon of psychoanalysis ever since I came," he remembered. "We had played at parlor games at 'associating' to lists of words, and had tried to unravel dreams by what we supposed to be the Freudian formula."[21] Cook and Glaspell's one-act comedy *Suppressed Desires* demonstrates the hazards of a too thoroughgoing and unreflective embrace of the New Psychology.

In their quest to create a new social order, the Greenwich Village radicals were ever on the lookout for new ways to envision the world and themselves as part of their rebellion against convention. They welcomed the concept of the unconscious and the belief that its hidden desires and drives could be revealed through the analysis of dreams, ostensibly as a way of employing Freudianism to achieve a more authentic relationship with reality and to see it more clearly. They also viewed Freudian psychology as a way of bettering society by ridding dysfunctional individuals of their complexes and neuroses. As Sanford Gifford concludes, "Early American Modernists saw no contradiction between turning inward toward self-understanding and outward toward political action to change society."[22]

Cook well exemplified this kind of double vision, imagining an "American Renaissance of the Twentieth Century." "I call upon the vital writers of America to attain a finer culture," he wrote. "It is for us or no one to prove that the finest culture is a possibility of democracy."[23] Just as Dell, Cook, Glaspell, and their contemporaries believed that the New Art and the New Psychology should inform and transform their lives and their society, they viewed the New Politics as another means to this end. It was as much a given for Greenwich Villagers to be Progressives and

Socialists as it was for their parents to be Democrats or Republicans, and it was through those movements that they sought to effect change. Dell and Cook were active in Socialist politics in Davenport. Glaspell was less of a political animal than Dell or Cook and certainly less of an activist, but her political sympathies also leaned leftward, as can be seen in her one-act comedy *The People,* which celebrates and satirizes a political magazine that closely resembles *The Masses,* and in her full-length play *Inheritors* (1921), which endorses the rights of political protestors, conscientious objectors, and proponents of academic freedom. As Douglas Clayton maintains, "Writers and artists within that chaotic, immensely productive vanguard mixed cultural and social rebellion in an effort to overturn the conventions and injustices they felt governed American life."[24]

One of the chief instruments of Socialist politics in Greenwich Village, *The Masses* exemplifies the kind of leftist cultural and social blend to which Clayton refers. In the words of editor Max Eastman, *The Masses* mixed "proletarian revolt with revolt against the genteel tradition."[25] After Dell became associate editor and wrote an article arguing against the US involvement in World War I, he was tried for violating the Espionage Act, along with his fellow editors Eastman and Jack Reed, cartoonist Art Young, and business manager Merrill Rogers. Accused of using *The Masses* to discourage men from enlisting in the armed forces, the defendants were finally freed after two trials that resulted in hung juries. The antiwar position of Dell and Cook during the World War I era is reflected in their plays *A Long Time Ago* (1917) and *The Athenian Women* (1918), respectively.

The New Science was perhaps less discussed on a daily basis by Greenwich Villagers than were other aspects of the New, but it was not any the less disruptive.[26] As Stuart Kauffman writes of the early twentieth century, "Paradise has been lost, not to sin, but to science."[27] Sir Charles Lyell's geological findings undermined the notion of a seven-day Creation, while Darwin's *On the Origin of Species by Means of Natural Selection* (1859) and *The Descent of Man* (1871) posited a new view of the human being as one species on the animal continuum, replacing the traditional notion of humanity as the apex of Creation. Regarding the latter work, one commentator remarked in the *Edinburgh Review* that "if these views be true, a revolution in thought is imminent, which will shake society to its very foundations by destroying the sanctity of the conscience and the religious sense."[28]

The game-changing effects of Lyell's and Darwin's research were amplified during the first decade of the twentieth century by physicists whose work further undermined long-held notions of God, humans, world, space, and time. Ludwig Boltzmann's research on the second law of thermodynamics shed new light on the concept of entropy; its central precept that all isolated systems tend toward disorder shook the beliefs of those who placed their faith in a Divine Creator who ordered the universe as well as their own lives. Niels Bohr, one of the founding fathers of quantum mechanics, postulated a solar-system model of the atom that helped convince others of its reality and introduced the layperson to the notion that the world of the very small was governed by different rules from those that regulated the larger world in which we live. Einstein's theory of special relativity had a similarly cataclysmic effect as it collapsed the concepts of discrete time and space into that of spacetime, which brought three spatial dimensions and one temporal dimension into a unified whole. Cook and Glaspell's *Tickless Time* and Cook's *The Spring* (1921) explore the effects of new theories of time and mind as they enact the conflict between forward-thinking moderns and those who were bound to tradition and convention.

Cook's vision of a new democratic America informed by art began to be realized during the summer of 1915 when a group of writers and artists staged Neith Boyce's *Constancy*, followed by Cook and Glaspell's *Suppressed Desires*, on the balcony of the Provincetown cottage Boyce shared with her husband, Hutchins Hapgood. These plays were also staged later that summer at the Wharf Theater, along with Cook's *Change Your Style* and Wilbur Daniel Steele's *Contemporaries*, and with those performances, the Provincetown Players was born. This amateur theatre group, of which Dell, Cook, and Glaspell were among the twenty-nine charter members and for which they cumulatively contributed eighteen plays, became such a source of excitement in Provincetown that the troupe launched a second summer season in 1916.

Many of the modernist innovations, issues, theories, and enthusiasms that were hallmarks of the New found their way to the stage of this theatre company. In *The Provincetown: A Story of the Theatre* (1931), Helen Deutsch and Stella Hanau describe the cultural milieu that stimulated and nourished the troupe: "They had been stirred by Isadora Duncan, had listened to Eugene Debs, had discovered Kraft-Ebbing. . . . Cubism was fighting it out with Futurism, and everybody wrote free verse. *The Little Review* was printing 'Ulysses' in installments, Gertrude Stein had discovered a new language, the old *Masses* was blazing away at injustice, *The New Republic* was in the first flush of its youth, Stieglitz was making magic with the camera. The International Exhibition had brought modern art to America, and a new set of text-books had appeared: 'Sister Carrie,' 'The Harbor,' 'The Spoon River Anthology.'"[29] Dell, Cook, and Glaspell believed, as Robert L. Dorman professes, that "artistic and intellectual production (especially social art) can in itself help to bring about dramatic social change," and they envisioned their theatre as a major vehicle of such change.[30]

Launched by Cook and Glaspell with early major assistance from Jack Reed, the Provincetown Players began as a loose association of writers, journalists, activists, and artists dedicated to producing new American plays and fostering new American playwrights. In the eight years of its brief existence, the company evolved from an impromptu summer experiment into an innovative Greenwich Village theatre club that featured plays by Eugene O'Neill, who contributed sixteen plays, and Glaspell, who mounted eleven. Cook wrote five plays for the group, two coauthored with Glaspell. Dell staged four of his plays with the Provincetown; earlier, he had written several plays for the Liberal Club in Greenwich Village.

The Provincetown Players—short-lived but influential—staged ninety-three plays by forty-seven American authors and, through its emphasis on collaboration, authenticity, experimentation, and social critique, became, according to Cheryl Black, "one of the most influential theatre groups in America." Among their contributions that Black enumerates are developing a noncommercial theatrical tradition; discovering two major American playwrights, O'Neill and Glaspell; promoting a nonhierarchical organizational structure; pioneering the use of racially integrated casts; and employing several scenic innovations, such as the plaster dome used for the first time in New York in O'Neill's *The Emperor Jones* (1920).[31]

The Provincetown Players' impact on the trajectory of American drama was noted by the theatre critics of their day as well as by contemporary theatre scholars. "The great hope of the future lies in the fertilization of the big by the little theatre, of Broadway by Provincetown . . . in the region of Washington Square or Greenwich Village—or ultimately among the sand dunes of Cape Cod—we must look for the birthplace of the New American Drama," declared William Archer.[32] Carl and Mark

Van Doren counted the Provincetown Players among the three little theatre groups of their day that were of historical importance: "The Provincetown Players . . . did an invaluable service in introducing original playwrights of purely local origin—and in two cases of unprecedented imaginative power."[33]

The three playwrights discussed in this book experienced life-changing encounters with the New during their formative years as writers in Davenport, Iowa, a Mississippi River town that was unusually fecund when it came to growing writers. Author, editor, and book critic Harry Hansen describes his native city as replete with authors:

> When Floyd Dell lived there and attended the high school Arthur Davison Ficke was writing his first book of lyrics; Susan Glaspell was toiling under the midnight lamp over short stories for the "Black Cat" and attempting musical comedies; George Cram Cook was living on a farm in the river lowlands to the south and basking in the sunshine of a local reputation won from writing with Charles Eugene Banks. Octave Thanet [Alice French] had been popular for years with the readers of "Scribner's" and "Harper's" as a writer of short stories and was about to emerge as a best seller with "The Man of the Hour." George Randolph Chester had slipped away; Charles Edward Russell and his son, John Russell, who was later to write "The Red Mark" and other tales had gone on to Chicago.[34]

The first of these playwrights, Floyd James Dell (June 28, 1887–July 23, 1969), moved to Davenport with his family in 1903. A sixteen-year-old poet and a voracious reader, he would become active with Davenport's Socialist local; edit his own Socialist periodical, the *Tri-City Workers Magazine*; run for county office on the Socialist ticket; and, with Cook, found the free-thinking Monist Society. Although he dropped out of high school to work in a candy factory to support his family, he continued to write, lucking into jobs as a reporter for the *Davenport Daily Times* and the *Davenport Democrat*.

Soon after his arrival in Davenport, he became acquainted with Cook, who had returned to his native city the same year after teaching English at Stanford University. The Dell chapter in this book chronicles his involvement with Davenport's Socialist Party, his friendship with Cook, and his later involvement in the Chicago Renaissance and in Greenwich Village bohemianism; it also traces the ways in which his acquaintance with leftist ideas gained through wide reading brought him to feminism and led to his exploration of gendered power relations in his later work. Dell's articles, essays, fiction, and drama demonstrate his feminist commitment and his dedication to the interrogation of traditional gender roles as seen in his Provincetown plays *King Arthur's Socks* (1916), *The Angel Intrudes* (1917), and *Sweet and Twenty* (1918). A fourth Provincetown play, *A Long Time Ago* (1917), reflects the antiwar spirit prevalent among Dell's peers in Provincetown and Greenwich Village during the decade of the First World War.[35]

Influenced by Dell, George Cram Cook (October 8, 1873–January 11, 1924) became active in Davenport leftist politics, leading to his involvement in the fight to prevent the extradition of a Russian dissident and his leadership in the Davenport censorship controversy that culminated in his run for Congress on the Socialist ticket in 1910. Cook's Socialist orientation shaped his fourth novel, *The Chasm* (1911), and his passionate belief in the New as a transformative force in American culture is seen in his five Provincetown plays: the two he cowrote with Susan Glaspell—*Suppressed Desires* (Freudian psychology) and *Tickless Time* (Einsteinian and Bergsonian theory)—and his three solo efforts, *Change Your Style* (postimpressionist art), *The Athenian Women* (pacifism), and *The Spring* (parapsychology).

Although he wrote only three one-act and two full-length plays for the Provincetown, his legacy was far-reaching. Establishing the Provincetown Players as a noncommercial theatre collective committed to the collaborative development of American plays that gave them the freedom to experiment without regard for the marketability of their work, Cook helmed what theatre scholar Brenda Murphy says is "the most significant and the most influential American theatre group of the early twentieth century."[36] During the eight years of the Provincetown's existence, Cook functioned as its unofficial artistic director—writing, directing, and acting in plays, building sets, and, most significantly, inspiring and encouraging his wife, friends, acquaintances, and neighbors to write and stage plays. Provincetown playwrights who achieved greater fame in other genres include Edna Ferber, Wallace Stevens, Jack Reed, Edna St. Vincent Millay, Theodore Dreiser, and Djuna Barnes.[37]

The best known of the Provincetown playwrights after O'Neill, Davenport native Susan Keating Glaspell (July 1, 1876–July 27, 1948) authored not only eleven plays for the troupe but also, after her Provincetown years, a Broadway play, *The Comic Artist* (1927), written with

Norman Matson, and *Alison's House* (1930), which won the 1931 Pulitzer Prize for drama. Glaspell also published six popular novels in addition to the three she wrote before the Provincetown period. *Brook Evans* (1928) was adapted for film by Zoe Akins as *The Right to Love*; another Glaspell novel, *The Morning Is Near Us* (1939), became a Literary Guild selection for 1940.

Glaspell's first solo dramatic effort, *Trifles* (1916), and its short story cognate, "A Jury of Her Peers" (1917), have been frequently anthologized and have inspired eleven stage, film, and television adaptations, ranging from a Vitaphone film in 1930 to an opera in 2010. The Glaspell chapter in this book chronicles how her involvement in the Davenport censorship controversy of 1910 contributed to her lifelong commitment to advocating for First Amendment freedoms as the bulwark of our democracy, a commitment that resulted in three of her best full-length plays— *Inheritors*, *Chains of Dew*, and *The Verge*—as well as the one-act plays *The People*, *Trifles*, and *Close the Book*. Glaspell's belief in free speech and the power of literature and language dates back to her debate and oratory activities at Drake University and to her subsequent career as a journalist in Des Moines and short-story writer in Davenport.[38]

Dell, Cook, and Glaspell, and their contemporaries thought they could change the world with their love and their art and their politics—and they almost did! They were men and women of their time, and time soon caught up with them. Just a few years after the Provincetown Players ended their run, John Galsworthy wrote presciently in *A Modern Comedy* (1926) that the chance for revolution was fading fast in the Machine Age: "The unskilled multitude and the Communist visionaries . . . only had a chance now where machinery and means of communication were still undeveloped, as in Russia. Brains, ability, and technical skill were by nature on the side of capital and individual enterprise, and were gaining even more power."[39]

The Provincetown playwrights' day in the sun was heartbreakingly brief; they could not have known that the Russian Revolution, on which they had pinned such high hopes for a freer and more egalitarian social order, would degenerate into rule by dictators and oligarchs. Although some critics accused them of merely playing at revolution, they did accomplish many goals, perhaps less lofty than they had envisioned but nonetheless worthy.[40] They fell short of achieving their vision of a new way of life by means of a Socialist revolution in which men and women could live, love, and work as equals in a free society that offered its bene-fits and protections to all. Instead, they unchained American theatre from commercial Broadway interests and established a theatre legacy in Provincetown that endures to this day. They fought to keep alive our First Amendment freedoms; laid the groundwork for laws that guaran-teed sexual equality; promoted the ideal of peace in a time of war; liber-ated Americans from constraining Victorian values, beliefs, mores, and cultural standards by embracing the New; and promoted authenticity by revealing its limitations.

It all began in Davenport, Iowa.

2

Three Midwestern Playwrights Arrive in a Romantic and Miraculous City

In those days . . . I lived in Davenport, which I hated, worked in a law office, which I loathed, was accountable for my every action to my father, whom I feared, and was married to a bad-tempered society woman.

—ARTHUR DAVISON FICKE

Davenport as a Literary Center is too precious a thought to be marred by a comment of mine. I pass it on to you in all its virgin beauty.

—SUSAN GLASPELL TO FLOYD DELL

But Davenport was in many ways a romantic and miraculous city . . . the fabulous capital of Haroun al Raschid. . . . In this Baghdad-on-the-Mississippi a truck farmer could be a poet-philosopher and a young factory hand could plot with him the overthrow of ancient tyrannies and the inauguration of a new world.

—FLOYD DELL

DURING THE SUMMER OF 1903, while Pope Leo XIII lay dying in Rome and President Theodore Roosevelt was denouncing racial discrimination, lynching, and mob violence, residents of Davenport, Iowa, were experiencing a fairly ordinary summer. Booth Tarkington's *The Two Van Revels* was serialized in the *Davenport Daily Times*. *Sweet Clover* was playing at the Burtis Opera House. The Dickens Club was reading *Martin Chuzzlewit*.

The Mozart Club held its annual recital. Former mayor C. A. Ficke took his family—including son Arthur, a rising Harvard senior and budding poet—to Mackinac Island to escape the hot, muggy Iowa weather, while novelist Alice French (Octave Thanet) headed east for the same purpose. Harry Hansen, who would make his mark as an author, editor, and book reviewer, was newly graduated from high school and working as a cub reporter for the *Times*. On August 22, Josephine Bickel Drechsler of Princeton, Iowa, boarded the packet boat Winona to visit friends and shop in Davenport, where she could buy ladies' tailored suits for $6.98 at the Bee Hive for daughters Adelheide, Carrye, and Ada Emielle. Rob Moore was working nearby as an engineer on the *J. W. Van Sant*, unaware that his future mother-in-law was in town shopping for his future wife.[1]

To most Davenporters, that summer of 1903 may have seemed fairly ordinary, but it would prove to be especially consequential for three writers who would change American theatre history. In June, twenty-nine-year-old George Cram (Jig) Cook left his teaching position at Stanford University to return to his native Davenport, preceded by his new wife, Chicagoan Sara Herndon Swain, who had been staying with his parents since April. Also in June, twenty-five-year-old Susan Glaspell, another native Davenporter, returned to her family home after spending five months in Chicago. And in early September, sixteen-year-old Floyd Dell moved to 306 East Sixth Street with his family just in time to begin his junior year of high school.[2]

That November, a headline in the *Times* proclaimed "Davenport a Kicking Town," and stories published in the paper that year verified that the city was indeed a happening place. Live theatre could be seen at the Grand Opera House in Turner Hall, where productions of *Othello*, *Hamlet*, and *Macbeth* were staged (as well as German-language plays), and at the aforementioned Burtis Opera House, where Lillian Russell, Ethel Barrymore, Billie Burke, Eddie Foy, Maude Adams, Chauncey Olcott, Wallace Beery, May Robson, and Sarah Bernhardt performed throughout the early twentieth century. George Bernard Shaw's *Candida* and the operas *Aida*, *Lucia di Lammermoor*, and *Il Trovatore* were among the works staged there. Jacob Strasser's band offered Sunday afternoon concerts in parks and beer gardens; other musical events featured the Davenport Zither Quartette and Miss Poddie Ross, "Davenport's Nightingale."[3]

Residents also enjoyed moonlight steamboat excursions, river carnivals, and regattas in the summer; torchlight parades in the fall; and skating and sleighing parties followed by oyster suppers in the winter. There were dances and masquerade balls at Lahrmann's Hall and the Outing Club, as well as progressive dinners, recitals, luncheons, card parties, and teas. For a nickel, adventurous Davenporters could take the trolley across the Mississippi to Black Hawk's Watch Tower, where for a ten-cent admission they could enjoy a recreation complex comprising a restaurant, a dancing pavilion, and a bathing beach; other available amusements included a Japanese penny arcade, a merry-go-round, a roller coaster, burro rides, and a shoot-the-chutes into the Rock River.

Free movies and lantern slides were offered for those in search of popular entertainment, while T. D. Mackey's Light Opera Company staged *The Mikado*, *The Pirates of Penzance*, and *The H. M. S. Pinafore* there for those with slightly higher brows.[4] R. C. Smith describes "trolley parties to Black Hawk Park where we sat in the grass high above the Rock River and listened to the band concert and then rode home in the open trolley and topped off the evening around the dining room table with cherry phosphates."[5] By 1908, Davenporters could conclude such an evening of amusements with Green Rivers at the new Lagomarcino's Confectionary in nearby Moline, which is still operating today.

In addition to the church groups and lodges that could be found in most midwestern towns and cities at that time, Davenport offered a plethora of clubs and societies. There were clubs for music lovers, gun enthusiasts, card players, theatre aficionados, history buffs, politicos, foodies, boaters, singers, bowlers, dancers, and readers. There were even clubs for people with no hobbies or interests who just wanted to be in a club. A very partial list of these associations includes the Idle Hours Club, the Sandwich Club, the Canoe Club, the Cumberland Gun Club, the Cuisine Club, the Harmonie Club, the Golden Eagle Social Club, the Euterpe Club, the Davenport Shooting Association, the Parliamentary Law Club, the Golden Rod Social Club, the Etude Club, the Lincoln Club, the Jolly Cinch Club, the Excelsior Rifle Club, the Bobby Burns Society, the Dickens Club, the Clionian Club, the Contemporary Club, and the Tuesday Club.

Of these organizations, the four study clubs at the end of that list would have had the strongest appeal for Dell, Cook, and Glaspell. Harvard-educated Cook was the author or coauthor of several books, and Dell was a teenaged prodigy whose poems would soon be published in the *Century*, *Harper's*, and *McClure's* as well as in the local periodicals

Trident, the *Tri-City Workers Magazine*, and the *Times*. Glaspell, a champion orator in college, had recently worked as a reporter and columnist for the *Des Moines Daily News* after she graduated from Drake University; before entering college, she had been a reporter for Charles Eugene Bank's *Davenport Morning Republican* as well as a columnist and society editor for his *Weekly Outlook*. After publishing a series of high-profile stories on an Iowa murder case that would inspire her first and best-known play, *Trifles*, Glaspell left journalism to concentrate on writing fiction and found early success, placing stories in *Authors Magazine, Black Cat, Harper's*, and *Youth's Companion*. Dell, Cook, and Glaspell would find themselves in Greenwich Village ten years later and, during the summer of 1915, would join several other writers and artists in Provincetown, Massachusetts, to found the Provincetown Players. Their plays, as well as the defining characteristics of their theatre practice, would be significantly informed by their involvement in Davenport cultural and political activities and events during the first decade of the twentieth century.

Early twentieth-century Davenport's cosmopolitan and progressive cultural milieu distinguished it from other midwestern cities of its size. By 1903, the town had grown exponentially. First platted in 1836 (ten years before Iowa became a state) and incorporated in 1839, nascent Davenport was described by J. M. D. Burrows as "a beautiful little hamlet of fifteen houses with a population of about one hundred and fifty persons."[6] However, this tiny town began to develop a cultural infrastructure from its first decade of existence. A lecture society for men, the Davenport Lyceum, was inaugurated during the year of its incorporation, as was the Carey Library Association. The previous year had seen the first issue of the *Iowa Sun, and Davenport and Rock Island News*, followed by Alfred Sanders's Whig newspaper, the *Davenport Gazette*, in 1841.[7]

The 1840s saw the establishment of the Davenport Literary Society; Iowa College, a private school founded by Congregationalists; and a Ladies Benevolent Society. The next decade brought to Davenport a Young Men's Library Association; the Pioneer Settlers' Association of Scott County; and Griswold College, an Episcopalian institution founded in 1859 that housed an eight-thousand-volume library and hosted a lecture series that was open to the public. Also in 1859, Davenporters of Scottish ancestry organized the Bobby Burns Society to mark the centenary of the poet's birth. The Davenport Academy of Natural Sciences and the

Burtis Opera House opened in 1867, and congregation B'nai Israel was organized in 1861; its successor, the Reform Temple Emanuel, was home for eleven years to Rabbi William H. Fineshriber, who became a leading civic and intellectual leader during the first decade of the twentieth century.

The Davenport Art Association, a forerunner of the Davenport Municipal Art Gallery and, later, the Figge Art Museum, was established in 1878. St. Ambrose College, a Catholic institution still in existence today as St. Ambrose University, was founded in 1882, and in 1885 a library with a free reading room was instituted. This library became a free public library in 1900, and a new building for the library was constructed in 1904, with $75,000 provided by Andrew Carnegie at the behest of Alice French. National and international figures—including Ralph Waldo Emerson, Horace Mann, Horace Greeley, Frederick Douglass, Wendell Phillips, Susan B. Anthony, William Jennings Bryan, Roald Amundsen, Mother Jones, Henry Ward Beecher, Jane Addams, Teddy Roosevelt, and Mark Twain—typically generated large turnouts when they lectured in Davenport; one thousand people came out to hear Twain and novelist George Washington Cable on a double bill in 1885. The 1890s saw the birth of two elite study clubs that still meet today: the Tuesday Club (for women) in 1892 and the Contemporary Club (for men) in 1896.[8]

This rich cultural infrastructure was due in part to the city's robust economy. "Economic development was, in every town, the basis on which social development proceeded," asserts Timothy R. Mahoney.[9] He argues that prosperity came early to Davenport partly because a small group of very rich men owned a significant percentage of the wealth: "The town economy was controlled throughout the 1840s and 1850s by a small oligarchy of early settlers, who, in turn, controlled the nature of economic competition on Main Street." During this period, Davenport's ten richest men owned 47 percent of the town's wealth, and the two richest, Colonel George Davenport and Antoine LeClaire, owned 25 percent. "Oligarchic economic rule, by intensifying the alignment between personal welfare and town economic development, thus clarified economic decisions and actions," concludes Mahoney.[10]

LeClaire, in particular, was heavily invested in the town, building a wharf, a hotel, a post office, and a number of private houses as well as donating land for school buildings and churches and subsidizing merchants and the Rock Island Railroad. Mahoney points out that this largess also increased LeClaire's personal wealth from over \$100,000 to \$250,000 between 1853 and 1855.[11] Marlys A. Svendsen and Martha H. Bowers enumerate other factors that, at midcentury, had turned Davenport into "the boom town of eastern Iowa and the Great West": "Proximity to new local and regional markets, a labor supply, raw materials, water power, river transportation, and rail connections." The mid-1850s brought the railroad to Davenport, which shifted its commercial axis from St. Louis to Chicago and brought new economic actors to town that forced out local businesses and manufacturers. However, despite this development and the economic crises of the 1850s, forty years later, the *Davenport Weekly Outlook* would note that "the city of Davenport has been called the money metropolis of Iowa."[12]

That description would hold true into the early twentieth century. William L. Bowers observes that in 1906, over 200 factories and 174 business and financial institutions created jobs that enabled Davenporters to enjoy a high standard of living. Davenport had become "the second leading city in per capita wealth in the United States, and of cities in Iowa it had the most invested capital, one of the highest assessed property valuations, and the lowest per capita debt."[13] It was and still is the largest freshwater port on the Mississippi River.

Another factor that contributed to Davenport's unique social and cultural milieu was its ethnic makeup. The city in which Dell, Cook, and Glaspell arrived in 1903 comprised nearly thirty-five thousand inhabitants, 25–36 percent of whom were German. The political-intellectual climate skewed progressive in part due to the influence of these free-thinking immigrants, who cherished personal liberty and fostered an environment of tolerance and openness, civic virtues promoted by two German-language newspapers: *Der Demokrat*, founded in 1851, and the *Iowa Reform*, founded in 1884. At midcentury, Theodor Gulich published articles on immigration and Socialism in *Der Democrat*, and civic-minded German Americans delivered stimulating lectures on political topics at Turner Hall. From pioneer days, this progressive orientation was evident, growing stronger with each decade.

Despite the heavily German makeup of the city, the temperance movement had early roots in Davenport. A temperance society was organized there in 1839, Hiram Price established a Davenport chapter of the Sons of Temperance in 1847, and soon a Sons of Temperance Hall was in evidence. An editorial in the December 24, 1857, edition of the

Gazette urged citizens to leave the alcoholic punch off the buffet table at the traditional New Year's Day open house.[14] An early (if short-lived) temperance newspaper, the *Blue Ribbon News*, appeared in 1878, named for the Blue Ribbon Temperance Society, which was formed the previous year.[15]

The antislavery campaign, too, found adherents in Davenport and Scott County; the former was a stop on the Underground Railroad during the city's early decades. In 1856, abolitionist Benjamin Gue helped found the Iowa Republican Party, representing Scott County at its convention in Iowa City.[16] Gue and *Gazette* editor Edward Russell fought fiercely to persuade Iowa voters to pass a Negro suffrage amendment to the state constitution, achieving success in 1868. The amendment passed in Scott County with 65 percent of the vote.[17] Davenport's German population was strongly antislavery; in 1860, the Turnverein came out against the Fugitive Slave Law, and after John Brown was hanged, he was eulogized in *Der Demokrat* and the German theatre was draped in black.[18]

As the decades rolled on, several Davenport women were key in the city's development, some attaining national and even international renown. Their activism in social welfare work, publishing, education, public health, and social movements such as temperance and suffrage advanced the cause of women, enriched the cultural milieu of the city, and contributed to its social betterment. It might be a stretch to call Clarissa Cook (1811–79) a feminist, but it would be accurate to call her a philanthropist who engaged in "women's work for women."[19] Wife of pioneer settler, banker, and mayor Ebenezer Cook and great-aunt by marriage of Jig Cook, she provided seed money for early Davenport institutions, such as Trinity Episcopal Church; the Clarissa C. Cook Memorial Library, founded in 1885; and the Clarissa C. Cook Home for the Friendless.

Founded in 1882, the latter institution, commonly referred to as the "Cook Home for Old Ladies," was notable for its nondiscriminatory admissions policy, established by Clarissa Cook herself, which extended not only to elderly African American and white women but also to younger transient women of good character. Sharon E. Wood notes that "Clarissa Cook's will established not just a home for elderly women, it created an enduring institution staffed and managed by women who became self-supporting as a result."[20]

Mary Louisa Duncan Putnam (1832–1903) focused her philanthropic efforts on the Davenport Academy of Natural Sciences, becoming its first female member and serving as its first female president in 1879. Although not a scientist herself, Putnam put her gifts for organization and administration to work in support of the academy, promoting membership among community women, facilitating the publication and distribution of its scientific papers, promoting its public lectures, strengthening ties between the academy and the public schools, and, most significantly, raising funds for the academy and its museum, which would later be named for the Putnam family. A respected member of the community, she was one of three women chosen by the Charitable Alliance in 1889 to appear before the city council in support of hiring a police matron and establishing a separate jail for women and children.[21]

Maria Purdy Peck (1840–1913), the wife of Dr. Washington Freeman Peck, drew on her medical background to focus her activism on the realm of public health and social welfare, helping found St. Luke's Hospital and St. Luke's Training School for Nurses and serving as the first president of the former. Her interest in child welfare led to her service on the state's child labor committee and her work for the kindergarten department of the People's Union Mission. Mrs. Peck helped found a free kindergarten in Davenport at a time when the public schools lacked a kindergarten program, and she paid its teachers' salaries for one year.[22]

Maria Peck's keen intellectual interests bore fruit when she founded the Clionian Club, one of Davenport's elite study clubs, of which she served as president for ten years; she was also president of the Scott County Historical Society for two years and president of the library board. A talented writer and eloquent speaker, she published a series of articles, "Davenport and Its Environs," for the national magazine of the American Historical Society and wrote articles on Fort Armstrong and Chief Black Hawk for the *Annals of Iowa* as well as a travel piece on Italy for the *Weekly Outlook*.[23] A descendent of Stephen Hopkins (a signer of the Declaration of Independence), she was active in the Daughters of the American Revolution, one of the founders and the first regent of Davenport's Hannah Caldwell chapter. She also served as regent of the Iowa DAR, writing the State Regent's Report for the Iowa DAR's Fourth Annual Conference in 1903.[24]

Peck also spearheaded causes that advanced the status of women. A strong supporter of women's clubs because she believed that they developed "breadth of character" in women and made them "logical thinkers and ready speakers," she was one of the founders and the first president of the Davenport Women's Club and was active in the Iowa Federation of Women's Clubs, traveling to London in 1899 as a delegate to the International Council of Women and serving on its legislative committee in 1909 and on its civil service and social reform committees in 1910. She was also active in the Association for the Advancement of Women as well as in Frances Willard's National Council of Women, serving as vice-president-at-large in the early 1890s. A strong supporter of women's suffrage, at the Lend a Hand Club's 1897 suffrage convention, she spoke for the affirmative on the question, "Does the Tax-Paying Woman Need It?" In a letter published in the *Davenport Democrat*, she asserted that the opponents of women's suffrage were "party bosses, gamblers, prize-fighters, wreckers of homes, despoilers of women's virtue, the frail sisterhood, criminals, and law breakers of all sorts."[25]

Sarah Ann (Annie) Turner Wittenmyer (1827–1900) arrived in Davenport after service as a Civil War battlefield nurse. After founding homes for war orphans in Van Buren County and Cedar Falls, Iowa, Wittenmyer established a residential facility in Davenport for 150 soldiers' orphans, founding the Iowa Soldiers Orphans Home (later the Iowa Annie Wittenmyer Home) in 1865 on the former site of Camp Kinsman and Camp Roberts northeast of the city and serving as its first matron. In 1876, the mission of the home was broadened to accommodate any child in need, and it became a state-tax-supported institution in 1866. Wittenmyer was active in the temperance movement as well as in social welfare work. In 1874, she helped found the Women's Christian Temperance Union and served as its first president for five years before Frances Willard assumed that role. She also wrote several books, including *History of the Women's Temperance Crusade* (1878).[26]

Born near Kalamazoo, Michigan, Ella Grace Bushnell-Hamlin (1860–1936) taught school and then ventured into journalism, writing for the *Muscatine News-Tribune* and the *Des Moines News* before moving to Davenport in 1902 to become society editor for the *Morning Republican*. In January 1904, she and Mary Harrah founded *Trident*, a weekly magazine owned and staffed by women. Termed "Davenport's busiest little woman" by the *Davenport Democrat and Leader*, Bushnell-Hamlin was a suffragist and temperance advocate who was also a proponent of public playgrounds, public baths, and public kindergartens. She was a delegate to the 1900 National Women's Suffrage Association's convention in Washington, DC, and spoke on April 8, 1904, at a meeting of the

Rock Island chapter of the Women's Christian Temperance Union on "How to Win." In 1909, she was among the Davenport delegates to the second District Convention of the Iowa Federation of Women's Clubs, and in 1910 she served as the delegate to that convention, representing the Altruistic Circle, one of twelve Davenport women's organizations that were affiliated with the Iowa Federation.[27]

Bushnell-Hamlin never hesitated to speak her mind on local as well as national issues. She cited taxation without representation as grounds for her refusal to pay a city license tax, challenging Mayor Alfred Mueller to incarcerate her. Although she denied that she was "a militant suffragette," her response to President Taft's concern that bad women would get the vote if the suffrage amendment passed was forthright: "If Taft will take care of the bad men, we will take care of the bad women, and we will have a very much smaller job on our hands." She further pointed out that "there is a large colony of men bankers in Leavenworth prison [but] not a single woman banker to be found there," although Kansas could boast four women bank presidents and five hundred women bank employees, all of whom had managed to stay out of jail.[28]

Bushnell-Hamlin and Harrah's magazine, *Trident*, although nonpartisan, was progressive in orientation, pledging to "deal with political questions, being careful to distinguish between politics and partisanship; patriotism and cant."[29] *Trident* published editorials favoring women's participation in electoral politics and articles about the achievements of nationally known feminists such as Susan B. Anthony and temperance leader Frances Willard, as well as such locally prominent women as Susan Glaspell, Phebe W. Sudlow, Dr. Jennie C. McCowen, and Moline poet Marjorie Allen Seiffert. The December 31, 1910, issue featured an opinion piece, "Why Should a Man Not Marry a Suffragette?" To appeal to a broad-based audience, *Trident* ran romance fiction, poetry, book reviews, pictorial features, fashion articles, and Madame Zuleine's Beauty Column alongside prosuffrage, protemperance, and prolabor articles.

Like Bushnell-Hamlin, Phebe W. Sudlow (1831–1922) began her career as a teacher, first in Ohio at the age of fifteen and later in Iowa, where she relocated in 1856. In 1858, she began her meteoric rise through the ranks of the Davenport public school system. First named an assistant principal and later principal of several schools, including the high school and the Training School for Teachers, she became Davenport's first female superintendent of schools in 1874, overseeing eight grammar schools, a high school, the teacher training school, ninety teachers and principals, and more than twenty-five hundred students. When she learned that the school board planned to pay her less than her male predecessor, she took a firm stand: "Gentlemen, if you are cutting the salary because of my experience, I have nothing to say; but if you are doing this because I'm a woman, I'll have nothing to do with it."

Subsequently, Phebe received the salary that was due her and served in the post for four years, a self-reliant woman whose career reflected her priorities: women's issues and child development. The litany of firsts that follows her name includes first woman principal in Davenport, first woman superintendent in Iowa and probably in the nation, and first woman president of the Iowa State Teachers Association. While superintendent, she pushed for equal pay for male and female teachers, a proposal that the Davenport Board of Education subsequently adopted. Throughout her career, Sudlow was a vocal advocate, not only of equal pay for teachers regardless of gender but also of kindergartens, social services for working mothers, and technical and vocational education.[30]

In addition to her groundbreaking professional achievements, Sudlow demonstrated exemplary leadership in civic and church circles. In 1889, she founded a women's reading circle and history club, the Club of '89, and for fifteen years she was president of the Ladies Industrial Relief Society. Founded in 1878 and incorporated in 1891, this agency provided essential services for working-class women with its day care, sewing and cooking classes, laundry, lunchroom, and working women's club. In his history of Davenport, Harry Downer names Phebe Sudlow, a long-serving member of the library board, as one of the Davenport women most responsible for the library's success.[31]

Sudlow's church work was as extensive as her work as an educator and civic leader. A member of St. John's Methodist Episcopal Church, she served as the first treasurer of the Women's Foreign Missionary Society, speaking in 1904 on Russia's role in the Russian-Japanese war then being waged and urging her listeners to sympathize with the Japanese. Sudlow served as president of both the Missionary Society and the Ladies Aid at St. John's; she also taught Sunday school there and prepared the church's history for its cornerstone box. In 1921, the name of the East Intermediate School was changed to Phebe W. Sudlow Intermediate School to honor her civic and professional accomplishments.[32]

Like Bushnell-Hamlin and Sudlow, Dr. Jennie C. McCowen (1845–1924) began her career teaching school; also like Sudlow, she became self-reliant early in life. The daughter of an Ohio physician, she began teaching at age sixteen and then went on to a distinguished career in medicine and public service, focusing on women's issues and mental health. She graduated with honors from the University of Iowa, earning a medical degree in 1876, and worked with female patients at the State Hospital for the Insane in Mount Pleasant, Iowa, for almost three years. In 1880, she relocated to Davenport, where she would practice medicine for forty years.

Dr. McCowen was active in state and national medical societies and frequently read papers on social welfare and mental health topics at national meetings, arguing in one article against the uterine-reflex theory of insanity (the theory that women who rejected domesticity were prone to madness). She was elected the first female president of the Scott County Medical Society in 1884, serving two terms. She also wrote newspaper columns on medicine and hygiene for the *Gazette* and the *Times*, as well as for the *Woman's Tribune* (a national suffrage paper), and served on the editorial staff of the *Pan American Women's Medical Journal*.

In 1885, McCowen was elected to the New York Medico-Legal Society, becoming vice president in 1888. She was named a vice president of the International Congress of Medical Jurisprudence in 1889 and 1904. In 1906, she represented the Medico-Legal Society at the International Medical Congress in Lisbon, Portugal, contributing a paper, "The Effect of Rest and Recreation on Mental Health." She was also a founder of the Iowa State Society of Medical Women, serving as its president in 1893 and 1894.[33]

McCowen's tireless efforts for social betterment bore fruit not only in the arena of medicine but also in the Davenport community and, later, the state and the nation. In 1882, the governor named her a delegate to the National Conference of Charities and Corrections. For the National Association for the Advancement of Women, she wrote a report, "Women in Iowa"; in 1884, she published a version in the *Annals of Iowa* and served as vice president for Iowa for that organization. In 1889, she was elected president of the Davenport Academy of Sciences and helped found the Hadlai Heights Hospital Charitable Alliance.[34]

McCowen's most enduring contribution to Davenport's quality of life was her work for the Lend a Hand Club, an institution that, like the

Ladies Industrial Relief Society, offered support for Davenport's working women. McCowen had been advocating for women for her entire career; these efforts came to fruition in 1888 when, with Eliza F. "Lil" Bickford (her longtime companion), Electa "Lettie" Meacham, May Santry, and Anna McCrum, she founded the Lend a Hand Club and served as its president for twenty-five years. The club's membership eventually rose to two thousand women; its mission was inspired by Edward Everett Hale's verses, "Look up not down, / Look forward and not back, / Look out and not in, / Lend a hand."

McCowen led the Lend a Hand Club in its efforts to help working women find "better opportunities for self-improvement and social recreation of a desirable character." Dedicated to inclusiveness, the Lend a Hand Club pledged to "stimulate an interest in every kind of women's work and a spirit of mutual helpfulness among all women workers. It has no class distinctions, no religious test of membership, but all meet on a common ground for the common good."[35] At a time when some Davenport girls worked from 7:00 a.m. until 10:00 p.m. six days a week and until noon on Sunday to earn forty cents a day, Dr. McCowen's helping hand was sorely needed. The Lend a Hand Club's noon rest/lunch program and daily suppers in its downtown clubrooms offered working women six meals for one dollar, as well as recipes and cooking instructions.[36]

Dr. McCowen did not limit her efforts on behalf of Davenport's working women to the Lend a Hand Club; she also worked to improve downtown conditions for women who continually confronted the iniquities of Davenport's Bucktown, a riverfront red-light district that prompted Episcopal bishop Henry Cosgrove to call Davenport "the wickedest city for its size in America."[37] Bill Wundrum notes that in the early 1900s, the red-light district had "fifty-one bars, plus prostitution dens, dime-a-dance parlors, boxing rings and gaming spots for poker and faro games."[38] The neighboring Lend a Hand Club countered with classes in beginning German, American literature, travel and biography, domestic science, current events, parliamentary usage, arts and crafts, basketry, needlework, and crochet.[39]

Due to Dr. McCowen's efforts, the Lend a Hand Club could offer Davenport's working women alternatives to the saloons, dancing pavilions, and wine rooms of Bucktown; they could choose instead lectures and monthly discussion groups on such topics as "Bicycling: Detrimental

to Women?" and "Is the World Growing Better or Worse?" In a town
that had over two hundred saloons by the mid-1900s, the Lend a Hand
Club provided a much-needed alternate social space for women. "Where
young men turned to the saloon for sociability and services, the women
of the Lend a Hand created an alternative that did not jeopardize their
respectability," asserts Wood.[40]

In January 1889, Sudlow and McCowen, along with Martha Glaspell—
president of the local chapter of the Women's Christian Temperance
Union—tackled one of the most pressing social problems in Davenport:
the pervasive presence of prostitution in downtown Davenport and the
dangers they believed it posed for the women who worked, shopped, or
socialized nearby. Bill Roba reports that in 1890, of the 1,095 arrests in
the city that year, 438 of them were for prostitution, and in July 1904, 57
prostitutes were arrested as well as 16 keepers of houses of ill fame—a
total of 73 arrests for prostitution-related crimes in one month alone.
Added to this number were the 12 people arrested for assault and battery, totaling 85 such arrests in all, a number reflective of an urban environment that was unsavory, if not unsafe, for women who frequented
downtown Davenport.[41]

Much of this activity took place in Bucktown, its boundaries stretch-
ing from the Government Bridge to Perry Street and encompassing First
and Second Streets. In *Them Was the Good Old Days in Davenport, Scott
County, Iowa,* W. L. Purcell relishes the good time that was had by all in
Bucktown:

> We had some corkin' variety theatres and dance halls in Bucktown in
> the old days, too—Jack McPartland's "Bijou," Perl Galvin's "Standard,"
> Oscar Raphael's "Orpheon," Brick Munro's "Pavilion," and Jocky Man-
> waring's "Dance Hall." Them enterprisin' amusement places catered
> especially to the needs of restless rounders lookin' for speedy entertain-
> ment. They toplined the cheesy slapstickers and raspy-voiced crowbaits
> that could take a rise outa soused rubes. Operatin' on the all-night
> schedule and glucose circuit, things didn't hit the right stride till the
> clock in the steeple struck a dozen or so. Brick Munro originated the
> cabaret at his "Pavilion," and it spread over the country like wildfire.[42]

Sudlow, McCowen, Martha Glaspell, and other civic leaders believed that
the proximity of these entertainment establishments to Davenport's
stores, restaurants, and factories was a threat to Davenport womanhood. Wood observes that "the expanding urban workforce disrupted

the old geography of gender and class. Middle-class girls and women now mixed on the streets with their working-class sisters."[43] Cleaning up crime there would prove to be a Sisyphean task. Although Iowa had enacted prohibition in 1884, by the middle of the first decade of the 1900s, Scott County officials were collecting fees from 240 saloons at the same time that they were telling the state that they didn't know how many saloons they had, and by 1907, Davenport alone had 188 such establishments—one for every 200 inhabitants.

In 1893, the election of twenty-five-year-old Henry Vollmer, "the boy mayor of Davenport," marked the beginning of legalized vice in the eyes of reformers, for Vollmer, a German American, was inclined to take a libertarian attitude toward alcohol and prostitution. Instead of ordering a police crackdown on saloons and brothels, Vollmer's approach was to charge operating fees for saloons and a fine that served as a license fee for brothels, as well as to require registration and health certificates for prostitutes, stating in his inaugural address that "candid, thinking men will admit that the best method of dealing with these evils is rigid regulation and control."[44] Vollmer recognized that sex and booze were here to stay; rather than beat his head against a brick wall trying to extirpate them, he chose to focus on mitigating any harm that they might do while deriving all possible benefits from their existence. It was rumored that the new Davenport City Hall, built in 1895 for $100,000 without raising anyone's taxes or issuing any bonds, was funded by fees from the saloons and brothels.[45]

Sudlow, McCowen, Martha Glaspell, and a number of other women active in civic affairs believed that this laissez-faire policy toward what Vollmer and his supporters might have characterized as victimless crimes created an environment of vice that posed risks for Davenport women, risks for which the Lend a Hand Club could only be a partial solution. In 1889, they coordinated the efforts of ten civic organizations that came together to found the Charitable Alliance with the aim of persuading the city council to hire a police matron and establish a separate house of detention for women and children to ensure their privacy and protect them from assault. "The campaign for a police matron was not a radical step but a cautious strategy to claim downtown space for respectable women," argues Wood.[46]

The Charitable Alliance circulated petitions in support of their proposal and then chose McCowen, Mary Louisa Duncan Putnam, and

Sarah Foote Sheldon (secretary of the Academy of Sciences) to present it to the city council. Their petition specified that "every woman arrested should be given into [the matron's] hands to be searched and cared for," including "all girls and women who would otherwise be committed to jail."[47] The women of the alliance argued that the police matron could not only protect women detainees from illicit male advances but also from unjust prosecution. They also hoped that the police matron would discourage the women in her care from working as prostitutes. Although opponents of their proposal presented countering petitions, the Charitable Alliance's campaign for a police matron and a women's detention center was ultimately successful.[48]

In addition to the contributions by these female civic leaders, Davenport enjoyed an early and vigorous history of trade union activity dating from the Civil War era that enhanced not only the material well-being of working-class Davenporters but also the quality of city life. In 1866, workers formed an Eight Hour Labor Day League, founded to combat the ten-hour workdays and five- to six-day workweeks that were common; two years later, the coachmakers and the tailors organized the city's first trade unions, soon to be joined by the typographical workers, the locomotive engineers, the blacksmiths, the brewers, and the cigar makers. In 1882, the latter group struck the Kuhnen Cigar Company for two months to protest a 25 percent pay cut.

The year 1882 also saw Thomas J. O'Meara organizing the Knights of Labor Assembly and the birth of the Davenport Trades and Labor Assembly. Two years later, the Eight Hour League persuaded the Davenport City Council to adopt the eight-hour day for city workers. The Tri-City Labor Congress was organized in the 1890s, and the Workman's Industrial Home Association, which grew out of the Knights of Labor, was established in 1896. The Tri-City Federation of Labor was inaugurated in 1900. As the new century dawned, Svendsen and Bowers observe, "trade unions had become firmly entrenched in the local industrial fabric."[49]

In 1890, the Iowa Legislature passed a bill naming the first Monday in September "Labor Day," four years ahead of Congress. The governor issued a proclamation urging Iowans to suspend their usual activities and observe the new holiday "designed to honor those whose strong arms are the shield of our nation as well as the source of our wealth."[50] The first Labor Day observance in Davenport was an elaborate affair:

The morning feature was the parade, headed by several hundred delegates from the Farmers' Alliance. Then came the military divisions, composed of State militia, the Grand Army of the Republic, and the Sons of Veterans. These were followed by representatives of the German charitable institutes, the singing societies, and the Turners. . . . The employees of the Rock Island Arsenal, iron moulders, printers, painters, tailors, stone cutters, and members of other organizations followed, including 200 commercial travelers. The industrial section was made up of four hundred floats, showing the various lines of goods manufactured. There were more than 5,000 men in the column, and two hours were required for them to pass a given point. In the afternoon thousands were welcomed by mayor Charles A. Ficke at Schuetzen Park where Governor Horace Boies gave a bold and courageous Labor Day address.[51]

Unions continued to thrive in early twentieth-century Davenport, as workers made advances through collective bargaining and job actions. In 1904, twenty-eight union plumbers and fifteen steam fitters at Dunker and Company walked out to protest the hiring of a nonunion worker whom the union said was incompetent, and the next year the Electrical Workers struck to obtain an eight-hour day and a wage of thirty-five cents an hour. By 1907, the journeymen plumbers were negotiating for a wage of four dollars per day plus one apprentice in shops that employed one plumber and two where more were employed, and the postal clerks were proposing that they work no more than six days in any one week and that six hours of night work be considered equivalent to eight hours of day work. Davenport's grocery clerks and teamsters were unionized in 1908, and in 1910 the carpenters working on the new First National Bank building walked off the job to protest the use of sashes manufactured by an antiunion company. Also that year, the Butchers' Local 279 protested that five area butcher shops were operating on Sunday in violation of the blue law. The butchers, who worked from 6:00 a.m. until 6:30 p.m. on weekdays and Saturdays, argued that they should have Sundays off "in view of the fact that we work longer than anyone else"; on April 29, they took Richard Burmeister to court for violating the Sunday closing law.[52]

The International Association of Machinists was one of the strongest and most colorfully active unions during this period, organized in 1893 as Tri-City Lodge No. 388, with fifty-five charter members. Never known to duck a fight, the machinists pulled together at the Locomotive Works on Rockingham Road in 1905, riding night foreman H. W. Miller out of the shop on an iron pole because he fired six day workers whom he alleged had shown up drunk and begun to cause trouble. The angry machinists rode the foreman down to the railroad tracks, looking to toss him through an open door on a passing train. Finding none, they then proposed to toss him into the quarry but desisted on learning that the police had been called. They then, with the foreman in tow, hopped aboard a D&S car, thus proving themselves the adaptable risk takers that Tocqueville found Americans to be.[53]

The machinists at the Rock Island Arsenal were goaded into action by the draconian measures of Major Stanhope Blunt, who assumed command in 1897. Blunt proceeded to cut wages to the level paid to area agricultural implement employees and instituted the piecework system to get more work out of the machinists. By 1897, most shops at the arsenal had been unionized, and the machinists had drawn up their own work rules, which controlled the pace, rate, and quality of the work. When they complained of Blunt's adoption of the Taylor system, he maintained that he was merely following the procedure set up by the Ordnance Department and his hands were tied.[54]

With their workforce down from twenty-six hundred to sixteen hundred, the machinists took their fight to the political arena, prompting Congressman James McKinney of Illinois to visit the arsenal to investigate their complaints. The machinists also visited the secretary of war and complained to presidents McKinley and Roosevelt, triggering a federal inspection that ultimately supported Blunt, whereupon the machinists brought in their national president, James O'Connell, who visited the area several times to publicize their grievances and urge the president and Congress to transfer Major Blunt. Getting nowhere with federal officials, the machinists then took their grievances (which included Blunt's outsourcing of machinist work to private contractors) to the American Federation of Labor, which condemned the arsenal as a sweat shop where men were forced to operate as many as seven or eight machines simultaneously in unsanitary, unventilated conditions. The machinists continued their fight until Blunt was relieved of his command in 1907.[55]

Life was not always a matter of strikes and boycotts for these early Davenport trade unions, many of which offered an appealing program of social events and good and welfare efforts. The *Times* reported in 1905 that the aforementioned machinists "gave an enjoyable dancing party at Armory Hall. Music for a long program of waltzes and two steps was furnished by Brockman's orchestra and the affair proved to be one of the most enjoyable ever given in the hall." A month later, the *Times* stated that "the Carpenters' Union Local no. 554 is making extensive preparations for the annual picnic which will be given at Schuetzen Park, Davenport, June 25. . . . Strasser's band has been engaged to give concerts both afternoon and evening and special vaudeville entertainment has been planned."[56]

Such social activities were enjoyed by members of the major unions in Davenport. The Tri-City Garment Workers gave a masquerade ball for three hundred people in February 1903; the Retail Clerks gave a dancing party at Black Hawk's Watch Tower and planned a regular series of monthly dances there from May through September. That union also gave a Thanksgiving Ball at Library Hall on Thanksgiving night in 1905 with Strasser's orchestra supplying twenty-one selections of dance music. The harness makers picnicked in Schuetzen Park in June 1904, and the cigar makers organized a ball in December of that year to raise money for a sick relief society. In 1910, approximately one hundred members of the Tri-City Typographical Union celebrated their silver anniversary with a banquet at Rock Island's Harper House.[57]

The unions became politically active during the first decade of the twentieth century. In 1904, the Tri-City Labor Congress pledged to defeat two Illinois politicians who were unfriendly to labor, and in 1908, the Davenport Trade Assembly came out against William Howard Taft's candidacy for president. The early years of the twentieth century saw Labor Day parades in which hundreds of trade unionists marched and elected officials spoke. In 1905, one thousand men and women participated in the biggest Labor Day parade ever, later gathering at Suburban Park to hear addresses by mayors Olson (Moline), McCaskin (Rock Island), and Phillips (Davenport), as well as a speech by ex-congressman Wade Judge (Iowa City). In February 1910, the Davenport Trades and Labor Assembly announced plans for a weeklong labor revival, coordinating their efforts with those in fifteen other Iowa cities, with speakers traveling a circuit from one city to the next. Davenport's revival, held at the end of March, featured labor leaders from around the state. "This movement is one which is found in every part of the country at the present time, and the meetings here represent but the local end of the work of enlarging the membership of the labor organizations," noted the *Times*.[58]

Davenport's hospitality to trade unions was due in some measure to the free-thinking atmosphere created by its large German population. Although there were Germans in Davenport as early as the year of its founding, the first major wave of immigrants from that country began in 1847, when 250 Germans from Schleswig-Holstein fleeing Danish despotism arrived in the city. One of those immigrants was Mathias J. Rohlfs, who founded a "private German school based on liberal principles for the children of other free-thinking parents in the community," as well as Davenport's first German singing society. In addition to his leadership in the German community, Rohlfs served three terms in the Iowa state legislature and was later elected Scott County Treasurer, serving for fourteen years. Hildegard Binder Johnson writes that "Rohlfs was a typical forty-eighter in his untiring promotion of liberal and democratic ideas, of educational facilities for youth and adults, and in his wariness of infringements on personal liberties." The Germans' commitment to religious freedom and civil liberties was also evident in brewery owner Mathias Frahm's will, which left money to his grandson with the stipulation that the latter's education be free of religious influence.[59]

Another large group of German immigrants followed through the early years of the next decade. They founded the Freier Deutscher Schulverein in 1851 and the Sozialistischer Turnverein in 1852 and, like Rohlfs, shouldered many civic responsibilities. They were joined a few decades later by German veterans of the Franco-Prussian war and by men escaping the compulsory military service that Prussia imposed. Germany was the country that sent by far the largest group of immigrants to Iowa, over 120,000 between 1820 and 1920; by 1890, the Davenport population was nearly one-third German.[60]

Christine Stansell points out that "the German forty-eighters bequeathed the town a tradition of reform politics, intellectual inquiry, tolerance, and love of high culture."[61] This German cultural infrastructure comprised the Claus Groth Gilde (1843), the Liedertafel singing society (1848), the German Literary Society (1851), the Mannerchor (1851), Der Deutsche Liebhaber Theater Verein (1855), the Schutzenverein (1862), and the Turnverein (1852), later called the Turngemeinde (1882), among other groups and institutions.

The latter organization, often referred to simply as the Turners, sought to cultivate strong bodies and free minds. An equally important part of its mission was "to induce by all possible means a true understanding of efforts for radical reforms in the social, political and religious field, and to work for the realization and preservation of inalienable human rights."[62] Additional goals were to promote the introduction of gymnastics and German language classes in the public schools, to keep religious influences out of the German American schools, to persuade all members to become American citizens, and to work against military conscription.[63] Forty-eighter Theodor Gulich, speaking at the fiftieth anniversary of the Turnverein, pledged that the Davenport Turners would fight against "church domination and nativism, and for 'freedom, enlightenment and welfare for all' as well as women's rights."[64]

Most German cultural societies met at Turner Hall, owned by the Turngemeinde, with its theatre, library, restaurant, gymnasium, and meeting rooms serving as the nucleus of German culture in Davenport. At Turner Hall, the Turngemeinde sponsored activities and events organized into three main sections: physical training, music, and mental training. Gymnastics classes often gave exhibitions there featuring calisthenics, Indian clubs, barbells, and work on the parallel bars and horse. Singing societies also performed at Turner Hall, where operas and operettas were staged, as well as plays in English and German. And in 1857, four decades before the prestigious Contemporary Club was founded, the mental training section of the Turngemeinde inaugurated a lecture and debate series that ran for sixty years, featuring topics such as "The Status of Women" (Theodor Gulich, 1857), "The Abolition of Capital Punishment" (Christophe Ficke, 1873), and "The Social Development of the Christian Church and the Socialistic State of the Future" (Gustav Donald, 1901). Debate topics included "Are the labor movements of the present to the advantage of the working class?" (1874) and "Is the procedure of the German government against socialists justified and wise?" (1878).[65]

Harry Hansen calls Turner Hall "the most influential organization west of Main Street before the First World War," and by 1900, Davenport was known as "the most German city, not only in Iowa, but in all the Middle West, the center of all German activities in the State," according to editor and publisher Joseph Eiboeck.[66] In 1952, William J. Petersen estimated that nine-tenths of the land in Scott County was German-owned.[67] Roba writes that "although Germans ran for political offices, sat on boards and commissions, and participated in the social life of the city, a substantially separate German-American culture persisted well into the twentieth century. For thousands of working-class Germans, their world consisted of *Der Demokrat*, downtown saloons, residential neighborhoods in the west end of Davenport, and Sunday outings to the privately owned Schuetzen Park."[68]

In Dell's autobiographical first novel, *Moon-Calf*, Rabbi Nathan (the William H. Fineshriber character) says that "Port Royal [Davenport] has a quality of its own. I suppose this is partly due to the pioneers from New England, who brought with them ideals and a respect for learning, but it is more due, I think, to the Germans, who left home because they loved liberty, and brought with them a taste for music, discussion, and good beer."[69] A particularly appealing German social space in Davenport in which all three of these delights were readily on hand was Schuetzen Park, a twenty-two-acre pleasure resort whose 1870 grand opening was attended by five thousand people. The park was owned and managed by the two-hundred-member Schuetzengesellschaft, which organized shooting tournaments and concerts there.

Although the primary focus there was target shooting, Schuetzen Park also comprised a restaurant, a bowling alley, and dancing and music pavilions. The park's grounds, with its herds of bison and deer, were "interestingly diversified with hill, dale, groves, tortuous ravines, nooks, dells, and splendid old trees" that were appealing to walkers and picnickers.[70] The park was also the scene of the Vogelschiessen, a children's shooting contest in which boys using crossbows competed for prizes for shooting off a wooden bird's wing, beak, and tail; the boy who brought down the body was named king.[71]

The park also proved to be a congenial venue for musical events. Over twelve hundred singers participated in the eighteenth annual National Sangerfest there in 1898, and in 1901, the Davenport Mannerchor, founded in 1851, celebrated its golden anniversary there with a concert for five thousand people. The following year, Schuetzen Park hosted the Davenport Turngemeinde's golden anniversary celebration, which featured a "Summer Night Festival" of "orchestra music, songs, plays, and competitions." The German custom of Pentecostal concerts, thought to be the first held in the United States, was observed in Schuetzen Park each Sunday morning of May and June in 1906, followed by breakfast in the grove.

Unsurprisingly, Germans dominated the music scene in Davenport. In Harry Downer's *History of Davenport and Scott County, Iowa*, Adolph

Petersen notes that "more than nine-tenths of the professional musicians here at all times have been Germans" and that 150 of the 170-member Tri-City Musical Society were German. However, Schuetzen Park was more than a place for shooting contests and concerts; for Davenport's German Americans, "it had come to symbolize what remained of their rich and beloved German culture," a place "reminiscent of their old 'Heimat' (homeland)," where "they could partake of their own culture and speak the 'Muttersprache' (mother tongue)."[72]

These Germans brought more to Davenport than their love of gymnastics, music, and intellectual pursuits; many of the refugees from the revolutions of 1848, along with later immigrants who came from a free-thinking tradition, were ready candidates for Socialism. Gerhard Bach observes that "Davenport has more to claim for itself in the latter half of the nineteenth century than an economically sound location on the Mississippi River: the largely German immigrant population give it one of the first municipal opera houses in the Midwest, but they also give it a home base in socialism."[73] Even from Davenport's early days, Socialism and German culture were entangled. *Der Demokrat* ran articles on Socialism in the 1850s, and the earliest incarnation of the Turnverein, inaugurated in 1852, was called the Sozialistischer Turnverein, although "Sozialistischer" was later dropped from the organization's name. The Socialist periodical the *Tri-City Workers Magazine* included German-language articles in most of its issues.[74]

A local of the Socialist Party was organized in Davenport in the spring of 1885, and the following year a Socialist meeting "held under the red flag" was routed by Police Chief Frank Kessler.[75] Davenport's Socialist Party sponsored a full complement of intellectual, social, and political activities, particularly after Floyd Dell joined the local. Its meetings, under Dell's influence, became lively affairs where members gave papers, discussed theorists such as Ferdinand La Salle and Herbert Spencer, and hosted prominent Socialists and labor leaders. W. D. "Big Bill" Haywood, David Wallace, John M. Work, Ida Crouch-Hazlet, Dr. W. C. Hills, May Wood-Simons, Eugene V. Debs, and Carl Liebernecht (Socialist member of the German Reichstag) spoke in Davenport. During the first decade of the twentieth century, the Socialists regularly fielded candidates for state, county, and municipal offices, as well as for Congress.

In 1902, the *Morning Republican* noted that the Socialists in nearby Dubuque had done surprisingly well in that city's election, garnering over seven hundred votes, "many more votes than was expected, even by them." The reporter concluded with the understatement, "It looks as though Socialism would bear watching."[76] Writing about early twentieth-century Davenport, Bowers describes the Socialist Party as "small but well-organized" and concludes that "the party had a platform and ran candidates for all municipal and school elections in Davenport during 1906–1907." Bowers notes that "while their main premise was that the capitalist system and its attendant evils were the source of most of the problems of government in the United States, they did support such worthwhile reforms as public kindergarten, night classes for those who were forced to leave school before finishing, abolition of child labor, better wages, employer's liability laws, and old-age assistance."[77]

By 1905, the Socialists had their own monthly publication, the *Tri-City Workers Magazine*, edited by Dell. Its inaugural issue stated that "the Socialist party comes to the workers with a plan of union, with a philosophy and a principle. Our union includes every worker on earth, without reference to race, color, or religious belief. Our philosophy accepts every fact of nature and history. Our principle is universal brotherhood."[78] The second number of the magazine offered two colorful aphorisms on its masthead: "When the beef trust gets all the cow hides cornered they will proceed to skin the public" and "Rockefelder's new overcoat has cost the dear people half a cent per gallon."[79] A later masthead asked the question, "What is the difference between Socialists and Reformers?" and provided the answer: "Well, Reformers wish to remove results, while Socialists wish to remove causes."[80] This lively monthly magazine featured informative articles on Socialism, muckraking articles on local issues, and a series of articles on working-class occupations written by an employee; readers were invited inside a candy factory, a cigar factory, a department store, a corn planter works, and a button factory.

The Socialists continued to be active on a number of fronts throughout the first decade of the twentieth century. In 1906, the Socialists' city convention, held on February 9 at Claus Groth Hall, was deemed "the largest gathering of Socialists in convention in the history of the city movement." The platform adopted at that convention stated that the Socialist Party of Davenport "adheres to the principles of international socialism, stands for the overthrow of capitalism by the working class through the capture of the political machinery of the nation and the reorganization of industry on a cooperative basis, the ownership of the means of production and distribution by the working class, and the democratic management of them with equal opportunity for all."

Among its many planks were those supporting the eight-hour workday; child labor laws; the initiative, referendum, and recall; public kindergarten; properly equipped public parks, playgrounds, gymnasia, and bathing places; and city ownership of street railways, waterworks, gas plants, coal and wood yards, and power houses. In June 1906, the Davenport local organized a bazaar to raise money for their propaganda fund, and in 1907, when Professor R. H. Peck of Brown's Business College criticized the Socialist press in his commercial law classes, party members challenged him to a public debate, offering to pay all expenses connected with the event.[81]

This potent mélange of feminism, trade unionism, German libertarianism, and Socialism invigorated a cultural matrix that nourished in Dell, Cook, and Glaspell a progressive mindset, one that would bear fruit in their fiction, plays, and theatre practice. All three writers reflected appreciatively in later years on the city's strong impact on their aesthetic and intellectual development. Glaspell set many of her stories, novels, and plays in Davenport and its environs; in his commentary on one of her best-known plays, *Inheritors* (1921), Bartholow V. Crawford observed that "Susan Glaspell is still at heart a daughter of Iowa."[82] Writing from her Cape Cod home, Glaspell corroborated his statement, reminiscing about her Davenport days: "I live by the sea, but the body of water that I have the most feeling about is the Mississippi River, where I used to row and skate, ride the ferry in childhood, watch the logs or just dream."[83]

Dell always fondly remembered the five years he spent in the city. He set *Moon-Calf* in Port Royal, Iowa, a thinly disguised Davenport, writing that the city "had been built for young men and girls to be happy in, to adventure in, and to think strange and free and perilous thoughts."[84] And Dell recalled that the last time he saw Jig Cook, he had put his arms around Dell, asking that they "gather the old Davenport crowd together, and go back there, and make it a new Athens."[85] For Floyd Dell, George Cram Cook, and Susan Glaspell, Davenport was the romantic and miraculous city that would change their lives as well as the course of American theatre history.

3

Floyd Dell Embraces Feminism in Port Royal

Floyd Dell was in high school when I first heard of him;
the story was that the high school had a freak poet, who actually
sold verses to "McClure's" but was eternally damned because
he was a Socialist.

—HARRY HANSEN

IN THE LATE SUMMER of 1903, sixteen-year-old Floyd Dell, newly relocated to Davenport, Iowa, was surprised to find himself giving a public lecture on Socialism. He had ventured to an African American church because a talk on that topic had been advertised, and he had hoped to meet some Socialists there, having thus far failed to locate the Socialist local in town. The invited speaker was Michael T. Kennedy, the Davenport Socialists' perennial candidate for Congress; however, Kennedy hadn't shown up to give his scheduled lecture. "Everybody waited and waited," Dell recalled in his autobiography, *Homecoming* (1933):

> I had taken my place in one of the front pews. I was the only white person there. Finally, the pastor came to me and asked if I were a Socialist.
> "Why, yes," I said.
> "It doesn't look as if Mr. Kennedy was going to get here," said the pastor, "and I was wondering if you would give us a little speech on Socialism."
> "Well, all right," I said.

This rising high school junior proceeded to deliver an extemporaneous talk on dialectical materialism, the class struggle, and the Socialist agenda, thus beginning a long career as an activist, writer, lecturer, and editor fueled largely by his ability to leap through the door when Opportunity knocked, seize it by the throat, and bend it to his will.[1]

This approach to life was next in evidence when Dell finally became involved with Davenport's Socialist Party. He had earlier joined up with the Socialists when he lived in Quincy, Illinois, so he went looking for them shortly after he moved to Davenport. After searching for them in vain at the German community's Turner Hall, he finally found them on a street corner when he observed none other than Michael T. Kennedy making a speech to the passersby. Here Dell first met Socialist mail carrier Frederick (Fritz) Feuchter, who would introduce him to Davenport's Socialists—in *Homecoming* he asserts that "my friendship with Fred Feuchter was the most important thing that had happened in my life" (*Homecoming*, 116–17, 119).[2]

After finally connecting with Kennedy and Feuchter, Dell swiftly became an active Socialist. He was accepted into the leadership of Davenport's Socialist local, became a member of the program committee, frequently contributed to the monthly program, and served as financial secretary and as a delegate to the state convention, where he was appointed to the platform committee. He also leafleted at factory gates for Eugene V. Debs, read his poem "The Builders" at the Tri-City Socialists' May Day celebration in 1905, and recited one of Robert Ingersoll's poems at the local's May 6, 1905, meeting. In the fall of 1906, the sample ballot published by the *Davenport Daily Times* listed the Socialist candidate for Scott County auditor as F. J. Dell.[3]

In his autobiographical first novel, *Moon-Calf,* Dell likened the Central Socialist Local of Port Royal (the fictional Davenport) to "a small, unpopular, semi-respectable heretical church which continued to exist because it is in the nature of institutions, once started, to keep on existing" (*Moon-Calf,* 214). In the novel, Felix Fay (the Dell character), armed with the chutzpah that only a sixteen-year-old newcomer can muster, breathes new life into the local by taking over the leadership, minimizing its business proceedings, and encouraging members to give lively talks on current political and social issues to stimulate discussion. Felix also stages a coup at the state convention by pushing out the local's perennial nominee for the district's Congressional seat in favor of a more charismatic candidate.

Dell amped up his activism during the summer of 1906 when he became the editor of the *Tri-City Workers Magazine*, a Socialist periodical published in nearby Moline, Illinois. Although he didn't find much muck to rake, Dell, usually writing as "Thersites," exposed a Moline garbage dump as a noxious hazard and argued for public kindergarten and more space for the Children's Department in the Davenport Public Library, in addition to writing articles about Socialism. He was thrilled when one of his muckraking articles actually effected change: the members of the Library Board read his piece about the Children's Department and moved it from the basement to the top floor (*Homecoming*, 112–13). But Dell's standout piece was "Why People Go to Brick Munro's," his first published feminist polemic, in which he explores the links among capitalism, feminism, and Socialism, connections that he would examine in more depth in his later writings.[4]

Although Socialism viewed gender inequality as a byproduct of capitalism that would disappear when the classless society came into being and abolished private property, in practice the party embraced feminist principles. From its inception in 1901, the Socialist Party of America developed platforms that endorsed women's suffrage and equal political rights for men and women.[5] Many Socialist candidates ran on issues that would benefit women and children; Meyer London, elected to Congress in 1914 as a Socialist from New York City's Twelfth District, advocated paid maternity leave, and Eugene V. Debs, the five-time Socialist candidate for president, espoused feminist principles in his pamphlet *Woman—Comrade and Equal*.[6] Female speakers traveled throughout the United States to spread the Socialist message; Sally M. Miller reports that "Socialists throughout the country always had a visible number of women activists, organizers, and convention delegates."[7] During Dell's time in Davenport, women held positions of responsibility in the Davenport local and ran for municipal and county offices on the Socialist ticket.

"Why People Go to Brick Munro's" is ostensibly focused on the dangers that Munro's entertainment complex posed for working-class women in downtown Davenport, but Dell's analysis goes deeper. "In this article I sought to implicate the respectable classes of Davenport in the flourishing industry of making prostitutes," Dell recalled (*Homecoming*, 132). Brick Munro's dining and dancing establishment was located in Davenport's red-light district, Bucktown, a four-square-mile riverfront area where saloons, dance halls, gaming houses, and brothels operated

freely. In *Moon-Calf*, Rabbi Nathan (the William H. Fineshriber character) describes Port Royal as a wide-open town:

> Port Royal does not hide its vices; in fact, it does not regard them as
> vices. . . . In the great days of river-traffic it was a Pleasure City, famous
> all over the Mississippi region. It has a long record of defiance of laws
> passed by the puritanical state legislature, and more than once the state
> militia has been sent in to enforce obedience. Just a few years ago the
> legislature passed a law forbidding prize-fights, and Port Royal kept on
> having them. So finally a company of farmer-boys with bayonets was
> marched into the Coliseum—and were told that it was all right, that
> there wasn't going to be any prize-fight, just a little boxing-match, and
> they were invited to take ringside seats. They did, and under the eyes of
> the state national guard sent to enforce the law, the biggest prize-fight
> ever held in the state was pulled off![8]

The foundation of Dell's case against Brick Munro's establishment is
that it required male patrons to pay a cover charge but admitted women
for free. To Dell, this was tantamount to prostitution, as the male cus-
tomers were mainly middle-class businessmen while the female patrons
comprised, for the most part, working-class shop clerks and factory
workers who labored for ten to fourteen hours a day and found there
what little fun they could manage to have in their difficult lives.

The problem of girls getting into trouble in dance halls found its way
into a story that the *Times* ran two years before Dell's article was published. The *Times* reported that four girls were arrested for "leading
immoral lives" and given ten days in the house of detention. "The police
are determined to stop the practice which it seems a number of working
girls have got into, of going to the dance halls in Bucktown, and it was
thought best to make an example of the four arrested that night," the
Times stated. Dell's concern was buttressed by arrest statistics: fifty-
seven inmates of houses of ill fame and sixteen keepers of such houses
were arrested during July 1904, as well as twelve others for assault and
battery.[9]

Dell thus finds two answers to the question posed by his title: people
go to Brick Munro's because both the owner and the patrons profit from
the establishment—"The men go there because of Capitalism . . . they go
there because under Capitalism the women of the working class are the
prey of the men of the business and professional classes."[10] Dell clearly
perceived that the economic success of places like Brick Munro's was
founded on the commodification of women:

I knew the attitude of the young men who went hunting for girls at parks and amusement places, and boasted that a girl could be had for a glass of beer . . . the fundamental sexual contempt which underlay the men's admiration . . . the implicit attitude of the lords of the earth toward a slave class. . . . Girls were things. And this was an old role for girls; church and state joined in denying them rights as individuals, and employers kept them in a position of helplessness by cheap wages; when all these had done their work, Nick Bingo [Dell's pseudonym for Brick Munro] gave them a good time in his dance-hall, and so they were gathered into the houses of prostitution down the street—well trained by then to accept their destiny of being used for pleasure and profit, with no say-so of their own. (*Homecoming*, 96)

While Dell's article accurately emphasizes that Brick Munro's establishment prospered because it satisfied working-class girls' need for fun and middle-class men's need for girls, he neglects to mention another motive: some girls went there hoping to attract middle-class husbands who would rescue them from their lives of drudgery, as was the case with Rose Pastor, who worked in a Manhattan cigar factory until James Graham Phelps Stokes, a wealthy investment banker, met and married her in 1905. That fact would have been additional grist for his Socialist mill.

Undergirding Dell's Socialist-based feminism was the wide spectrum of reading in which he engaged from childhood. Born in Barry, Illinois, in 1887, Dell had taught himself to read at age five and discovered the town's public library at age seven, thus beginning an ambitious program of reading in libraries, first in Barry and later in Quincy, Illinois, where the family moved when he was twelve to find better-paying work for his father and brothers. While books offered an escape from the realities of living for a child whose family was too poor to celebrate Christmas, they also gave Dell an educational program that he would continue in Davenport.

This wide reading would enable him to lay the foundation for a lifetime of letters as a poet, journalist, book reviewer, novelist, literary scholar, polemicist, playwright, and social critic. Under the guidance of the Davenport Public Library's Marilla Freeman, his reading would gain in breadth and depth, reinforce his Socialist beliefs, and help him develop the cogent feminist polemics that he would later publish in the *Friday Literary Review* of the *Chicago Evening Post*, the *New Review*, and the *Masses*. This feminist perspective, which opposed capitalism's commodification of women, illuminated gendered power relations, and advocated equal rights and freedoms for women, would inform his books and pamphlets, as well as the plays that he would write for the Liberal Club and the Provincetown Players. Three key issues pervading Dell's writings that he saw as fundamental to the cause of women's freedom were legalized birth control, companionate marriage, and free love.

Dell's early fondness for romantic tales gave way to a more realist sensibility; his early acquaintance with Mark Twain's *The Prince and the Pauper* (1881) laid the groundwork for his later embrace of Socialism. As a youth, Dell also read Socialist classics such as Friedrich Engels's *Socialism, Utopian and Scientific* (1880) and parts of *Das Capital* (1867), finding Socialism to be "the greatest intellectual and imaginative stimulus which existed in the world" (*Homecoming*, 146). In *Moon-Calf*, Felix Fay becomes enamored of the many new ideas he finds in books, such as evolution and "that other theory, of which his books furnished him vague hints, that in a final battle against kings and capitalists and priests, mankind should become free" (*Moon-Calf*, 111).

In Davenport, as in Barry and Quincy, the public library was Dell's portal to a rich intellectual, political, and emotional life; moreover, Dell's wide reading enabled him to imagine and aspire to possibilities beyond his Davenport working-class life. Freeman mentored Dell, helping him publish his poetry in prestigious national magazines, such as *Century*, *Harper's*, and *McClure's*, and introducing him to literary Davenporters such as George Cram (Jig) Cook, scion of an old Davenport family, who wrote fiction and poetry and had taught English at Stanford University and the University of Iowa; and Charles Eugene Banks, former editor of the *Davenport Morning Republican* and the *Davenport Weekly Outlook*, who also wrote fiction, poetry, and drama and whom Dell credited with teaching him how to criticize and revise his own work (*Homecoming*, 92).

Dell also met William H. Fineshriber, the popular young rabbi of Davenport's Reform congregation. Dell had become involved with Davenport's Unitarian Church, led by the Reverend Arthur Markley Judy, but also began attending services at Temple Emanuel, remarking in *Moon-Calf* that Rabbi Nathan exhibited during his sermons "the qualities of quick and free intelligence which made his private conversation so delightful" (253). Harry Hansen, Dell's colleague on the *Times*, sometimes joined him on his evening rambles through Davenport, remembering "a walk with Floyd Dell to that Vandervelde [*sic*] park of which he speaks in 'Moon Calf.'" The two teenaged reporters would talk books on their walks; Dell introduced Hansen to the works of Huneker and Housman, and Hansen found Dell to be "the best and most fluent talker of all if you hit his subject."[11] And Dell also was introduced to Arthur Davison Ficke, son of former mayor C. A. Ficke. As he recounts in *Looking at Life* (1924), he did not immediately warm to this rising Harvard senior: "In the same Middle-Western town in which I lived, there was a young man who was supposed to be a poet. I disliked him. I considered that one poet was enough for a small town; and I had staked out my claim. Besides, I was poor, and he was rich. He was indifferent to politics, and I was passionately a member of the Socialist Party. So, naturally, I despised him."[12]

In 1904, Dell dropped out of high school shortly before his senior year would have begun and took a job in a candy factory to help support his family and enhance his Socialist activism with working-class job experience. However, he continued his education at the public library to compensate for not going back to high school. Three utopian novels in particular helped him solidify his commitment to Socialism, further refined his feminist consciousness, and revealed to him that what linked the two was exploitative capitalism: Edward Bellamy's *Looking Backward* (1888), Ignatius Donnelly's *Caesar's Column* (1890), and William Morris's *News from Nowhere* (1891).

Dell's first encounter with a feminist concept had come by way of a book. Ik. Marvel's *Reveries of a Bachelor* (1850) was a revelation to Dell because it advanced the notion that women were people who were capable of being more than wives and mothers. The books by Bellamy, Donnelly, and Morris took him further. These Socialist polemics, thinly disguised as fiction, are set in the late twentieth and twentieth-first centuries, showcasing ideal societies that have vanquished capitalism and thereby eliminated strikes, poverty, crime, and, of course, gender inequality, as well as a host of other social problems that plagued the late nineteenth century of Dell's youth.

But these books did more than facilitate Dell's development as a Socialist activist; they also facilitated his metamorphosis into a self-proclaimed "ardent feminist" who would go on to interrogate gendered power relations and explore current issues such as legalized birth control, free love, companionate marriage, and women's suffrage in periodical essays and articles, as well as in books such as *Women as World Builders* (1913), *The Briary-Bush* (1921), and *Janet March* (1923) and plays such as *King Arthur's Socks* (1916), *The Angel Intrudes* (1917), and *Sweet and Twenty* (1918).

   Looking Backward, set in Boston in the year 2000, introduces protagonist Julian West to a society in which "the industry and commerce of the country . . . were intrusted [*sic*] to a single syndicate representing the people, to be conducted in the common interest for the common profit."[13] Bellamy's Socialist utopia frees women from housekeeping chores, gives them the same national service obligation as men, and enables them to work at jobs that make best use of their abilities: "The reason that women nowadays are much more efficient co-laborers with the men, and at the same time are so happy, is that, in regard to their work as well as men's, we follow the principle of providing every one the kind of occupation that he or she is best adapted to" (*Looking Backward*, 124). Women as well as men are issued credit cards and have equal access to credit. Women are not dependent on men for their support; thus, there is no prostitution. "The sexes now meet with the ease of perfect equals, suitors to each other for nothing but love," explains West's guide, Dr. Leete (*Looking Backward*, 128). Moreover, women raised in this society are well positioned to assume leadership positions: there are female generals, cabinet officers, and judges. "Our women have risen to the full height of their responsibility as the wardens of the world to come, to whose keeping the keys to the future are confided" (*Looking Backward*, 131).

   In Donnelly's *Caesar's Column*, the utopian community is founded in 1988 high on a plateau in Uganda, where Gabriel Weltstein and his nearest and dearest have escaped after a worldwide revolution led by the Brotherhood of Destruction against the totalitarian capitalists, who have oppressed multitudes. Although Donnelly spends less time on his utopian vision than do Bellamy and Morris, like them, he advocates such Socialist projects as land reform, the abolition of the gold standard, and expanded government; his social critique anticipates that of Thorstein Veblen in his articulation of what Veblen would later term *invidious comparison, conspicuous waste*, and *conspicuous consumption*.

   Although *Caesar's Column* is less explicitly feminist than the other two works, Gabriel's Socialist utopia in Uganda is based on a constitution that guarantees universal suffrage and public education for both males and females and a living wage for all workers. Moreover, Donnelly ascribes a central role to his female characters, who exercise considerable agency in facilitating the revolution and consequent removal to Uganda. Gabriel's lady love, Estella Washington, escapes from Prince Cabano's harem to join the revolutionaries; the Brotherhood's leader, Maximilian Petion, enlists in the cause his sweetheart, Christina Carlson, a professional singer who supports her family with her talent.

A stronger feminist orientation informs William Morris's *News from Nowhere*, a novel in which the protagonist wakes up in a classless and largely agrarian England of 2090 where private property has been abolished and happy, friendly, and harmonious "neighbours" are engaged in arts and crafts in charming cottages surrounded by bounteous gardens, untroubled by politics, government, crime, prisons, poverty, schools, or industrial blight. The status of women, of course, is much improved; as an old man explains, "The men no longer have any opportunity of tyrannizing over the women, or the women over the men. . . . The women do what they can do best, and what they like best, and the men are neither jealous of it or injured by it." The old man then explains how this gender equality has come about: "Again, many violent acts came from the artificial perversion of the sexual passions, which cause over-weening jealousy and the like miseries. . . . What lay at the bottom of them was mainly the idea . . . of the woman being the property of the man, whether he were husband, father, brother, or what not. That idea has, of course vanished with private property, as well as certain follies about the 'ruin' of women for following their natural desires in an illegal way, which was of course a convention caused by the laws of private property."[14]

Dell had ample time to continue his program of reading after he was laid off from the candy factory after the Christmas rush. However, he soon found a better job. The "Watch the Tri-Cities Grow" edition that the *Times* published in November 1905 praised Dell, now one of its reporters, as "a young man of good education—an industrious reader that gives him a good command of the language. . . . He has been employed by the *Times* as a reporter for several months and has developed a talent not only as a gatherer of routine news, but as a writer of human interest reports that every once in a while attracts [*sic*] special attention."[15] Here Dell once again seized an opportunity to leverage his chutzpah when he created a job for himself reviewing German-language plays at Turner Hall, even though he didn't speak German. After he was fired from the *Times*, he moved to the rival paper, the *Davenport Democrat*, in 1906, but he was terminated the next year by that paper.

After Dell left his reporter's job on the *Democrat*, he moved to nearby Buffalo, Iowa, a few miles downriver from Davenport, to help his friend Jig Cook, who was operating a truck farm there. In Buffalo, he met an actual feminist. Cook's friend, Susan Glaspell, also a Davenport native, was a Drake University graduate who had recently left a job as a reporter in Des Moines to return to her hometown and launch a career as a fiction writer. Glaspell was a frequent visitor to the Cabin, as the Cook family's Buffalo estate was called, and eagerly joined Cook and Dell in creative collaboration. Their projected New Woman novel never came to fruition, but another joint endeavor did come to come to pass when, in 1907, Cook and Dell, with the enthusiastic participation of Glaspell, founded a society of free thinkers, the Monist Society, described in *Moon-Calf* as "a new free-thought society" comprising about fifty members (*Moon-Calf*, 283, 297).

Cook and Dell composed a manifesto for the society that reflected Ernst Haeckel's theory of the essential oneness of the universe. In *Moon-Calf*, Felix Fay and Tom Alden (the Jig Cook character) toss ideas back and forth:

> "We live in a world . . . where people are fooled by their dualistic habits of language. We think in terms of pairs of opposites. Day-and-night seems a reality and heat-and-cold; so why not good-and-bad? It's a primitive way of thinking; but it isn't true. The world isn't like that."
>
> "Sliced up into neat little categories," nodded Tom Alden. . . . "Balanced! Heaven and Hell! Chaste and unchaste women! It's just a logomachy—a war of words."
>
> "The universe isn't two things," said Felix. "It's one thing. Let's assert that. Monism!" (*Moon-Calf*, 288).

The Monist Society was also one of the Davenport influences that led Dell to feminism. In *Moon-Calf*, Felix and Tom, while discussing their favorite subject, women, experience a revelation. Tom wonders if women might not be like the universe, and Felix replies, "Perhaps it's humanity that is monistic. . . . Perhaps the trouble is that we try to think that men and women are opposed categories" (*Moon-Calf*, 292).

After voting for Debs in the 1908 presidential election, twenty-one-year-old Dell moved on to Chicago. He had done all he could do in Davenport; moreover, perhaps Cook's wife Mollie, with whom he had fallen in love, had proved to be too much of a temptation for him to remain. However, he took with him fond memories of the city where he had served his literary and journalistic apprenticeships and deepened his commitment to Socialism and feminism. Near the end of *Moon-Calf*, after he decides to move to Chicago, Felix Fay notes that he "had been happy in Port Royal: it had given him love, and painful wisdom, and the joy of struggle." Reflecting on the town's heritage, he observes that Port Royal was different from other midwestern towns: "No, it had a history of its own—from the first it had been a rebellious place. It had been founded so, by men who were different from others. . . . Port Royal had been built for such purposes—for growing up in" (*Moon-Calf*, 394).

In Chicago, Dell would continue to develop as a writer, editor, activist, and feminist. He became friends with and later the husband of feminist Margery Currey, a Davenport English teacher and Evanston, Illinois, native whom he had met when she was a guest of the Cooks at the Cabin in Buffalo. Margery relocated to Chicago and married Dell in 1909. The Dells' companionate marriage reflected their feminist values; as Dell put it, "We were equals, each contributing to the support of the home. . . . I was assistant homemaker and very much on the job" (*Homecoming*, 198).

Although he didn't think much of the way the Chicago local did its business, Dell continued to be an active Socialist. Margery's father, J. Seymour Currey, was writing a history of Chicago to which Dell contributed "Socialism and Anarchism in Chicago" and several other chapters. Dell also became friends with editorial writer Charles Hallinan and literary editor Francis Hackett, both Socialists who wrote for the *Chicago Evening Post*, where Dell had once again talked his way into a reporter's job. He was promoted to assistant in 1909 and, the next year, to associate editor of the paper's new supplement, the *Friday Literary Review*, becoming editor in 1911 when Hackett, the founding editor, left Chicago (*Homecoming*, 186).

When Dell moved to Chicago, he found a city that was becoming a leading cultural metropolis. Theodore Thomas's Chicago Symphony Orchestra; Daniel Burnham's, Thomas Wellborn Root's, and Louis Sullivan's architecture; the Art Institute's superlative collection; and the scholarly resources of the University of Chicago and the Newberry Library helped transform the city formerly derided as "Porkopolis" into one with cultural cachet. In particular, Chicago writers and critics were starting to put the city on the literary map. "For a short time, a half century ago the Second City became the first city of American literature," observes Robert Sklar.[16] Even curmudgeonly H. L. Mencken recognized

Chicago's cultural progress, proclaiming the city to be the literary capital of the United States: "In Chicago there is the mysterious something that makes for individuality, personality, charm; in Chicago a spirit broods upon the face of the waters. Find a writer who is . . . an American who has something new and peculiarly American to say and who says it in an unmistakable American way, and nine times out of ten you will find that he has some sort of connection with the gargantuan and inordinate abattoir by Lake Michigan."[17]

Dell was now the editor of a literary publication that was sold in many American cities as well as in London, Paris, and Berlin, soon to become, according to Douglas Clayton, "one of the nation's few important and genuinely influential literary publications."[18] Under his editorship, the *Friday Literary Review* grew in influence, and Dell became the leader of a literary movement—the Chicago Renaissance. First in the *Friday Literary Review* and later in the *Bookman*, Dell published a series, "Chicago in Fiction," as well as many book reviews, essays, and articles. Soon his work attracted national and even international notice. "For fifteen years I have been saying that Floyd Dell is the best critic of books in America," wrote Upton Sinclair, a sentiment that was echoed by Ezra Pound.[19]

Dell frequented one of Chicago's premiere literary clubs, the Little Room, and presided with Margery Currey over a literary salon, first in Rogers Park and later in Jackson Park, where Chicago's writers, artists, and intellectuals could find good talk, camaraderie, and literary advice. Eunice Tietjens, associate editor of *Poetry* magazine and a poet in her own right, recalled taking her poems to Dell and Currey's salon and getting some much-needed encouragement from Cook: "It was George Cook who said the thing that released me, as the right thing said at the moment has the power to do." She also sought help from Arthur Ficke, remarking that "he would put his finger with an unerring instinct on any thing slack or careless in my work and drive his point home with a fastidious irony that was devastating, but salutary."[20] Clayton concludes, "Two years after he had arrived in Chicago, still a mere twenty-three years of age, Dell had established himself as one of the most powerful figures on the city's cultural scene."[21]

However, the nascent literary lion had not abandoned his politics. Dell continued to espouse the positions on Socialism and feminism that he first articulated in the *Tri-City Workers Magazine* and later developed and refined in the book reviews and opinion pieces he published in the *Friday Literary Review* and other periodicals. R. Craig Sautter notes that in the *Friday Literary Review*, "Dell regularly examined origins and developments of the socialist movement in America and Europe. He also probed and promoted the emerging international women's movement and sought to examine psychological implications of changing sexual relations on characters and situations in the literature and society."[22]

Soon Dell's fame grew to the point where his contemporaries began putting him in their novels: he appears as Gardner Knowles in Theodore Dreiser's *The Titan* (1914) and as Hugh Brace in Dorothy Day's *The Eleventh Virgin* (1924). However, he maintained his Chicago relationships even after he left the city, contributing a review of Olive Shreiner's *Women and Labor* to the inaugural issue of the *Little Review* and two poems to *Poetry* magazine. He helped Sherwood Anderson, a regular at Dell and Currey's salon, find a publisher for his first novel, *Windy McPherson's Son* (1916), and assisted Dreiser, another regular, with revisions of *The Genius* (1915).

During the second decade of the twentieth century, Dell began to focus more narrowly on feminism and gender issues. "Feminism was in the air as well as in my mind," observed Dell. "Men and women were thinking about it, and eager to read about it" (*Homecoming*, 199). In 1912, Dell launched a front-page series on feminist leaders in the *Friday Literary Review* that was published the following year as *Women as World Builders*. The *Friday Literary Review*'s wide scope of readership and growing reputation exposed these feminist profiles to a large audience and, of equal importance, associated the women's movement of that day with optimism and progress.[23]

The common denominator that Dell found in the work of all of these women was their advocacy of freedom. "Men are tired of subservient women," claims Dell in the first chapter of *Women as World Builders*. "What men desire are real individuals who have achieved their own freedom."[24] Dell's commentary on Beatrice Webb and Emma Goldman acclaims the former's "statistical habit of mind" in the service of revolution and the latter for "holding before our eyes the ideal of freedom."[25]

Dell praises Charlotte Perkins Gilman for skewering "the ideal of love that is founded on masculine privilege."[26] He champions Emmeline Pankhurst's and Jane Addam's suffrage advocacy, stating that "there is only one argument for woman suffrage: women want it; there are no arguments against it."[27] In his discussion of Olive Shreiner and Isadora Duncan, Dell articulates a theory of embodied feminism that was decades ahead of its time, calling the two "sister workers in the woman's movement. They have each shown the way to a new freedom of the body and the soul. . . . It is to the body that one looks for the Magna Carta of feminism."[28]

Dell explains that while Shreiner liberated woman's hand from idleness, Duncan liberated woman's foot for play. Dell commends Margaret Dreier Robins for her work with the Women's Trade Union League, lauds Swedish feminist Ellen Key for advancing the argument that sex has a spiritual dimension, and concludes with an essay that applauds social worker Dora Marsden for her work in the cause of women's freedom, saying that "she makes women understand for the first time what freedom means. She makes them want to be free. She nerves them to the effort of emancipation."[29]

In a second feminist polemic, *The Outline of Marriage* (1926), Dell identifies and advocates the key to such freedom: legalized birth control, of which Dell had long been a proponent. The Comstock Act of 1873, as well as a number of state laws, prohibited distributing birth control information and disseminating it through the mail; a number of people, including Margaret Sanger's husband, William, had been arrested for their birth control advocacy. Dell, believing it to be his moral duty to violate such laws, surreptitiously passed along all the requests he received for birth control information to "other private individuals" who would send the letter writers the information that they requested (*Homecoming*, 252).

The Outline of Marriage promotes using birth control to enable companionate marriage and sets up a series of fictional interviews with "expert witnesses" to create and sustain interest. Says one of the characters, "I wanted somebody at breakfast who would make life more interesting for me all day, just seeing and talking with him; and somebody who would make me forget that I was tired when I met him again at night."[30] Dell's main strategy is to undermine the notion that sex in marriage must inevitably entail reproduction. "The modernity of marriage consists in the degree to which familiarly associated ideas of sex and reproduction are separated, in theory as well as in practice," argues Dell, and throughout the pamphlet, he emphasizes birth control as the means by which this goal is to be achieved.[31]

Dell's support for companionate marriage was due in no small part to his immersion in Socialist thought. As Kathleen Kennedy points out, "Socialists advocated a type of companionate marriage in which men and women formed relationships from their common commitment to political and social causes. Such relationships were ideally based on affection and a mutual respect. . . . The revolutionary man saw his wife as his companion, as an intellectual and political equal. Together, husband and wife worked for economic and political democracy."[32] Despite his own failed companionate marriage to Currey, Dell was no less of a believer in the principle and explored this topic in *Janet March* (1923), *Love without Money* (1931), and *Diana Stair* (1932).

Although he was a passionate advocate of freedom for women and the means through which they would be able to exercise that freedom—birth control, free love, and companionate marriage—Dell was not oblivious of what feminism had to offer men. "Feminism is going to make it possible for the first time for men to be free," he declares in "Feminism for Men."[33] Once again, Dell employs a materialist analysis to the woman question, reasoning that if women were given the opportunity to work at well-paying jobs, men would be free of the burden of supporting them. "At present the ordinary man has the choice between being a slave and a scoundrel," Dell asserts.[34] In this article, he endorses "social insurance for motherhood" that would "enable women to have children without taking away a man's freedom from him," a feminist goal that he predicts will be the last one to be achieved.[35]

Dell continues to explore the issue of female as well as male oppression with a materialist analysis: "Capitalism does not want free men," Dell claims. "It wants men with wives and children who are dependent on them for support."[36] He also ties men's reluctance to support gender equality to their need for power and control in a capitalist society that offers them little of either in the world of work: "Men don't want the freedom that women are thrusting upon them. . . . Men want the sense of power more than they want the sense of freedom. They want the feeling that comes to them as providers for women more than they want the feeling that comes to them as free men. . . . In short, they are afraid that they will cease to be sultans in little monogamic harems."[37] Dell contends that feminism would eliminate the harem and offer both men and women the freedom to live life fully in the world.

Dell is concerned for women's and men's emotional as well as economic well-being, arguing that feminism would free wives to be sweethearts and companions to men: "When you have got a woman in a box, and you pay rent on the box, her relationship to you insensibly changes character. . . . It ceases to be companionship, for companionship is only possible in a democracy. It is no longer a sharing of life together—it is a breaking of life apart."[38] Dell reasons that feminism, in offering women opportunities for equal pay for equal work, would free them from the box of domesticity. Once financially independent, they would be able to be sweethearts and companions of men in the wider world: "When she has left that box and gone back into the great world, a citizen and a worker, then with surprise and delight he will discover her again, and never let her go."[39]

Dell does not seem to realize that the domestic "box"—with its "cooking, clothes, and children"—would not magically vanish with the achievement of gender equality; it would still be there for women to come home to and deal with after working in the "great world." Moreover, he never mentions the most impactful benefit that feminism offers to men: more sex for them when legal birth control and social acceptance of free love and companionate marriage remove existing barriers to sexual freedom. In *Intellectual Vagabondage* (1926), he touches on this subject, writing that the progressive men of his generation supported feminist goals because "what we wanted was something for ourselves— a Glorious Playfellow."[40]

Despite these shortcomings, "Feminism for Men" is insightful in several respects. In the last section of the essay, he demonstrates that gender inequality is enabled by masculine privilege and presciently predicts that when male prerogatives are abolished, they will be replaced by a comradeship in which males and females will equally enjoy formerly male pursuits such as smoking, drinking, swearing, participating in athletic games, and voting.[41] Dell wasn't always so prescient; in another essay in *Looking at Life*, "Dolls and Abraham Lincoln," he poses what he believes to be a rhetorical question: "Can you imagine an actor running for President?"[42]

When it came to free love, Dell practiced what he preached. He fell in love, as the song goes, too easily, too fast, and, one might add, much too often. When Jig Cook brought Mollie Price home to Davenport, Dell had promptly become infatuated with Cook's "happy and sparkling and delightfully talkative" bride (*Homecoming*, 172). In Chicago he was involved with photographer Marjorie Jones; the actress Kirah Markham, also wooed by Theodore Dreiser; and several other women in his circle. A series of adulterous affairs contributed to the breakup of his marriage to Currey.

Dell left Chicago in 1913 and relocated to Greenwich Village, in Ludwig Lewisohn's words an "already full-fledged radical, poet and stylist."[43] Dell quickly became the center of Village intellectual life as he had been in Chicago—writing plays for the Liberal Club, frequenting Mabel Dodge's salon, hanging out at Polly Holladay's restaurant, giving talks on feminism around town, and organizing dances called Pagan Routs to benefit the *Masses*, a radical magazine at which he had become, in editor Max Eastman's words, "my superbly gifted associate editor."[44]

The *Masses*, under Eastman and Dell, published fiction, poetry, essays, cartoons, and articles, blending politics and culture to bring its Socialist message to a popular audience and, in its mingling of art and politics, exemplifying the Greenwich Villagers' holistic approach to social change.[45] As Dell put it, the *Masses* was dedicated "to fun, truth, beauty, realism, freedom, peace, feminism, revolution" (*Homecoming*, 251). Upon discovering that the magazine's contributors weren't paid, Dell told Eastman that the first time that he wasn't paid, he wouldn't say anything, but if it happened a second time, he'd be gone. This materialistic stance, however, is balanced by the tribute that Eastman wrote to Dell in *The Enjoyment of Living*:

> Floyd Dell may have some faults as a human being, and I have even thought at times that I detected one or two, but as a friend in need to a man who has dragged down upon himself through sheer foolhardy zest for life the job of running a co-operative magazine, he is without a flaw. I never knew a more reasonable or dependable person, more variously intelligent, more agile in combining sociability with industry, and I never knew a writer who had his talents in such complete command. . . . Floyd brought to *The Masses* a gift of literary criticism as fine as we had in the country.[46]

At that time, many Greenwich Villagers summered in Provincetown, Massachusetts, and Dell showed up there—Forrest Gump-like—during the summer of 1916, just in time to participate in another historic cultural movement. His Davenport friendship with Cook and Glaspell drew him to their new amateur theatre company, the Provincetown Players, and later that summer, Dell became one of its twenty-nine charter members. The four one-act plays that Dell staged at the Provincetown reflect his commitment to egalitarian leftist politics but enact views that are more nuanced and ambivalent than those he articulated in his earlier writings. According to Clayton, Dell "felt that the behavior and ideas of his generation of young rebels was, sadly enough, best treated ironically."[47] His three comedies are described by Helen Deutsch and Stella Hanau as "civilized little plays, clever, polished and really funny," and by G. Thomas Tanselle as "charming bits of foolishness with some skillful sophisticated dialogue."[48] However, there is more to them than Deutsch, Hanau, and Tanselle acknowledge. They freely employ the irony Clayton mentions to interrogate the positions on love, romance, sex, marriage, and gender roles that their characters espouse and acknowledge the ambiguities and complexities of the gender issues that they explore. The themes that link them are the tenuousness of the romantic ideal, the ephemeral nature of love, the power of desire, and the equally strong pull of conventionally gendered mores.

King Arthur's Socks, the first of Dell's one-act comedies to be staged by the Provincetown, is thematically similar to *The Angel Intrudes* and, like that play, mixes temporalities to convey the universality of its concerns. Clayton says that the play's theme reflects a perennial paradox for Dell: "That the rebellious generation of which he was a part was also traditional in its underlying desires and principles."[49] Set in Camden, Maine, the comedy draws on the King Arthur legends, with leads named Lancelot Jones and Guinevere Robinson, to demonstrate that radical beliefs about love and romance did not originate with Socialism or bohemianism. Christine Stansell makes this point, writing that many of the Village radicals were unaware that they were not inventing the free love wheel: "Their elevation of sex outside of marriage to a point of principle derived from a long political and intellectual tradition, going back to utopian socialists in France and England in the early nineteenth century."[50]

Guinevere, who sits at home darning socks while her husband, Arthur, is away on a trip, disparages seemingly progressive approaches to love to her friend Vivien: "Don't tell me you're going in for this modern, free-love stuff, because I won't believe it. You're not that kind of fool, Vivien."[51] As it turns out, Vivien is in love with the artist Lancelot Jones, as are Guinevere and her housemaid, Mary, who has canoodled with him in his studio but, true to free love principles, denies that their tryst gives her a claim on him. Lancelot, played by Eastman, professes love for both Vivien and Guinevere; the latter's response is "I'm not in love with you. And you're not in love with me. We're just two wicked people who want to kiss each other."[52] In *King Arthur's Socks*, Dell represents the bourgeois and radical positions on love and marriage without taking sides.

The most interesting and well-crafted of the three comedies, *The Angel Intrudes*, is, in Clayton's words, "a satiric spoof on the transience of youthful love and idealism."[53] However, the ambiguous character of the Angel gives it additional depth. Mounted on December 28, 1917 (a little over a year after *King Arthur's Socks* was staged), *The Angel Intrudes*, according to what Dell told Dreiser, uses Anatole France's novel *Le revolte des anges* (1904) as an intertext to examine the multidimensional nature of love, deriving its energy from the juxtaposition of the sacred and the profane, the conventional and the radical. Like his other Provincetown comedies, *The Angel Intrudes* endorses neither the bohemian nor the conventional view of love, romance, and marriage but enacts the competing claims of committed love and passionate romance.

This three-hander's protagonist is forty-year-old Jimmy Pendleton, a jaded sybarite who acknowledges the ephemeral nature of love and is planning to run off with his sweetheart, young Annabelle. For Jimmy, love is "a blithering, blathering folly," while Annabelle believes in a true love that is an eternal love, the kind of love she thinks that she feels for Jimmy.[54] However, comic reversals ensue when Jimmy's guardian angel shows up and seduces Annabelle, who becomes smitten with the Angel and decides to abandon Jimmy, her erstwhile true love, while Jimmy is moved by this state of affairs to profess undying love for Annabelle.

The reversals in the play satirize those who hold uncompromising views of love: the bohemian who subscribes to free love and the more conventional proponent of everlasting, unchanging love. The most intriguing character in the play is the Angel, who has come to Earth because he is "attending to important business" and then flies off to Jimmy's apartment to try on a mortal identity.[55] After he smokes a cigarette and drinks a cocktail for the first time, he dons a spare suit of Jimmy's and proceeds to seduce Annabelle and run off with her. However, in the final and decisive action of the play, the Angel returns to Jimmy's apartment to retrieve his wings.

Although the Angel had found immortality tiresome and longed to become a mortal human who could enjoy earthly pleasures, his return for his wings demonstrates his uncertainty about relinquishing eternal glory to experience human sexuality. His ambivalence about love and sex reflects the ambivalence and instability of beliefs about love shared by Jimmy, Annabelle, and Dell's Greenwich Village peers. For all his polemicizing about feminism, free love, birth control, and companionate marriage, Dell, in this play, is taking a more nuanced position as he emphasizes and illuminates the complexities of modern love and sexuality.

A one-act comedy that Dell produced with the Provincetown in 1918, *Sweet and Twenty*, also explores the questions of whether love is true and eternal or ephemeral and fleeting, and whether passion and romance are stronger than the quotidian banalities that threaten to destroy modern relationships. The play nods to Chekov in its cherry orchard setting, where the young protagonists, Helen and George, fall in love. As in Chekov's play, this cherry orchard is for sale along with the estate of which it is a part; however, unlike the feckless aristocrats of *The Cherry Orchard*, who are living in the past, Helen and George are very much people who make the most of the present.

The play's title alludes to Shakespeare's *Twelfth Night*, a comedy that, like Dell's play, interrogates many kinds of love and includes the lines, "In delay there lies no plenty / Then come kiss me, sweet and twenty."[56] Each character thinks the other is married; then they kiss and learn that they are single. Yet the fact that they thought each other to be married and still indulged their desire proves an obstacle to their betrothal, as does their discovery of incompatibility: despite their mutual physical attraction, his passion is Socialism and hers is dancing. "If we married we might be happy for a month," he tells her, acknowledging the transitory nature of romantic love.[57] The bohemian critique of marriage is further articulated by the Agent, who, like the Angel in Dell's earlier comedy, intrudes, admonishing them: "Marriage, my young friends, is an iniquitous arrangement devised by the Devil himself for driving all the love out of the hearts of lovers" (95).

The Agent puts the case bluntly: romantic love, when consummated in marriage, proves incompatible with the realities of daily living. He uses the analogy of a picnic—something that's fun once in a while but that no one wants to do every day: "How many books would you write, young man, if you had to go back to the campfire every day for your lunch? And how many new dances would *you* invent if you lived eternally in the picnic stage of civilization? No! The picnic is incompatible with everyday living. As incompatible as marriage" (96). Although the Agent urges George and Helen not to "stifle love with civilization, nor encumber civilization with love," his views are hilariously undermined when he turns out to be a bigamist with fourteen wives and an escaped mental patient who was driven mad by the works of George Bernard Shaw (98). Well, as Joe E. Brown remarked to Jack Lemmon in *Some Like It Hot*, "Nobody's perfect!"

Like Dell's three Provincetown comedies, *A Long Time Ago* deals with both timeless and very timely concerns, yet this play is quite different in tone, theme, and theatrical mode. Mounted in 1917 and ostensibly set in the ancient past, *A Long Time Ago* evokes, with its ironic title, a very contemporary situation: the entry of the United States into World War I and the resistance to that action that was pervasive in Dell's Greenwich Village. Here Dell's pacifism, grounded in the Socialist Party's historic opposition to all wars and, more specifically, in the *Masses'* opposition to the United States' involvement in World War I, is much in evidence. The Fool's early remark, "What do you suppose all that fighting was for if it wasn't to put an end to quarreling for all time," evokes the shibboleths of the day: that World War I would be the war to end all wars and that it would make the world safe for democracy.[58] The play's allegorical characters—a pacifist and love-besotted Fool, an adventurous Prince, an amorous Queen, and a war-mongering Old Woman—universalize its theme beyond the events of 1917. Thus, the play not only critiques the politics of Dell's day but also examines questions that have confounded Western civilization for centuries: whether the human lust for warfare is part of human nature and whether war can bring about peace. Moreover, like Cook's *The Athenian Women*, it enacts the age-old conflict between the proponents of love and peace and those who relish warfare and believe that conquest is a prerequisite for peace and love.

As with *The Angel Intrudes*, Dell builds this one-act play on role reversal. The Fool, who professes pacifism and love early in the play, is transformed by three kisses from the Queen into a would-be hero eager for battle. The Prince, who had set sail for war, returns to his Queen, stating, "I know that the only thing that is real in all the world is love."[59] Thus, the action of the play is governed by peripeteia: love makes a hero out of the Fool and a fool out of the Prince. The play ends on a cynical note with the Prince dead; the Fool still eager for battle; the Old Woman egging him on; and the Queen renouncing love for war, suggesting the futility and yet the inevitability of war and the moral vacuity of jingoism.

Dell found himself in a pacifist drama of his own the following year when he and other *Masses* staffers were brought to trial by the federal government for violating the Espionage Act of 1917. Accompanied by his current girlfriend, the poet-playwright Edna St. Vincent Millay, Dell, as well as Eastman, cartoonist Art Young, and business manager Merrill Rogers, came to court every day to hear themselves described by the prosecution as dangerous radicals.[60] Dell, who had published an article in the *Masses* in support of conscientious objectors, was accused of thwarting military recruitment efforts.

Writing about this experience in "Not without Dust and Heat," he describes the trial as a grim joke: "The Government of the United States was going to devote its energies, its time, and its money to the task of sending us to prison for the next twenty years."[61] Dell frames the controversy as a free speech issue: "We were Socialists. We were pacifists of a sort. And we were, most particularly, believers in free speech and the rights of individual opinion. . . . We were fully agreed only upon one point, that it was a good thing to have a magazine in which we could freely express our individual thoughts and feelings. . . . And so—here we were, on trial."[62]

As prosecutors read from the *Masses*, Dell observes ironically that "I felt a certain pride as an author in having my own writings, among others, treated as matters of social and political importance. . . . There are different ways in which the State may encourage its young writers; if this present ceremonial was open to criticism from some points of view, yet it could not be said that it was lacking in impressiveness."[63] With his tongue firmly in his cheek, he notes that as Eastman took the stand and proceeded with a crash course in Socialist theory, the men of the jury "were having a spiritual adventure as gratifying as it was doubtless unique in their experience."[64]

The *Masses* defendants were tried twice and twice reprieved when two hung juries failed to convict them. Although they would not go to prison, the trials put an end to their magazine, which was unable to survive its suppression by the United States Post Office, one of more than four hundred such publications that the Post Office refused to mail out during World War I.[65] The following year, Dell left his Greenwich Village life behind when he married Socialist and suffragist Berta (B. Marie) Gage;

moved to Croton-on-Hudson, New York; fathered two sons; and began lecturing locally and throughout the country on child-raising, progressive education, love and marriage, and the complexities of the Machine Age and publishing prolifically in a variety of genres throughout the 1920s and into the 1930s.

Although he was an editor of the short-lived *Liberator* (which Eastman and his sister Crystal had kindled from the ashes of the *Masses*) and served as a contributing editor on the *New Masses*, by the late 1920s he had developed other priorities, and when he resigned as contributing editor from the latter publication in 1929, editor Mike Gold took him to task for selling out as soon as he had made some money from *Little Accident*, the Broadway hit he had had the year before, and abandoning the Socialist cause. In 1935, Dell began working as a writer and editor for the Federal Writers Project, a program of the Works Progress Administration; he also wrote speeches for WPA director Harry Hopkins, WPA assistant commissioner Florence Kerr, and United Mine Workers president John L. Lewis, and he wrote the final report on the WPA when that program was legislated out of existence in 1943. He later worked for the United States Information Agency, retiring from government service in 1947.

Dell's biggest success was his first novel, *Moon-Calf*, which went through eleven printings and sold over thirty-eight thousand copies. Clayton attributes *Moon-Calf*'s success in part to Dell's ability "to capture that delicate balance between alienation and affection that had always characterized his feelings for the Midwest."[66] Except in *Moon-Calf* and *Homecoming*, Davenport never featured largely in the books he published during the twenties and thirties. Nevertheless, the spirit of early twentieth-century Davenport was present in nearly everything he wrote. "In Davenport Dell found the community, the intellectual resources, and the opportunities that allowed him to think of himself as a politically committed aesthete," concludes Timothy H. Spears.[67]

Cherishing the memories of the city he called Port Royal, Dell never failed to give it credit for helping make him the writer he became. In a letter to Davenport journalist Ralph Cram, he wrote, "I seem to remember that our poetry and our youth did not fail to find something of old Athens in Davenport. . . . When I hear about the drab life of the Middle West, I think to myself, 'Davenport was never like that!' I remember that I was out of a job and looking for work at times; but I found beauty there, and the splendor of ideas, and friendship, and love."[68]

4

George Cram Cook Runs for Congress in the Red City of Iowa

It is difficult to write even a review that concerns Cook without emotion, for his glowing, rich, child-sweet personality haunts, like the echoes of a bell, the memories of all who knew him.

—ARTHUR DAVISON FICKE

George Cram Cook had always been temperamentally at odds with the world he lived in, and with the respectable class into which he was born.

—FLOYD DELL

ON OCTOBER 1, 1908, George Cram (Jig) Cook, author and activist, got his comeuppance at a meeting of Davenport's exclusive Contemporary Club. He and his Socialist friends—poet Floyd Dell and mail carrier Frederick (Fritz) Feuchter—had stopped by to raise the consciousness of the city's intelligentsia. In his autobiography, *Homecoming*, Dell frames the incident as a clash between old guard members and the enlightened Socialist guests: "George, of course, was bringing Fred and me to put the conservatives to rout and the liberals to shame with devastating Socialist argument." Poet Arthur Davison Ficke, now practicing law with his father (former mayor C. A. Ficke), read a paper on the use of the injunction in labor disputes, a factual, objective paper that Dell termed "intellectual pablum." Dell relates how Cook then got up to critique Ficke's paper:

> But it wasn't the George that Fred and I knew who got up. It was the George who belonged to respectable Davenport, hated it, feared it, was morbidly sensitive about what it thought of his eccentricities—the George who had been brought up as a gentleman, whose father was there looking on and wishing to be proud of his big, handsome son—it was *that* George, never seen clearly by Fred or me before, who got up, tried to modulate his voice to the right tone, a tone implying that it wasn't anything to be excited about, the tone of an amiable, academic discussion between gentlemen—got the tone, lost it, and then said his say like a schoolboy in the presence of his father with the family clergyman looking on.

Then it was Dell's turn, and by his account he did no better, characterizing his own commentary as "merely ill-tempered, bad-mannered, foolishly rude." After he became incoherent, he looked to Fritz for help. But Fritz, too, struck out: "He sputtered. He grew ponderous. Then, overcome by righteous and ineffective anger, he burst into vehement broken English. . . . He ended in furious unintelligibility, sat down, and wilted." Dell reports that after the meeting, he and Cook drank away the evening's humiliations and then repaired to Cook's house, where his wife, Mollie, asked them if they had overthrown the capitalist system. Cook replied, "We met the enemy and we are theirs."[1]

Dell's storytelling gifts are evident when his account of the Contemporary Club fiasco is compared to those of others. E. E. Cook's version was laconic and devoid of drama: "There were 20 present, Arthur Ficke read a very able paper on 'Injunctions Against Labor' and a long and interesting discussion followed."[2] The *Davenport Daily Times*'s account was more informative, hinting at the evening's drama but saying nothing about the Socialists' failure to articulate their critique effectively and terming the discussion "a rousing reception by both the pros and the cons." The story went on to note that "opinions were expressed in about as many ways as there were members present and if there is any point relative to the injunction question that was not given an airing last evening, it still remains to be brought to light. The Republican, Democratic, Socialistic, and, in fact, all political views were considered from every standpoint."[3]

In *Homecoming*, Dell recollects that he became well acquainted with Jig Cook via the Monist Society, a group of free thinkers founded in

1907 that was grounded in the philosophy of Ernst Haeckel, whose best-selling *The Riddle of the Universe at the Close of the Nineteenth Century* (1899) argued for the essential oneness of reality. Cook wrote to author-journalist Charles Eugene Banks, who had recently left Davenport for Chicago, that "Floyd Dell and I have formed—or are—the Monist Society of Davenport for the propagation of our philosophy in the guise of religion, or religion in the guise of philosophy" (*Homecoming*, 191). He and Cook were asked to write the society's manifesto, which stated, "We welcome all who are ready to reject conventional beliefs which are in contradiction to their intellectual convictions; believing that the forces of progress may be strengthened" (*Homecoming*, 193). In her biography of Cook, *The Road to the Temple*, Davenport novelist Susan Glaspell paints an arresting picture of Monist Society members:

> A few of the more fearless clubwomen, wanting to know all that should be known about education, even though it involved "certain matters of sex"; a number of free-thinking Germans—long since more interested in free-thinking than in thinking; the town atheist, who had filled that position for so many years that he was viewed as having a certain solidity, even with something like gratitude—giving us an atheist without doing us much harm; disappointed politicians quite ready to identify themselves with the new movement; young people always to be seen at the Public Library, people glad to have some place to go on Sunday, and various lonely souls who hoped in this bare hall of the Monist Society to find their own, for they had not found their own in Davenport.[4]

The Monist Society was not the only progressive organization with which Cook had become affiliated. Before he met Dell, Cook was an enthusiastic proponent of what Dell termed a "Nietzschean-aristocratic-anarchist philosophy," but Dell persuasively explained and advocated his Socialist politics, and Cook became a member of the Socialist Party in 1907. Dell characterized Cook's political evolution as he made "a new picture of the world for him": "The theory of historical materialism, or economic determinism was new to him, and gave him a fresh imaginative grasp of history, politics, and social movements" (*Homecoming*, 150–51).

Jig's background was hardly that of a proletarian. Born in 1873, he was the great-grandson of pioneer settler Ira Cook, grandson of Congressman John P. Cook, and son of E. E. Cook, the attorney for the Chicago, Rock Island, and Pacific Railroad. The younger of two sons, he apparently was never expected, as were his brother Ruel and Arthur Ficke, to become a lawyer and join the family law firm. Brought up by

Ellen (Ma-Mie) Dodge Cook to revere the art and literature of ancient Greece, the music of Beethoven, and the writings of Ruskin, he was then educated at Davenport's Griswold College, the University of Iowa, Harvard College, and the universities of Heidelberg and Geneva.

After teaching stints at Iowa and Stanford, he returned to Davenport in 1903 with his new wife, Sara Herndon Swain, to live on his family's country estate in Buffalo, called the Cabin, a few miles downriver from Davenport. The author of two historical novels—*Roderick Taliaferro* (1903) and *In Hampton Roads* (1899), the latter coauthored with Banks—as well as a nonfiction book that chronicled his experiences in a Spanish-American War training camp, *Company B of Davenport* (1899), Cook planned to combine farming with writing. If he could support himself as a farmer, Cook reasoned, he would be free to write what he wanted rather than be obliged to write for money.

Cook's life took a turn for the worse when his wife left him in 1905 and his third novel, *The Balm of Life*, failed to find a publisher. However, a bright spot on the horizon was his burgeoning friendship with Dell, who moved to Buffalo to live with Cook at the Cabin and work on the farm with him after Dell was fired from his reporter's job at the Davenport *Democrat*. "In the whole history of Iowa there has probably not been so stimulating a hired man," remarks Glaspell. "I do not know how good Floyd was for the farm, but he was good for the farmer. . . . The cock-sure young Socialist, for whom Herbert Spencer had synthetized knowledge, kept biting at this Nietzschean, anarchist, profound and lazy man of God, the way a terrier would worry a St. Bernard" (*RTT*, 181–82).

For his part, Dell appreciated what his Harvard-educated friend could bring to his own intellectual development, his formal education having ended with his junior year of high school. The two sat each evening by the fireplace, smoking their corncob pipes and talking of poetry, science, history, and world politics: "What I wanted from George was something gentler and more mellowed than my raw youthful brew of tonic ideas— the wine of an older vintage of thought, a more urbane and ironic and doubtful wisdom" (*Homecoming*, 156).

Dell also believed that each man represented the other's lost youth— Cook envying Dell's youthful potential and Dell seeing in Cook the educated man he could have become had he not dropped out of high school. This arrangement gave the two friends ample opportunity to discuss politics as they hoed potatoes and cucumbers and drove them to market;

these discussions led to further collaboration, and, led by Dell, Cook soon became further involved in leftist politics. In 1908, he became one of the leaders of a local effort to prevent the extradition to Russia of dissident Christian A. Rudowitz, whose case had become a cause célèbre because, if extradited, Rudowitz could face the death penalty.

Earlier that month, Davenport's Reform rabbi, William H. Fineshriber, had interrupted his series of sermons on Jewish American problems to speak on Rudowitz's plight, taking for his text Job 34:37: "For he addeth rebellion unto his sins."[5] On December 16, a citizens' meeting was held in Armory Hall "to express the sentiment of liberty-loving American citizens of Davenport about Russia's attempt to extradite political refugees from the United States." A Davenport Political Refugees Defense League was organized, and Cook was elected secretary-treasurer of the two-hundred-member group, working on a steering committee alongside Fineshriber, former mayor Henry Vollmer, Baptist minister Dr. H. O. Rowlands, Congregationalist pastor R. K. Atkinson, and attorney and district deputy of the Knights of Columbus E. M. Sharon.[6]

The league adopted resolutions opposing Rudowitz's extradition, addressing them to the president of the United States; in so doing, the league joined the efforts of the Tri-City Social Service Club, which had passed a similar resolution the previous week. The league also resolved to seek additional information on other such political dissidents currently residing in the United States and charged Cook with communicating with the Political Refugees Defense League of Chicago to seek abrogation of the United States' extradition convention with Russia and with circulating a petition to send to President Roosevelt.[7] The December 28 issue of the *Times* carried a front-page story on the Chicago group's resolution that asked Secretary of State Elihu Root to review all evidence before extraditing Rudowitz. A month later, the *Times* reported success for the opponents of Rudowitz's extradition: Root refused to extradite Rudowitz, stating that the nation's treaty with Russia prohibited political extraditions.[8]

Jig's venture into politics was not the only new undertaking on which he embarked in 1908; that spring, he married twenty-two-year-old Mollie Price, whom he had met two years earlier when she visited the Tri-Cities on an excursion with the Chicago Press Club. E. E. Cook, a member of Davenport's Commercial Club, was serving on a committee that helped the local press club with the arrangements for the excursion.

Jig tagged along to help his father play host to the Chicago journalists, and Banks (at that time third vice president of the Chicago Press Club) introduced him to Mollie, a feminist who had worked on Emma Goldman's magazine, *Mother Earth*.

Mollie was perfect for Jig both politically and personally, and she made a welcome addition to the Monist Society crowd. His friends were charmed by her, especially Dell, who was still living at the Cabin when Cook brought his bride to Buffalo. Cook was busy writing *The Chasm*, so Mollie and Dell began spending a lot of time together. She was everything that Tom Alden and Felix Fay had fantasized about when they talked of "The Very Improbable She" in *Moon-Calf*. Now, quite improbably, She had arrived. "I want a girl that can be talked to, and that can be kissed. And I want it to be the same girl," Felix declared (252–53). Dell found that girl in Mollie and promptly fell in love with her.

College educated and adventurous, Mollie was an anarchist who had posed nude for a sculptor and acted with a road company. "Mollie and I talked and laughed together happily," remembered Dell. "Neither of us guessed how mournfully superannuated a husband in his middle thirties could feel as he looked from his study window and saw his young wife with his young friend, a girl with a boy, eager, happy, care-free. He brooded, twisting his forelock" (*Homecoming*, 175). The two became so close that Cook, hearing them argue, remarked, "Anybody would think, to hear you two quarreling, that it was you who were the married couple." During the summer of 1911, Floyd and Mollie finally consummated their relationship when he was back in Davenport for a visit. By then both Glaspell and Cook had moved on while Mollie remained at the Cabin. Floyd and Mollie went joyfully to bed, agreeing that their sexual liaison would last only for that one night (*Homecoming*, 173, 176; Ben-Zvi, *Susan Glaspell: Her Life and Times*, 110).

Cook's life, never free of complications, remained fraught. During his engagement to Mollie, he fell in love with Susan Glaspell, with whom he had become better acquainted through the Monist Society; a few years later, they would play leading roles in the censorship battle waged by Davenport's Ethical Society. In *The Road to the Temple*, Glaspell reprints his account of the night that friendship became love: "They stood close together in snow-covered Central Park, beneath the illimitable white blaze of the winter stars. . . . The two human minds were filled with the wonder of it, as though they had never before looked out upon the universe through the cone of night. . . . His hand moved suddenly toward her in gratitude. She drew hers from her muff. There in the starlit night their fingers exchanged a quick pressure. It sealed something between them—wide as the stars, long as time" (*RTT*, 200–201). During Cook and Glaspell's romance in Davenport, Mollie gave birth to Nilla in 1908 and Harl in 1910. Free love can get complicated.

On October 6, 1910, Cook took his leftist politics to Davenport's intelligentsia when he delivered "Some Modest Remarks on Socialism" to the Contemporary Club, a group he had addressed in 1906 with a paper on evolution. Fortunately, he was a bit more eloquent this time than he had been in 1908 when he attempted to critique Ficke's paper on injunctions. Yet the confident tone of the talk belies its title; Cook was anything but modest in his claims for the future of Socialism. "We do not think we need give you more than twelve more years," he told Davenport's power wielders.[9] Cook did make an effort, though, to rebut the common misconception that a Socialist government would eliminate current social and political structures, stating that while society was constantly evolving and changes would be made, nothing that worked well would be destroyed by Socialism and no change would be made without reason.

The main change that Socialism would effect, according to Cook, would be to make America's nominally democratic institutions more democratic: "Democracy, as we all know, has never been tried in America. We intend to try it. We are not blind to the fact that at present the proposal to introduce democracy is red-hot revolutionary Socialism."[10] As he wrote in a brief essay for the *Masses* two years later, "Let the government own the trusts, and the people own the government."[11] He enumerated the benefits of a Socialist government: it would eliminate graft and fraud, more efficiently administer government functions, reduce inequality, destroy the trusts, and eradicate wage-slavery.

As he endeavored to convince his father, Ficke's father, Mayor Mueller, former mayor Vollmer, and other Davenport dignitaries that the control of the city's industries and utilities should be handed over to cigar makers, brewery workers, plumbers, and carpenters, Cook asked the following question: "If Socialism *is* inevitable and if it really is the one remedy for the ills developed by the uncheckable concentration of the bulk of the national wealth in a few socially irresponsible private hands, why should anyone desirous of social improvement shilly-shally along any longer with demonstrably inadequate measures and programs which offer everything but the two things needful—transformation of the privately owned trust into the publicly owned industry, and control of government by the people?"[12]

The previous two years had found Comrade Cook, as Glaspell liked to call him, getting increasingly involved in Socialist Party activities. "Soon there were Socialist picnics at the Cabin," wrote Glaspell, "the class-conscious working-men and their wives coming down on the 'Firefly' which once brought the young people of 'the master class' for suppers or week-ends. The old log-house received the proletariat as serenely as it had the bourgeoisie" (RTT, 190). In the election of 1908, Cook ran as the Socialist candidate for Scott County superintendent of schools, and in March 1910, Davenport's Socialists nominated him as their candidate for Congress from the Second Congressional District of Iowa.

Glaspell describes his campaign as thoroughly rooted in the Iowa soil: "Congressman Cook's grandson ran on the Socialist ticket. When he made a speech he might talk about cucumbers and baby rabbits" (188). Cook's rallies were literally down-to-earth: "As a truck-farmer receiving for my vegetables about fifty per cent of the price the eater pays, with expense of production taking another twenty-five per cent, I am not inclined to regard surplus value as a myth. They might at least give the Socialist farmer, who for four or five months fertilizes, plows, plants, fights striped bugs and hauls cucumbers to town, the satisfaction of naming the fifty cents he doesn't get. I can think of lots worse names to call it than surplus value" (RTT, 189).

Cook's campaign for Congress was ignored by the Times, as was that of the Prohibition Party candidate, John Bernet. The Times campaigned vigorously and relentlessly for Republican Charles Grilk, publishing weekly stories on his run for office throughout the fall. Grilk's major opponent, Democrat I. S. Pepper, was mentioned only when it was to Grilk's advantage. One story described Grilk as if he had already won the election: "Mr. Grilk is demonstrating his splendid qualities as a speaker and thinker. The Second District will have no reason to regret its determination to send Mr. Grilk to Congress as its representative."[13] The Harvard-educated Grilk enjoyed not only the unwavering support of the Times but also that of no less a Republican luminary than former president Theodore Roosevelt, who, after a breakfast of fish and game with local dignitaries hosted by Alice French, shilled for Grilk before a crowd of thousands in Davenport's Central Park.[14]

Nevertheless, Grilk managed to snatch defeat from the jaws of victory. Pepper carried every county in the district, garnering 19,815 votes to Grilk's 16, 971. Socialist Cook was able to win a mere 1,507 votes, although he did handily prevail over Bernet and got twice as many votes as the previous Socialist candidate for Congress, Michael T. Kennedy, got in the 1908 election.[15] Davenport's Socialists would share a small triumph in the presidential election of 1912; their candidate, Eugene V. Debs, would garner 11 percent of the vote there compared to 6 percent in the nation at large, earning Davenport the nickname of "the Red City of Iowa."[16]

The following spring saw the publication of Glaspell's and Cook's Socialist novels. Cook's *The Chasm* was published by the Frederick A. Stokes Company in 1911, as was Glaspell's *The Visioning*. Both stories are set partly in the Illinois-Iowa Tri-Cities and their environs, and the books' premises are essentially the same: an entitled young woman steeped in upper-middle-class values and prejudices is converted to Socialism by a working-class man with whom she becomes romantically involved. But the parallels end there. Glaspell's Katie Wayneworth Jones lives with her brother, an army captain who is stationed on Arsenal Island, located in the middle of the Mississippi River across from Davenport. Her novel is fast-paced and lively with engaging dialogue, sharply drawn characters, and arresting and occasionally melodramatic events, culminating in Katie's introduction to the New by Socialist handyman Alan Mann.

Susan C. Kemper characterizes *The Chasm* as "primarily a Bildungsroman, tracing the intellectual and emotional growth of a spoiled only child, a member of America's privileged elite, into a courageous humanitarian capable of bold action in the cause of social justice."[17] However, Cook's problem, as Kemper points out, is that he attempts to accomplish this transformation via a dialectic that does not resolve easily into a synthesis, complicated as it is by a third ideological position represented by Marion Moulton's Russian suitor and future husband, Count De Hohenfels, who is an admirer of Friedrich Nietzsche and his theory of the Superman.[18] Moreover, the historical romance that structures the story is heavy with preachy political debates between Marion (the daughter of a Moline, Illinois, plow manufacturer loosely modeled on John and C. H. Deere) and one of the gardeners on her family's estate, Walt Bradfield. These debates slow down the action, although the novel does become more eventful toward the end, as Marion and Walt escape from Russia in a fishing boat headed for Finland. "It is a book of thrills and theories," pronounced *Literary Digest*.[19]

Marion's status in Moline is similar to that of Cook in Davenport, and her interest in radical ideas initially seems to be motivated by her rebellion against her father and the restrictions that his power and social standing place on her freedom, just as Cook's early fascination with Socialism may have been, in part, a means of breaking away from his father to establish his own identity. The plot hinges on Mr. Moulton's breaking Marion's engagement to De Hohenfels; Marion retaliates by making friends with Bradfield. Their conversations suggest those Dell and Cook probably engaged in that brought Cook into the Socialist fold, as well as the mental gymnastics Cook may have undergone before he embraced Socialism:

> "Do you know your father sells a plow costing him seven and a half for labor and materials, for thirty-five dollars? Do you know he has crushed the union which stands for a little better pay, a little better house, a little better life for all these workingmen? Do you know these working-men receive less than one-fifth the value of their labor?"
>
> "I don't know just what proportion of the total value they receive. Did these workmen buy the steel and wood to make the plows?"
>
> "No, the steel was mined and made, the wood cut and sawed by other workers who received only a fraction of the value they created out of the natural earth."
>
> "Why didn't your workers organize the United States Plow Company themselves? Why did they leave that to my father and grandfather?"
>
> "The time was not then ripe. They had not learned how to work together in great factories. They know how now; your grandfather did perform a service to society. Was it so great that society should give him and his heirs forever despotic power over their labor and life?"[20]

Marion's dialogues with Bradfield are interrupted by De Hohenfels's arrival in Moline. De Hohenfels believes that the evolution of a biologically superior race of men is as inevitable as Bradfield believes the dictatorship of the proletariat to be. Thus, in De Hohenfels, Marion, and Bradfield, Cook represents the three stages of his own intellectual development: the Nietzschean elitist, the rebellious free thinker, and the radical activist, respectively. The Marion-Bradfield-De Hohenfels triangle also allows Cook, according to Walter Rideout, "to argue the inferiority of Nietzsche to Marx with the drama of dialogue and action, even though the two male characters rarely come out from behind the philosophies respectively assigned to them."[21] After the Nietzschean triumphs over the Socialist in the contest for Marion's hand, the newly-weds journey to the count's estate in Russia. There Marion witnesses for herself the beginnings of the Russian Revolution and the poverty and oppression that precipitated it. Finally converted to Socialism, she becomes a spy for a band of revolutionaries headquartered in her husband's village. After De Hohenfels learns of her radical activities and divorces her, Marion is discovered to be a spy by the Russian government and flees to Riga, where she is reunited with Bradfield; the two then make their escape.

The two novels' contemporaneous reception is also where the parallels end. *The Visioning* garnered a thoughtfully appreciative review in the *Davenport Daily Times* that faulted Glaspell only for insufficiently developed minor characters.[22] The novel also attracted quite a bit of national attention. While not all of it was positive, *The Visioning* earned kind words from the *Bookman*, the *New York Times*, the American Library Association's bulletin, the *Outlook*, the *North American Review*, and the *Chicago Evening Post*.[23]

The Chasm, by contrast, appears not to have been as widely reviewed, with *Book Review Digest* citing only one entry in 1911 and none for the following two years.[24] The novel did receive some laudatory comments from Glaspell's friend Sinclair Lewis, at that time employed on the editorial staff of the Frederick A. Stokes Publishing Company when *The Chasm* was being considered for publication there.[25] But *The Chasm* has not worn well, despite Lewis's admiration for it. "Indeed, it is difficult to conceive of the book as a novel, for it seems to have been written solely to convey certain socialist ideas," argues G. Thomas Tanselle. "No opportunity is overlooked for inserting a socialistic reference or parallel." Tanselle believes that the difference between *Roderick Taliaferro* and *The Chasm* indicates the degree of Dell's influence on Cook.[26]

Cook soon found that it was time to leave Davenport. Friends who had been sympathetic to his first divorce and remarriage were less supportive of his romance with Glaspell. When Dell and his wife, Margery Currey, visited Davenport during the summer of 1910, Cook confessed his love for Glaspell, and Dell, still enamored of Mollie and concerned for the Cook children, was less than enthusiastic. The next year, when George asked for Dell's support, he replied, "How many times are you going to ask me to believe in your eternal love for some girl?" (*Homecoming*, 205). Fineshriber was also disapproving, writing to Dell that "the whole miserable conventional liaison down here has ruffled my smooth feathers." "I wish I were going to be in your home tonight! Davenport is lonely," wrote Glaspell to Dell in May 1911.[27] The obliquity and brevity of her comments about the uncomfortable situation in which she found herself reveal her bitterness and disappointment: "For both of us, there were old friends who were friends no longer" (*RTT*, 219).

Cook headed for Chicago, as Dell had done in 1908; early on, he found work on a dictionary and became part of the literary coterie revolving around Dell that would later be called the Chicago Renaissance. He attended productions of Maurice Browne's Chicago Little Theatre and those of the Irish Players during their American tour, was introduced to postimpressionist art, and enjoyed the good talk at Dell and Currey's salon, also frequented by Sherwood Anderson, Theodore Dreiser, and Arthur Ficke, who made regular visits to Chicago to socialize with the *Poetry* magazine crowd and nourish his poetic gift. When Dell was promoted to editor of the *Friday Literary Review* of the *Chicago Evening Post*, Cook left his dictionary job to become Dell's associate editor, writing many book reviews and essays and later sending back a weekly "New York Letter" after he relocated to Greenwich Village.

Cook's sojourn in Chicago was not lengthy. He moved on to New York City in the fall of 1912, and soon there was good news. He wrote Dell on April 13, 1913, that "tomorrow, Floyd dear, I shall be on the Fall River boat, en route to Provincetown. With Susan. The mayor of Weehauken across the river is going to give us permission at noon tomorrow. . . . Susan and I are happy people."[28] As Cook indicated, the two were married on April 14, 1913; they then settled down in Milligan Place in Greenwich Village.

Their ten-year marriage was not without its trials. Cook, claiming that alcohol freed his creative spirit and encouraged collaboration, became increasingly dependent on wine and liquor and was often publicly and obstreperously drunk. This kind of behavior must have been difficult for Glaspell to live with, although she makes the amazing statement in *The Road to the Temple* that "a woman who has never lived with a man who sometimes 'drinks to excess' has missed one of the satisfactions that is like a gift—taking care of the man she loves when he has this sweetness as of a newborn soul" (*RTT*, 324). And it must have been difficult for Glaspell, who believed in the enduring power of true love, to countenance Cook's continual dalliances with actresses and writers in Provincetown and Greenwich Village, most notably Ida Rauh, known as the Duse of MacDougal Street, who was widely viewed as Cook's mistress.

Two years later, Dell, Cook, and Glaspell would make American theatre history when they founded the Provincetown Players. The journalists, activists, writers, and artists who joined this amateur group had one thing in common: they were committed to social change. As Leona Rust Egan explains, "For these versatile bohemians, writing plays was just another experiment in trying to change the world."[29]

Everything from the problems of the homeless to academic freedom to World War I to birth control inspired the Provincetown playwrights. Some of their plays focused on the personal lives and loves of the Players themselves, such as Neith Boyce's *Constancy*, which spoofed the love affair between Jack Reed and Mabel Dodge, and *Enemies*, by Boyce and Hutchins Hapgood, which drew on their marriage. "The Provincetown Players' lives became their public art," asserts Egan. "What they talked about in their bedrooms and private salons was grist for their scenarios. . . . There were few perceptible boundaries between what they did and what they wrote."[30]

A pertinent example in support of Egan's assertion is *Suppressed Desires*, a one-act comedy that Cook and Glaspell had written in their home in Milligan Place and then submitted to the Washington Square Players. When it was rejected because it was "too special," Cook and Glaspell staged it informally during the summer of 1915 at the Hapgood home, with Cook, Glaspell, and Glaspell's college friend Lucy (Lulu) Huffaker playing Stephen Brewster, Henrietta Brewster, and Henrietta's sister Mabel, respectively (*RTT*, 250–51). *Constancy* had been done there earlier that evening; a more formal production of both plays was mounted later that summer, along with Wilbur Daniel Steele's *Contemporaries* and Cook's *Change Your Style*, on the Provincetown Players' first stage, the Wharf Theater.

Although derided by C. W. E. Bigsby as "an inconsequential comic satire in two scenes" and by Tanselle as "a rather shallow satire on psychoanalysis," *Suppressed Desires* has become a favorite of community theatre groups and college dramatic programs and was a mainstay of the Provincetown Players' review bills.[31] Robert Karoly Sarlos believes that *Suppressed Desires* has held up fairly well: "The script retains much of its flavor; . . . although the dialogue is repetitive and awkward in places, the puns supporting the comedy are lively and the theme is still timely."[32]

J. Ellen Gainor is even more appreciative, cautioning that *Suppressed Desires* should not be evaluated by aesthetic criteria alone; rather, the play's significance in terms of its historical and cultural contexts should be factored in as well. Gainor emphasizes the ways in which *Suppressed Desires* "critically examines contemporary marriage and heterosexual relationships . . . and reveals the tension between the lingering Victorian values of monogamous marriage and the emerging bohemian code of free love" and how it "epitomizes the remarkable synergy between the arts and the culture at large in Greenwich Village at this highly charged time."[33]

Like many of the Provincetown plays by Dell, Cook, and Glaspell, *Suppressed Desires* spoofs the pretensions and overblown enthusiasms of the Greenwich Village/Provincetown crowd for the New, whether it be the New Science, the New Art, or, in this case, the New Psychology. Brenda Murphy argues that a likely source for the play is Max Eastman's "Exploring the Soul and Healing the Body," in which he discusses one of Freud's cases, a woman who had a suppressed desire for her brother-in-law.[34] Egan traces the play to a story that Cook wrote at age ten in which he visited the Brewster family on Long Island and called young Stephen Brewster "Step-Hen."[35]

As Glaspell, Dell, and several others have related, Freudian psychology was so popular among early twentieth-century bohemians that it had become a fad, a way for Greenwich Villagers to show that they were au courant and authentically avant-garde. Helen Deutsch and Stella Hanau report that psychoanalysis was "being taken up seriously by every housewife and professor."[36] Edna Kenton, a member of the Provincetown Players' Executive Committee, asserts that "Freud and Jung and the minor psychoanalysts were just then beginning to be translated and Washington Square and its many radiating little streets bloomed into a jungle of misunderstood theory and misapplied terms."[37] Dell was especially taken with Freudianism; he underwent psychoanalysis and found the process to be quite beneficial, but, like

Glaspell and Cook, he deplored those who went overboard in their obsession with all things Freud.

Such a person is *Suppressed Desires*'s Henrietta Brewster; her love affair with psychoanalysis is driving her husband, Stephen, to the end of his tether: "Psychoanalysis. My work table groans with it. Books by Freud, the new Messiah; books by Jung, the new St. Paul."[38] Two weird dreams and a couple of Freudian slips later, Henrietta's sister Mabel, as well as Stephen, is off to the Freudian analyst.

But when it turns out that Stephen's dream of receding walls means that he has a suppressed desire to be free of his marriage and Mabel's dream of being a hen who is told to "Step, Hen" means that she has a suppressed desire for her brother-in-law, Henrietta, hoist on her own petard, falls out of love with psychoanalysis. Jig and Susan's send-up of the would-be bohemian who latches on to the latest craze only to become disillusioned with it when its ramifications are found to be incompatible with middle-class mores would be repeated a few years later in their second one-act comedy, *Tickless Time* (1918). Dell, too, would delight in scratching a radical to find a bourgeois who cherishes conventional values in *King Arthur's Socks* (1916), *The Angel Intrudes* (1917), and *Sweet and Twenty* (1918).

Cook's own five Provincetown plays were a mixed bag. His three one-act plays are witty satires that incisively skewer the overly enthusiastic proponents of the New who go off the deep end about psychoanalysis, postimpressionist art, and new scientific theories mainly because they *are* new and in vogue, perhaps making the point that many Greenwich Village bohemians were not all that different from those Midwestern conformists they were so eager to get away from. Eddy Knight, a character in *Tickless Time*, sums up this attitude succinctly: "If other people have got the wrong dope, you've got to have the wrong dope or be an off ox" (Ben-Zvi and Gainor, 87). Cook's solo effort, *Change Your Style*, demonstrates how this mindset drives reputations and prices in the art world.

First mounted on September 9, 1915, *Change Your Style* was one of the first four plays produced by the Provincetown Players during their inaugural year and the first to be staged in the first of their three theatres, Mary Heaton Vorse's fish house on Lewis Wharf. This one-act play was cleverly cast, with two practicing artists, both charter members of the Players, portraying artist characters: B. J. O. (Bror) Nordfeldt played himself, the postimpressionist Bordfelt, and Charles Demuth played the neophyte artist Marmaduke Marvin Jr. Max Eastman, editor of the *Masses*, played Bordfelt's opposite number, the academic painter Kenyon Crabtree, modeled on muralist Kenyon Cox and academic painter Charles Webster Hawthorne; Cook himself played Marmaduke Marvin Sr.

Deutsch and Hanau recall that the play "drew a hilarious picture of the differences between the academic and the modern schools of painting."[39] This deceptively simple play operates satirically on at least three levels. In depicting the fluctuating value of Marmaduke Jr.'s abstract painting, Cook is satirizing the false values that link commercial and artistic worth in the art world. A second target of satire is the faddishness of the New, here represented by Bordfelt's postimpressionist school of art. Third, a metatheatrical reading sees the play, with its scorn for commercialized painting, as Cook's indictment of a commercialized Broadway.

Like Cook and Glaspell's collaborative efforts, the action of *Change Your Style* is driven by reversals. Marmaduke Marvin Sr. decides to continue to fund his son, avant-garde artist Marmaduke Jr., after he learns that Crabtree hasn't sold a painting all year but one of his son's experimental paintings has been sold to Myrtle Dart (a thinly disguised Mabel Dodge) for $100. "This hectic stuff is all that gets talked about," Crabtree tells Marmaduke Sr.[40] While Marmaduke Jr. vows to change his style and join Crabtree's academic art school to avoid becoming commercialized, his father urges him to stay with Bordfelt and make more money.

However, Marmaduke Sr.'s newfound appreciation of postimpressionism is soon eroded by Dart, who demands her money back when she learns that the abstract painting represents not the sacred umbilicus, as she had thought, but the eye of God, and Crabtree tells him that the New Art's notoriety has not often been accompanied by financial gain for the artist. He complains of Bordfelt's school, "They are ruining us without in the least benefiting themselves. Nobody buys their stuff."[41] Marmaduke Sr. then reverses his decision to withdraw financial support from his son because "the revelation he has made of his business capacity forces me to the conclusion that I owe it to society to support him—as a defective!"[42]

Change Your Style premiered at the Provincetown before theatre critics started regularly reviewing their productions; however, a few twentieth-century scholars have weighed in on the play. Sarlos's opinion is mixed: "Despite its heavy-handed humor, the play is interesting because issues have hardly changed, and the clichés (e.g., the artist corrects a painting that was hung upside down) were presumably still fresh."[43] Murphy calls the play "a revealing look at some basic conflicts and values that prevailed in the group and its audience."[44]

Although Bigsby says that "several of Susan Glaspell's one-act plays for Provincetown were genuine trifles," surely *Tickless Time* is not one of them.[45] Of the three one-act plays in which Cook had a hand, *Tickless Time* is undoubtedly superior, in terms of both stagecraft and complexity of conception—an assessment shared by Heywood Broun, a newspaper critic who, after viewing the three plays on the bill for December 20, 1918, pronounced *Tickless Time* "easily the best," high praise as the bill included Eugene O'Neill's *The Moon of the Caribbees*.[46]

Directed by the authors, *Tickless Time* was inspired by a sundial that Cook had made for their Provincetown garden. Described by Tanselle as "a highly amusing way of pointing out the idealist's eternal dilemma of alienation or compromise" and by Dorothy Chansky as "captur[ing] the anxieties and pieties of a particular segment of American theatergoers—progressives, bohemians, left-wing intellectuals—even as it goes about deflating them," *Tickless Time* centers on Ian Joyce's plan to replace his household clocks with a sundial that he has constructed to establish "a first-hand relation with truth" and the obstacles placed in his way by his wife, Eloise; his friends Eddy and Alice; and his cook, Annie.[47]

As the film version of *Dinner at Eight* concludes, the veteran actress Carlotta, played by Marie Dressler, is visibly taken aback when Kitty, the platinum blonde floozy played by Jean Harlow, tells her that she has been reading a book. Kitty then informs her that according to the book, "machinery is going to take the place of every profession." "Oh, my dear," replies Carlotta. "That's something you need never worry about."[48] Carlotta and Kitty's exchange is indicative of the anxiety about the increasing industrialization and mechanization that was becoming prevalent in the culture. The words *machine* and *mechanical* recur throughout *Tickless Time*, evoking the term *machine age* with which contemporary observers characterized the twentieth century.

In *Love in the Machine Age* (1930), Dell elaborates on the term when he writes in his first chapter that "it is often said that the mechanization of our modern world is inevitably destroying romantic love and family life."[49] The term also calls to mind dramatic efforts by contemporaries of Glaspell and Cook that focus on the dehumanizing effects of industrialization, such as O'Neill's *The Hairy Ape* (1922), Elmer Rice's *The Adding Machine* (1923), and Sophie Treadwell's *Machinal* (1928). Unlike these plays, however, which enact the serious and in some cases tragic consequences of the machine age, *Tickless Time* responds to anxieties about the era with humor as Ian and Eloise bury, dig up, rebury, and dig up the clocks that represent a mechanized and standardized existence.

Another context that informs *Tickless Time* is that of science and philosophy. Staged thirteen years after Einstein published his theory of special relativity and two years after he developed his theory of general relativity, the play reflects contemporaneous interest in and concern about these new scientific advances as well as about time and space in general that stemmed from Einstein's work, as seen in Ian's statement that "space is rhythm and time is flow," which evokes Einstein's concept of the space-time continuum (Ben-Zvi and Gainor, 82).

Typical of the interest that laypeople of the day expressed in the New Science is this comment of Neith Boyce: "The 'new science' is marvelous and fairylike—all those things about light, and getting rid of matter, time and space (which only religious people could do before!)."[50] Other modern theories were referenced as well. Gainor writes that "it is more than likely that [Cook and Glaspell] wrote their short comedy as a dramatization of the philosophy of Henri Bergson. His 1889 treatise, *Essai sur les donnees immediates de la conscience*, 'was primarily an attempt to establish the notion of duration, or lived time, as opposed to what he viewed as the spatialized concept of time, measured by a clock, that is employed by science."[51]

Like *Change Your Style*, *Tickless Time* turns on reversals. At first Eloise is thrilled with the prospect of telling time by the sun but balks at burying her grandmother's clock, her alarm clock, their watches, and the cuckoo clock that their dinner guests (Eddy and Alice Knight) gave them as a wedding present. She tells her husband that she is afraid of tickless time and becomes even more skeptical when Eddy and Alice arrive and begin to question Ian's project. When she learns that the sundial is completely accurate only four times a year, Eloise digs up the clocks, and Ian buries the sundial.

Aghast at this latest development, Eloise begins to rebury the clocks. However, when Annie learns that she is doomed to a clockless kitchen, she walks off the job, whereupon the Joyces, confronted with this unthinkable calamity, proceed to dig up the clocks once again to bring her back, and a neighbor, Mrs. Stubbs, digs up the sundial, proclaiming her regard for truth. As with all comedies, the play ends in reconciliation, with both clocks and sundial accepted into the Joyces' lives as Mrs. Stubbs proclaims, "Let them that want sun time have sun time and them that want tick time have tick time" (Ben-Zvi and Gainor, 91).

Tickless Time joins *Suppressed Desires* and *Change Your Style* in satirizing radical pretensions that implode when they come in conflict with the realities of bourgeois culture. Ian's grand plan to rid himself of a mechanized and standardized middle-class lifestyle and align himself with the truth of sun time falls apart when it fails to accommodate the actualities of everyday life, such as catching trains and cooking dinner. As Kristina Hinz-Bode remarks, "The play hits home the notion that whoever insists on 'cosmic truth' when all other people live by 'standardized lies' will fall through the network of human relations."[52]

Linda Ben-Zvi, who, along with Gainor, has noted that Glaspell is always critical of extremism in any form, points out that "by carrying Ian's drive for truth to its extreme and situating it in opposition to the daily details of life, Susan and Jig are able to make a hilarious spoof of dreamers and the pitfalls they face."[53] And Aegyung Noh sees the play as poking fun at elitist modernists: "Ian's idiosyncratic notion of time delivered to the 'standardized' crowds evokes the proud elitism discovered in modernists who positioned themselves as visionary individuals in battle with the collective bourgeois culture."[54]

Noh makes a further point when she reads the play as a critique not merely of the modernist project but also of the male modernist project, calling the play "a revealing, though a bit hyperbolic, picture of gender politics within Modernism" and characterizing the movement of the play as "this male-female dynamic of the one pushing his idea and the other pressed and patronized to embrace it, or one dumping a wedding present—symbol of a blissful marriage—without a second thought and the other trying to salvage it."[55]

In viewing the play through the lens of gender, she is joined by Hinz-Bode and Gainor. Hinz-Bode points out "the obviously gendered contrast in which the play treats the concept of truth in the conflict between Ian and Eloise," and Gainor calls the play conservative in its reinscription of gender and class hierarchies, arguing that Glaspell and Cook have created "characters conforming to deeply rooted conventions of heterosexual gender behavior, including an intellectually domineering and condescending husband who masks his superiority through the guise of protectiveness . . . and a flighty, shallow, and emotional wife who relies on her husband for guidance."[56] Noh goes even further in arguing that the play's "caricatures of a modernist-type visionary and his less intellectual wife indeed call for a feminist reappraisal of the kind of Modernism led by artists such as Ian and his real model Cook" and in suggesting that if Ben-Zvi is correct in attributing the play mainly to Glaspell, *Tickless Time* is actually Glaspell's satirical critique of male modernists.[57]

Tickless Time's metatheatrical critique of representation is another way that the play interrogates modernism, questioning notions of absolute and unmediated truth as well as representation's ability to convey truth and transcend form. While Ian aspires to apprehend ideal time and rejects clocks as mere "approximations" of time, he learns during the play that he cannot escape such approximations. Like Claire Archer in Glaspell's *The Verge*, he cannot elude representation. And as the play demonstrates the inevitability of representation, it also critiques the modernist project of the New. Ezra Pound's instruction to "make it new" is shown in *Tickless Time* to be a hopeless dream.

Although new forms did indeed result from modernist experimentations, such as Picasso's Cubist paintings and Joyce's stream-of-consciousness fiction, they never completely transcended form. Like Claire, who attempts to get beyond form with her experimental plants, they merely end up with a different kind of form. The process of burying and reburying the clocks and the sundial interrogates the validity of representation itself and the likelihood of getting beyond it, as Ian learns that the sundial is merely another representation of time and truth and not the unmediated route to Ideal Time and Truth that he has envisioned.

The two full-length dramas that Cook wrote and staged for the Provincetown are as solemn and ponderous as his one-acts are lighthearted and witty; unlike Glaspell, he had not learned how to convey ideas through dramatic action, as she does so effectively in her best-known play, *Trifles*. The United States' entry into World War I prompted Cook to write his first full-length play, *The Athenian Women*, inspired by a performance of Euripides's *The Trojan Women* by Maurice Browne's Chicago

Little Theatre that he saw in 1912 and one of Aristophanes's *Lysistrata* that he attended in New York City in 1913, as well as by the veneration of all things Greek that he learned at his mother's knee. "Jig's life-long study and love of Greek life and thought bore fruit in this play," observe Deutsch and Hanau.[58]

The Provincetown Players mounted *The Athenian Women* in the spring of 1918. Their first full-length production, it comprises three acts in six scenes with three sets and thirty-three speaking parts, a nearly overwhelming effort for the small theatre company that was acclaimed by the *Boston Transcript* as "a real triumph in production against staggering physical odds."[59]

Like Cook's other plays, *The Athenian Women* reflects the context of its genesis. Although set in ancient Greece, it incorporates two elements of the New, pacifism and feminism, as it unites Athenian courtesans and wives in the Temple of Demeter who deny their husbands comfort until a looming war with the Peloponnesus is averted. Cook's critique of the United States' involvement in World War I is reflected in Lysicles's assertion that "the democracy of Athens cannot be safe until Spartan militarism is completely destroyed" and in Aspasia's response to Pericles's plan to build an iron circle of defense around Athens: "A ring of conquered neighbors will not make Attica safe. Conquer them as often as you please and they will still revolt. Another spear undoes what a spear has done."[60]

In his 1923 preface to the play, Cook calls it "a tragedy of the death of the possible beauty of life, ancient or modern, in war" (*Athenian Women*, 8). The play continually opposes war with beauty, as the dialogue between the protagonist, Aspasia, and the antagonist, Pericles, demonstrates. For Pericles, peace equals weakness and war equals security and strength, and security and strength are needed before beauty can bloom. For Aspasia, war is the enemy of beauty and peace is its nurturer, as evidenced by the flowering of the arts that Athens enjoyed during the fourteen years of peace between wars with the Peloponnesus and the destruction of the great works of art and architecture that ensued when war resumed, symbolized by the death of the artist Phidias.

Kemper points out that in this respect, "*The Athenian Women* transcends the simple category of 'anti-war play,' expressing as it does some of Cook's deepest perceptions about the ambivalence of human nature and the precarious position peace and beauty occupy in the affairs of men in the rare times they are able to prevail at all."[61] Tanselle agrees, stating that "the real theme of the play . . . is the senseless destruction in war of man's greatest achievements," and goes on to point out that "the play emphasizes that war is an unqualified evil, capable of destroying all the best in life."[62]

But does the play rise to the level of tragedy, as Cook asserts in his preface? Is the protagonist, Aspasia, a tragic heroine who attains self-awareness through suffering brought about by a flaw or error in judgment? Although Aspasia's efforts to establish a lasting peace are ultimately unsuccessful, the resulting horrors of the resumed war cannot be laid at her doorstep. The news that all of the Theban prisoners have been killed does not bring to Aspasia any self-knowledge but rather the knowledge that the dream of a beautiful, peaceful Athens that could be a beacon for the world has ended. "And it is we—we first—the nobler-minded—whose minds have first darkened back into barbaric hate," she laments. "O Pericles—our great bright circle—this life which has created beauty—we have been but a candle burning in the darkness—a point in space—a bright ripple on a black wave—a boat on a shoreless sea!" These lines return us to the play's contemporary context of an America engaged in a futile war to end all wars and make the world safe for democracy (Athenian Women, 320).

The Athenian Women suffers from two main faults: heavy-handed, tone-deaf dialogue and a dearth of dramatic action. Barbara Ozieblo concludes that "Cook was no Aristophanes, and the comedy inherent in the subject is expunged by his serious purpose and idealistic rhetoric, which ultimately fail him."[63] Unlike Dell's A Long Time Ago (1917), an allegorical staging of the futility of war, or Edna St. Vincent Millay's Aria da Capo (1919), a critique of war enacted in commedia dell'arte style, Cook failed to find an innovative mode of theatre to render its age-old ideas fresh and new.

Comprising little more than a series of speeches, The Athenian Women comes across at times as a tiresome antiwar polemic. Broun identified another problem with the play, pointing out that it enacted "the too obvious attempt to state present-day problems in terms of Greece."[64] Dell, whom Deutsch and Hanau list as playing the architect Ichtinos as well as Antiphon, leader of the Oligarchist Party, said that the play was "noble in idea and conception, but somehow not dramatic, though I tried to persuade myself that it was at the time" (Homecoming, 266).

The Spring, Cook's second full-length play (written during the year-long sabbatical that Cook and Glaspell took during the Players' 1919–20 season and staged on January 31, 1921), was rooted, like *The Athenian Women*, in Cook's boyhood experiences. Calling Cook "the strangest mixture of Red Indian-American Greek culture these strange young States have ever produced," Kenton describes the genesis of the play: "The Cooks' summer cabin, out from Davenport, was just off the forgotten old Indian road leading from the Mississippi inland to the Iowa Hills. His boyhood had been impressed with a sense of America's ancient life; he had absorbed Indian lore like a sponge."[65]

Set in what is now Rock Island, Illinois, on land where Chief Black Hawk's village, Saukenuk, once stood, the play juxtaposes Native American subject matter with psychic phenomena. Sarlos points out that the play is governed by the assumption that "a higher order of knowledge than is now thought possible can be achieved through actively seeking and encouraging unconscious (extrasensory) communication between the living."[66] The proponent of this view is a young psychology instructor, Elijah Robbins, who uses hypnosis to explore the psychic gifts of Esther Chantland, the emotionally fragile daughter of his department head. Esther has seen a vision of the past in the eponymous spring where Black Hawk's daughter, Namequa, saw visions one hundred years earlier and which is now part of the Robbins estate.

While Elijah wants to continue to work with Esther as a medium, Chantland vigorously opposes his plan, aware that people might view Esther's gift as mental illness. "I don't want people's tongues to start wagging over this relapse," he argues.[67] Thus, the play, like *Suppressed Desires*, *Change Your Style*, and *Tickless Time*, enacts the conflict between the Old and the New. Here the New is represented by Elijah, one of the proponents of new parapsychological theories and methodologies, such as extrasensory perception, mental telepathy, automatic writing, and hypnosis; Chantland, a traditional empiricist, stands for the Old.

Elijah presses his case because he believes that "there have not been more than five or six sensitives whose vision equals [Esther's]"; he is certain that if he continues to probe Esther's unconscious via hypnosis, their work will result in "a new unfolding of the human soul" that will reveal "the hidden oneness of all men" and thus precipitate all kinds of wonderful advances in human culture (*The Spring*, 45, 47, 49). Cook's Socialist worldview is evident when Elijah explains that these wonderful advances will include the extinction of war and "spiritual communism," which might even spark "communism of material wealth" (*The Spring*, 50). Professor Chantland just as vigorously opposes Elijah's plan and threatens to forbid Esther to see Elijah and have him fired if he persists.

The Spring earned some kind words from Cook's contemporaries that were reproduced on the circular that advertised the play. William Archer judged it to be "a work of arresting theme and highly imaginative workmanship," and Charles Darton praised the play's "poetic quality of fine strain."[68] Surprisingly, critic Kenneth Macgowan called *The Spring* the hit of the Provincetown season.[69] However, Alexander Woollcott dubbed it "less a play than a séance," and Dell believed that it "had a moving idea in it, muffled in an awkward plot."[70]

Deutsch and Hanau offered the most insightful critique of *The Spring* and *The Athenian Women*: "Jig's half-thoughts, so pregnant when spoken in his beautiful voice, with the weight of his unuttered associations behind them, were unfinished and aborted in the mouths of actors."[71] Ozieblo expresses a similar view: "Cook's effort to endow his characters with a poetic language reflecting the profound beauty of intrinsic unity results in a primitive—not to say childish—and highly stilted prose." Gainor calls the play melodramatic and contrived.[72]

Kemper views *The Spring* as indicative of Cook's continuing interest in human evolutionary potential, first seen in *The Chasm*: "In *The Spring*, Cook sought to portray the beginnings of a new evolutionary development in mankind—the first groping steps towards human unity and the ideal society of the future."[73] Esther's vision of Namequa and her subsequent transcription of Black Hawk's words via automatic writing demonstrate Faulkner's dictum that "the past is never dead. It isn't even past." Throughout its seven scenes, the play demonstrates how the past inhabits the present, reflecting Cook's Monistic philosophy.

Kemper calls the play a melodrama, as does Tanselle, for whom it exemplifies "Cook's desire to attack . . . the narrow-mindedness of college administrations and—by extension, the reluctance of the world at large to accept new ideas."[74] The views of Archer, Darton, and Macgowan were shared by the critic from the *New York Evening Post*, who compared Cook to Tolstoy and O'Neill in his theatrical experiments, stating that Cook had "produced a piece of sustained emotional and intellectual interest" and praising the poetic dialogue that Ozieblo criticized.[75]

These positive readings of *The Spring* become less persuasive, however, when the play is viewed through a feminist lens. Although Kemper argues that the play's theme is one of spiritual oneness and reconciliation, Cook's idealistic Monism is undercut by the toxic gendered power relations that are enacted when two strong male characters contend for control of an emotionally vulnerable female, one trying to commodify her to further the cause of science and, most likely, his own professional renown, and the other trying to "protect" her from what he believes to be dangerous parapsychological experiments, as well as from the gossip and scrutiny attracted by these experiments that might jeopardize his professional standing. "I see a gorgeous life-work, Miss Chantland—*if* I can find a good psychic sensitive," enthuses Elijah, while Chantland conspires to have Esther committed to a mental institution rather than surrender her to his ministrations (*The Spring*, 48).

Although the play places much emphasis on Esther's "powers," these powers prove to be very meager when confronted with those of the two men who are vying for control of her. Her resulting breakdown under the strain of being torn between the man she is falling in love with and the father to whom she owes filial obedience appears reversible only by Elijah, who again uses hypnosis to bring her to herself. "A conscious mind like mine directing unconscious powers like yours—two such as we might grow to be one person—one person in two minds—gifted as no one mind has been gifted—a new kind of genius—the end of loneliness!" he raves (*The Spring*, 50). In a culture that until fairly recently operated under the common law principle of coverture, in which a husband and wife were considered to be one person and that person the husband, there is little doubt here about who that one person would be, however sincere Cook's Monist beliefs. Elijah's repetition of the words "I want" four times in a seventy-nine-word speech belies his idealistic vision of a partnership between the two (*The Spring*, 51).

After its premiere at the Provincetown, *The Spring* was unwisely moved uptown to Broadway, where it closed after twenty-four performances because, according to Sarlos, "the artistic effect of *The Spring* did not keep step with its ambitious plan, and the staging did not and could not remedy the mediocrity of the script."[76] His comment about the staging underscores another problem with Cook's full-length plays: although he was strongly committed to experimentalism, there is nothing remotely experimental or innovative about the structure and stagecraft of *The Spring* and *The Athenian Women*. Despite his enthusiasm for and efforts to effect innovation in plays such as *The Emperor Jones* with its blue dome, *A Long Time Ago* with its buskin-like boots worn by the actors, and *The Game*, which featured Marguerite Zorach's postimpressionist-inspired set design, Cook was never as forward looking when it came to staging his own plays.

Although his literary output was not prodigious, George Cram Cook became a key interpreter of the New with his sparkling satires on the New Psychology, the New Art, and the New Science and with his theatre company that promoted innovation and experimentation. Nurtured in Davenport, Iowa, his Socialist politics, with its emphasis on collectivism and communitarianism, was the perfect complement to his devotion to the Greek ideal of art as the expression of a divine community. The conjoining of these two passions informed his theatre practice as he developed and led the first theatre collective in the United States. More-over, he had a lasting impact on the writers with whom he interacted, making his mark on American literature and theatre through the sheer power of his lived beliefs.

Cook's neighbor Hutchins Hapgood offers a sensitive description of Cook's process in his autobiography, *A Victorian in the Modern World* (1939): "It was perhaps in conversation that the creative quality of Jig's imagination was most entrancingly manifested. When four or six of us, or perhaps seven or eight, were sitting with our flagon of red wine, or slowly sipped whiskey, and the gentle excitement was suffused through Jig's being, then picturable ideas flowed like rippling streams from his laughing mouth. His eyes danced with the joy of ideas becoming poetic realities. The fact that he never paused an instant in quick transitions from one flashing thought or impulse to the next, made his talk a living reality."[77]

Arthur Davison Ficke echoed Hapgood's words in an encomium that he wrote after Cook's death: "Of all of them from a material standpoint Cook might have been called the only failure, for his few books had had only a limited sale. But his inspired words in the endless talk-fests, his enthusiasms, holding others to the line when they might have wavered, his insistence always upon artistic integrity, made him in the highest sense the leader of them all. And his grave in Greece stands now as a challenge to writers of talent who feel the pull away from their ideals."[78]

Later in the twentieth century, scholars evaluating Cook's career were no less generous. Tanselle concludes that he "engaged himself in a continual search for beauty, a search which made of his own life a work of art."[79] Arthur Waterman, Susan Glaspell's first biographer, writes that Cook's two main contributions were his vision and his idealism: "He reminds us by his life of other values which we have neglected: pioneer self-reliance, humanitarianism, a unified culture like that of ancient Greece, and of the possibilities of an artistic flowering rising from these values."[80] Bigsby acknowledges that "Cook was not an original thinker but he did combine a personal vision with practical energy and an inspirational power which makes him a crucial figure in the history of American drama."[81] Sarlos sums up Cook's impact succinctly: "The power to activate creativity in others was Jig's essential contribution to the Provincetown Players' collective."[82]

Cook may not have secured a place in the pantheon of American dramatists, but he did help shape the work of many American playwrights by giving them a theatre company that took them seriously, freeing them from commercial concerns, focusing on developing their talent, and encouraging their experimental stagecraft and unconventional themes, thus inspiring and facilitating some of their best work. O'Neill, who staged sixteen plays at the Provincetown, saw the value in Cook's contribution, remembering that "Cook was the big man, the dominating and inspiring genius of the Players. Always enthusiastic, vital, impatient with everything that smacked of falsity or compromise, he represented the spirit of revolt against the old worn-out traditions, the commercial theater, the tawdry artificialities of the stage."[83] Perhaps Dell, one of his oldest and closest friends, said it best: "He quickened with his companionship the sparks of belief and of courage in young minds—belief in the possibility of creating a new world and courage to begin now."[84]

5

Susan Glaspell Fights for Free Speech in Freeport

Saw Susie Glaspell last night. 'Twas grand to get such new mental pictures of you. Also, the girl herself is charming. I never realized it.

—GEORGE CRAM COOK TO MOLLIE PRICE

For the thunder of my anger rolls mostly for Susan. . . . I have come to the mature conclusion that the Third Party is an amateur vampire . . . [and] that G. C. C. is a child who tires of his toys too easily and who won't even attempt to mend them if they break or crack.

—RABBI W. H. FINESHRIBER TO FLOYD DELL

AT THE FEBRUARY 13, 1910, meeting of Davenport's Ethical Society, Susan Glaspell rose to ask a question of the speaker, sparking a censorship controversy that would impact the upcoming mayoral election, motivate her sweetheart, George Cram (Jig) Cook, to run for Congress, inspire one of her best stories, and strengthen her commitment to free speech and expression, a commitment that would animate and energize her dramaturgy as well as her life. When Glaspell asked Rabbi William H. Fineshriber what he thought about the library board's countermanding the librarian's decision to purchase George Burman Foster's *The Finality of the Christian Religion*, he replied that he thought the library board's action was "positively medieval."[1]

That Fineshriber's topic was "Religious Liberty" was probably no coincidence. In announcing their lecture series in early February, the Ethical Society was most likely setting the stage for a fight against censorship that they would mount in February and March 1910 against a library board that they believed was acting out of religious bias. Immediately after Fineshriber's talk, Glaspell, Cook, and their friends in the Ethical Society launched a campaign against this act of censorship perpetrated by four members of the library board, one of whom was a Catholic priest and another a district deputy of the Knights of Columbus, circulating petitions to persuade people to request the book at the library and writing letters to the *Davenport Democrat and Leader*. This letter-writing campaign, waged by members of both sides of the controversy, drew commentary from a number of prominent Davenport clergymen in addition to the Ethical Society members and other citizens.

After library board member E. M. Sharon published a screed in the *Democrat* denying that censorship was at issue, the first letters to appear there were by Glaspell and Cook. In her letter, Glaspell succinctly made the case for the library's purchase of *The Finality of the Christian Religion* as an important book dealing with issues of public interest. But beyond this rationale, she objected to the basis on which the library board had made its decision. "We live in an age of inquiry," she wrote. "In fiction, poetry, many critical fields, a large number of the best things being written stand upon that same ground upon which Prof. Foster wrote 'The Finality of the Christian Religion.' Are these books, too, to be excluded from the public library?" Glaspell concluded her letter with a rebuke to the library board for undertaking the "self-appointed task of religious censorship."[2]

In his letter, Cook, too, emphasized the importance of the book and its author, deploring how it had been mischaracterized as "the outcome of a row in the Baptist Church," objecting to the procensorship faction's tarring their opponents with the brush of Socialism, and echoing Fineshriber's charge of medievalism.[3] Next up were attorney Isaac Petersberger and J. F. Bredow, who challenged the defending faction's premise that the United States is a Christian nation.[4] The next issue of the *Democrat* featured another letter from Sharon, who appeared to be one of the primary movers behind the library board's decision, arguing that "controversial religious literature must be barred because its admission would violate the principles on which the library is established, and if one side of a controversy is given a hearing, in equity the same right should be granted others and that means more space than any library can afford without barring proper and suitable books." While denying the charge of censorship, Sharon nevertheless listed several authors—Balzac, Maupassant, Flaubert, Rousseau, Voltaire, Rabelais, and Defoe—some of whose works he deemed "unfit for general circulation." Sharon's lengthy letter concluded with a straw-man argument in which he quoted from one of Foster's sermons extolling George Sand's feminism, enumerated George Sand's transgressions against traditional morality, and then condemned Foster on the basis of guilt by association.[5]

The February 20 edition of the *Democrat* brought input from two clergymen into the controversy. Episcopalian bishop Theodore Morrison disparaged Foster's book but argued for its purchase on the ironic basis that if the library had bought the book in the first place, it would have been read by only a few people, thereby causing little harm. Morrison went on to advise against clergymen serving on the board of a public library. The Reverend Leroy M. Coffman, DD, weighed in for the affirmative on the question of whether the United States is a Christian nation, stating that while there is no state religion, the Christian religion of the Founding Fathers had shaped the country's social institutions and still informed most public policy positions. "Christianity, without being a state religion, is so rooted in our institutions, as to be perpetually a dominant factor in the life of the nation," he asserted.[6]

The debate continued in the pages of the *Democrat*, with Sharon, Petersberger, Bredow, and Cook trading blows and reinforcing the Ethical Society members' belief that the question was one of not only freedom of speech but freedom of religion as well. While the fight raged on, the paper published a statement by Monsignor James P. Ryan, the library board member whose objections to the book had initiated the controversy. Ryan asserted that "it is not necessary or proper to spend the people's money for books which attack the fundamental principles of Christianity or the fundamentals of government. So I object to infidel works and the extreme socialistic books." He further asserted that "it was not a Catholic conspiracy in any sense, as some seem to have intimated" and, following the example of E. M. Sharon, employed a guilt-by-association tactic, noting that a University of Chicago colleague of Foster's advocated free love.[7] In contrast to Monsignor Ryan's position was that of Unitarian minister Arthur Markley Judy, who contended that the library board's duty was "to provide a free and fair encounter of all views which are likely to command the attention of men's sober second thought . . . it is only through the process of receiving, weighing, and then accepting or discarding that the advancement of truth can be secured. And freedom for this process is the inalienable right of every adult."[8]

On February 24, the *Democrat* reported that news of the Davenport controversy had spread to "metropolitan centers," reprinting part of the *Chicago Evening Post*'s tongue-in-cheek editorial, which called Cook "a market gardner [*sic*]," Glaspell "the author of the season in Davenport," and Fineshriber "the cause of it all," speculating that he had requested the book at the library in the hope that it would assure him of Christianity's demise. The *Post* summarized Glaspell's criticism of the library board's decision as follows: "It was outrageous to have the most discussed book of the year barred from the library because it did not suit the religious views of certain members of the library board. It was undue censorship; nay, more, it was medievalism; it showed appalling ignorance. The town rang with the charges."[9]

At its next meeting, the Ethical Society took the dispute to the next level, protesting the library board's "extreme non-liberal course" and opposing its members' "religious zeal and bias in making book selections." Unitarian minister Manfred Lilliefors reviewed *The Finality of the Christian Religion* at the Labor Lyceum on March 6, attempting to shed some scholarly light on the controversy by explaining that the word *finality* in this case derived not from the Latin word meaning *end* but from the Greek word meaning *progress*. Unmoved by his explication, the library board again voted against the purchase of the book, even after being presented with a petition containing two hundred signatures endorsing its purchase.[10]

Not to be outdone by the Ethical Society, the Socialists also censured the library board at their February city convention. One plank in their platform advocated more money for the library; they also pledged that Michael T. Kennedy, the Socialist candidate for mayor, would, if elected, appoint to the library board "only such persons as are broad-minded enough to conduct the library as a public, nonsectarian, non-partisan institution from which no class of books that a library should contain shall be excluded, and in which the librarian shall be given greater freedom in all matters requiring expert knowledge."[11]

The battle rose to a climax on St. Patrick's Day, when Professor George Burman Foster came to town to defend his book, freedom of speech, and religious liberty and tolerance. Speaking before a crowd of nearly one thousand, Foster indicted the un-Christian economic system and the justice system based on property rights, asserted that the church was the enemy of freedom of thought, and deplored its missionary efforts, calling for "human justice, fair play, and cooperative endeavor." At this event, petitions that garnered nearly five hundred signatures were circulated that urged the library board to buy Foster's book.[12]

Although the controversy was quelled when the board's chairman, Judge C. M. Waterman, purchased *The Finality of the Christian Religion* and donated it to the library, its impact was far ranging. In *The Road to the Temple*, her biography of Cook, Glaspell declares that "we even became powerful and changed the city election. . . . We wrote the papers such stinging letters . . . that the short-sighted candidate for mayor who had first defended the [Library] Board was quite snowed under by enlightenment."[13] There was some truth to Glaspell's assertion. The incumbent, Democrat George W. Scott, was supported by the *Democrat*, which added fuel to the fire by publishing the flurry of letters from both sides. The *Times* backed the Republican challenger, Alfred C. Mueller, running a front-page banner headline on March 31: "Boost for a Greater Davenport—Elect Mueller." Floyd Dell, who had left Davenport for Chicago in 1908, wrote in *Homecoming* (his autobiography) that the conflict was an "epistolary war" centering on "the issue of freedom of thought" that was decisive in Davenport's 1910 mayoral election, stating that "a new mayor was elected on a pledge to appoint a library board that would put Dr. Foster's book in the public library."[14]

Did Scott's early support of the library board's censorship cost him his job? A more plausible reason for his defeat might be found in Republican Mueller's relentless attack on Democrat Scott's fiscal policies, thoroughly reported by the *Times*. Although the Democrats asserted that Scott had "brought order out of the chaos that has existed in the city finances, and in the municipal account of the city for a generation past," the *Times* lambasted "the financial and extravagant improvements program of the Democratic administration" and ran an especially pointed article on March 31 that charged Scott's administration with costing the city $166,164 more than it cost to run Sioux City and $172,990 more than it cost to run Dubuque. The article featured an interview with one C. H. Blair of West Liberty, Iowa, who stated that he had decided not to invest in Davenport property due to "heavy taxes and wasteful methods." Blair blamed "rotten city administrators," "vampires" who "suck dry city offices" and "an army of has-beens" who feed at the city trough.[15]

The time-honored Republican tactic of portraying Democrats as taxers and spenders worked as well as it usually does, and Mueller was narrowly elected by a margin of 212 votes. Yet another factor in Scott's defeat might have stemmed from the ethnic affiliation of his opponent. Although Scott ran stronger than he had two years earlier in the upper end of the city, when a candidate named Scott runs against a candidate named Mueller in German West Davenport, no one is surprised when the latter garners considerable support there.[16] The censorship controversy had further impact when Cook, who had waded into politics the previous year, was nominated as the Socialist Party's candidate for Congress.

The short story Glaspell published six years later, "'Finality' in Freeport," took a lighthearted approach to the subject, lampooning progressives as well as conservatives, as she would do in her Provincetown comedies. However, freedom of speech, authenticity of expression, and the power of the written word were principles that she took seriously, cherished, and advocated, not only in "'Finality' in Freeport" but also in stories such as "For Tomorrow: The Story of an Easter Sermon" (1905), "A Matter of Gesture" (1917), and "Poor Ed" (1918). As the twenty-year-old society editor of Charles Eugene Banks's *Davenport Weekly Outlook*, Glaspell endorsed reading, learning, and literature in her earliest writings in that periodical. In her October 1896 "Social Life" column, Glaspell asserted that "a woman who can talk politics intelligently has been proven to be more charming than she who can not." In a February 1897 column, she had some good advice for a society girl: "My dear girl, you are making an awful mistake in not reading anything. . . . Take an hour or two every day to read the best magazines. You have no idea of how you would add to your powers by being conversant with what is going on in the great world about you." A "Social Life" column later that month disparages women who, purporting to appear well informed, read book reviews instead of books and magazine headings instead of articles.[17]

For Glaspell, literacy was not just an individual achievement; it was the cornerstone of democracy, and censorship was a threat to the freedoms inherent in that democracy. These values were reflected in her choice of extracurricular activities at Drake University, where she served as vice president of the Debating Association, trounced her oratorical competitors with the speech "Bismarck and European Politics," contributed to Drake's literary magazine, the *Delphic*, and read her work at commencement events in 1899.[18]

After she returned to Davenport following her stint as a journalist in Des Moines, Glaspell continued to be engaged with intellectual inquiry. She was invited to join two elite women's study clubs: the Amateur Musical Society in 1905 and the Tuesday Club in 1906. For the former, she chaired the Literary Committee and read portions from the Oberammergau Passion Play at its November 10, 1905, meeting; for the latter, she contributed three papers, all of which centered on the power of language and its cultural work: "The Influence of the Press" (April 2, 1907), "Socialism—Present Day Theories and Activities" (February 18, 1908), and "Present Tendencies in Fiction" (June 8, 1909).[19]

Although Glaspells had been living in Scott County, Iowa, since the city's founding, Susan was not from one of the elite families of Davenport, unlike Alice French, who was the daughter of a wealthy steel magnate and the city's literary doyenne; Cook, a lawyer's son who could boast of a congressman in his family tree; or Arthur Davison Ficke, son of former mayor C. A. Ficke. Her father, Elmer Glaspell, was a feed dealer and sometime contractor who lost on his jobs almost as often as he made money, and his daughter had begun earning her keep by writing for local periodicals from the time of her high school graduation in 1894. During her years at Drake, she relied on freelance writing to bring in money, and after graduating with a PhB in 1899, she supported herself as a reporter for the *Des Moines Daily News*, covering the statehouse beat and writing a column, "The News Girl."[20]

Glaspell had some early success as a fiction writer, publishing short stories in national magazines after she gave up her career as a reporter in Des Moines and returned home to concentrate on writing fiction. In 1904, "For Love of the Hills" brought her $500 in prize money from *Black Cat* magazine and kudos from not only the *Daily Times* but also Alice French, who told the Tuesday Club that "I know of no story of the masters more perfectly told or one that has in it more true pathos."[21] Becoming something of a local celebrity, Glaspell was now known as "Davenport's promising young writer" and was featured in two articles in Ella Bushnell-Hamlin's magazine, *Trident*.[22]

In June 1904, Glaspell and Banks attended the nineteenth annual meeting of the Western Association of Writers at Winona Lake, Indiana, where Glaspell read a short story; the following year, she was elected as one of the vice presidents.[23] In October 1904, Glaspell read her short story "The Return of Rhoda" at a meeting of the Mothers Club of the People's Union Mission of Davenport, after which Banks spoke on "the sentiment of Miss Glaspell's story."[24] Five years later, her first novel, *The Glory of the Conquered* (1909), would get a rave review from Bettye Adler, the society editor of the *Times*, which would begin serializing the novel later that year.[25]

In June 1907, the *Times* covered Glaspell's first Tuesday Club talk, "The Influence of the Press," in a story that ran for three columns and included her picture and large excerpts from her paper. Speaking as a former columnist and reporter, she began with humorous dos and don'ts for dealing with journalists. "Don't give the reporter two tickets to the church supper and think you have done wonders. The reporter doesn't wish to go to the church supper. What the reporter wants is news," she admonished.

She then moved on to assertions that reflected her lifelong commitment to civil liberties and the key role that journalism plays in protecting them. Addressing the press's inclination to emphasize scandals, she had some blunt words for readers: "When the people want better newspapers, they will get them. But while the public is so yellow itself, and such a good patron of yellowness, it cannot expect anything else of the newspaper." Glaspell then dealt with First Amendment issues: "Everyone claims to believe in the freedom of the press, and everyone does—for other people. The school board believes in the freedom of the press as regards the city council, but a newspaper story criticizing the school board is sheer insolence. We all believe in the freedom of the press . . . but it is curious how the freedom of the press becomes 'none of their business' when it strikes home."

Glaspell concluded with words that could just as easily characterize what would become her view of the playwright's mission as well as the journalist's: "It is the province of the newspaper to criticize. It is the province of the newspaper to expose. . . . It is the business of the newspaper to tell the people when things are wrong." The reporter covering her talk approvingly concluded that "the writer knows how to hand out the real thing."[26]

The year 1907 was also a watershed year for Glaspell's intellectual development, as well as her personal life, for in March of that year, Cook and Dell founded the Monist Society of Davenport. Susan Glaspell soon became an enthusiastic member of this group of free thinkers that was grounded in the theories of Ernst Haeckel, who postulated the oneness of the universe. However, her involvement with that group created some internal conflict. Susan was personable and popular; she had the kind of captivating charm that could make men fall in love with her even after she was dead. When she competed in the *Democrat's* Free Trip to Europe contest in the spring of 1903, she accumulated enough votes to place as high as third out of twenty-two city contestants in one of the weekly tallies, close behind city winner Blanche Campbell and Ada Emielle Drechsler, a comely telephone operator from Princeton, Iowa, who won the country division.[27]

But however much she enjoyed her reputation as a charming young woman, her status as "one of Davenport's gifted daughters," and the social cachet that attached to her club memberships, she relished even more her participation in the Monist Society. Her description in *The Road to the Temple* suggests that the thrill she derived from her forays into Davenport radicalism came from her ability to épater le bourgeois: "Declining to go to church with my parents in the morning, I would ostentatiously set out for the Monist Society in the afternoon, down an obscure street which it seemed a little improper to be walking on, as everything was closed for Sunday, upstairs through a sort of side entrance over a saloon," she recalled (*RTT*, 191). But the Monist Society ultimately held an even bigger thrill for her. As Glaspell herself put it, "The Monist Society is important to me, for it was there that I first began to know Jig" (*RTT*, 191).

At the February 25, 1908, meeting of the Tuesday Club, Mrs. T. O. Swinby read Glaspell's paper "Socialism—Present Day Theories and Activities," as she was traveling and unable to attend. The subject of this paper reflects a leftist political orientation that would become a larger part of her identity throughout the decade, a bent that would be encouraged by Cook and Dell.[28] Through the Monist Society, and later through the Ethical Society, she became better acquainted with Davenport's progressives, such as Fineshriber, Dell, Socialist mail carrier Frederick "Fritz" Feuchter, and, of course, Cook, who often hosted gatherings of Socialists, trade unionists, writers, and intellectuals on his family's estate, the Cabin, in Buffalo, Iowa, a few miles downriver from Davenport. Throughout the decade, Glaspell juggled writing, traveling, and hobnobbing with socialites on Tuesdays and Socialists on Sundays, enjoying the frisson of transgression that these conflicting activities produced.

But soon a more personal priority began to govern her life. First the Monist Society, then the Ethical Society, and finally the censorship controversy of 1910 brought her in closer and closer contact with Cook, who had married his second wife, Chicago anarchist and feminist Mollie Price, in 1908; at the time of the censorship controversy, the Cooks had one child and were expecting another.

This political brouhaha threw Glaspell and Cook together, and they continued to meet after the issue was resolved. In his diary, Cook's father, E. E. Cook, recorded nine visits that Glaspell made to the Cabin from January 25 through June 22, 1910.[29] Susan and Jig were ostensibly collaborating on a Socialist work of fiction; however, this book never materialized, although each would publish a novel that featured a Socialist character the following year. Cook wrote in an undated letter to Dell that "Susan and I had a day of creative energy here about a girl going to the city to seek her social salvation."[30]

Perhaps this literary collaboration never bore fruit because Susan left Davenport to summer in Chicago, not returning until fall. As the 1910s came to a close and her relationship with Cook became known around town, Glaspell found that Davenport was no longer the welcoming haven that had nurtured her writing and celebrated her talent. "Davenport's gifted young story writer" was now the paramour of a married father with a toddler and an infant.

In *The Road to the Temple*, Glaspell recounts the onset of her love affair with Cook, which appears to have begun in late 1907 or early 1908:

> Jig and I became friends. He would come to me, or we would take walks, and talk of all the things there were to talk about. Now life was taking us different ways. I was about to embark on my first visit to New York. He would be married within a few months. But that last night something outside ourselves brought us together, and there was a new thing between us ever after. . . . The next few years were full ones for the two who had looked out through the cone of night with a cosmic emotion neither could have felt alone, but they were not experiences shared. And yet, separated though we were—I in New York, then Paris, and Jig married and living at the Cabin, we were never really separated after we came together that night of snow and stars. (*RTT*, 200–201)

Although Susan would spend much of the next two years away from Davenport, she and Jig sustained their relationship through letters and resumed it in person during the winter of 1909–10. The next year, she would leave Davenport for Chicago and then for New York City's Greenwich Village as gossip about the couple continued to spread throughout their native city. During the summer of 1912, Glaspell began her long continual residence in Provincetown, Massachusetts, where she and college friend Lucy (Lulu) Huffaker rented the Roseboro Cottage. There, Glaspell and her neighbor, Mary Heaton Vorse, mentored Sinclair Lewis as he struggled to write *Our Mr. Wrenn* (1914).

Glaspell had been valued in her native city as much for her magnetic personality as for her success as a writer. An article in the *Times* stated that "Miss Glaspell has the most engaging personality imaginable. She is tall and slender, with warm brown eyes, the color of a hazel nut and is vivacious and witty—as unfailingly so in conversation as in her books."[31] However, neither personal charm nor two successful novels trumped an adulterous affair in the eyes of many Davenporters. In *The Road to the Temple*, Glaspell expressed regret that "the present was . . . full of sorrow for the wrongs to others" (*RTT*, 209). But she also stated that "even more than disgrace you will face for love. You will violate your own sense of fairness and right. In a world that is falling around you love dwells as sure, as proud, as if life had come into being that this might be" (*RTT*, 208). Jig's reaction was more succinct: "Can't see S. at all here. Lovely situation. Mollie seems to have sloughed all bitterness."[32]

After she moved to the East Coast, Glaspell would make regular trips to Davenport to care for her aging parents, but she would never return there to live. However, her involvement with Davenport radicalism had taken deep root in more than one respect. On April 14, 1913, she and Cook married and settled in Greenwich Village, where they collaborated on a one-act comedy, *Suppressed Desires*, that satirized the radical adherents of Freudian psychology (i.e., their friends and neighbors). During the summer of 1915, they put on the play, first at Neith Boyce and Hutchins Hapgood's home in Provincetown, Massachusetts, and later that summer in a converted fish house, the Wharf Theater. The following summer, Glaspell began writing plays on her own for the nascent Provincetown Players, many of which centered on issues of language and free speech.

Glaspell's concerns about threats to free speech and expression were well justified in the America of her day. The fight to defend First Amendment freedoms—always ongoing—can be traced back to the John Peter Zenger case of 1734 in which Zenger, a printer and journalist, was brought to trial for seditious libel. His acquittal established the legal principle that truth is a complete defense against such charges—that is, speech thought to be defamatory or libelous is legal if it can be proved true.

While the case has been considered a landmark in the fight to defend civil liberties, that fight did not end when the colony became a nation with a First Amendment that guaranteed freedom of speech, assembly, religion, and the press. "For the first hundred years of its existence, the First Amendment did little to protect speech rights," asserts Laura Stein: "The amendment did not prevent some of America's founding fathers from enacting laws against speech that criticized government officials (the Sedition Act of 1790). Nor did it inhibit the city of Boston from denying a black minister the right to speak against racism in a public park (*Davis v. Massachusetts*, 1897). Indeed, history shows that for more than a hundred years after its enactment, the First Amendment failed to protect political dissent or the right to speak on public property."[33]

Free speech rights were very much a part of the New that so engaged Glaspell's Greenwich Village peers. As Christine Stansell observes, "Free speech was self-conscious, flashy, daring, ostentatiously honest and sexual. . . . The astonishing linguistic play of *Ulysses* and the urbane stream of consciousness of Greenwich Village talk were fostered by similar urban forms: a booming print culture, the spread of advertising, and the compression of polylingual populations, all touching off an explosion of language."[34]

However, the nineteenth century could boast few successful efforts to protect free speech. As the century turned, a number of pressing social issues cried out for debate and discussion—including immigration, women's suffrage, temperance, urbanization, Socialism, and the suppression of unions. "Free speech became a defining ethos of the radical milieu," concludes Stansell. "The rebellious talkers were buoyed by a cheerful conviction that language, unimpeded by convention or law, could create democratic communities with constituencies otherwise divided—men from women, the poor from the privileged, the untutored from the educated. . . . Free speech politics thus linked artists, writers, and professionals of a progressive bent to working-class militants."[35]

By 1902, a Free Speech League was organized to take cases of restrictions on free speech to court—just in time to combat the Anti-Anarchist Law of 1903. Spurred by Leon Czolgosz's assassination of President William McKinley, the proponents of this law were successful not only in prohibiting anarchist speech but also in creating a chilly climate for free speech in general. By the next decade, as the United States entered World War I, the Espionage and Sedition Acts further endangered free speech and expression. Stansell reports that "within five months after the Espionage Act took effect, every major left-wing publication in the country had been barred from the mails at least once, some for weeks at a time."[36] Several staffers from the *Masses*, a leftist periodical published in Greenwich Village, were charged with discouraging enlistment and registration for the draft. Editors Max Eastman and Floyd Dell, cartoonist Art Young, and business manager Merrill Rogers endured two trials that resulted in hung juries. While they were never convicted, the end of the *Masses* trial marked the end of "the country's premier venue for mixing labor and sex radicalism."[37]

Glaspell's commitment to freedom of speech, thought, and expression was energized by this political context. Few reviewers took note of the Provincetown Players in those early years; however, her 1917 one-act comedy *The People* earned critic Heywood Broun's praise for its humor and eloquence, although he thought it was too literary and needed to be condensed and simplified.[38] This satirical play brings subscribers from Cape Cod, Idaho, and Georgia to the offices of the *People*, a periodical that is easily recognizable as the *Masses*. Sidestepping the comical internecine quarrels and petty concerns of the New Yorkers in charge, the outlanders shame them into reassessing their priorities with the sincerity that shines through the expression of their faith in the power of the written word.

As the Woman from Idaho confesses, "Your great words carried me to other great words. I thought of Lincoln, and what he said of a few of the dead. . . . I said—'The truth—the truth—that opens from our lives as water opens from the rocks.' Then I knew what that truth was. . . . Let life become what it may become!—so beautiful that everything that is back of us is worth everything that it cost."[39] Inspired by the Woman from Idaho, the editor of the *People* commits himself anew to fight for the periodical's survival. As Kristina Hinz-Bode points out, in *The People*, "Susan Glaspell stresses the act of artistic creation as a communal act and presents an ideal which claims that change is brought about in communicative interaction."[40]

During the previous summer, in her very first solo effort for the Provincetown, Glaspell had taken communicative interaction one step further, composing a fugue of silence and speech that enacts the power of language and the consequences of its suppression and links that suppression to patriarchy. Hinz-Bode emphasizes the connection between patriarchy and women's silence: "No one encountering the plays of Susan Glaspell can fail to notice the central importance assigned to notions of language, self-expression, and communication. . . . Glaspell's Provincetown plays demonstrate that her concerns about free speech and her advocacy of language and literature as liberating and empowering tools have matured into an understanding of the patriarchal basis of restrictions on and repression of women's free expression."[41] Martha C. Carpentier and Emeline Jouve concur, stating that early scholarship on *Trifles* and "A Jury of Her Peers," the short story that Glaspell adapted from her play, "celebrated Glaspell's innovative use of women's language as a silenced sign system representing their marginalized realms of experience in patriarchal culture."[42]

By keeping her protagonist, Minnie Foster Wright, offstage throughout the entire play, Glaspell foregrounds Minnie's lack of presence in her marriage and community, as well as her inability to speak up on her own behalf. As Jouve concludes, in *Trifles*, Glaspell indicts the unfair justice system and its patriarchal underpinnings by "dramatizing domesticity as female invisibility."[43] Living on an isolated Iowa farmstead with no telephone, Minnie is little more than a cipher in her marriage to John Wright, a taciturn farmer who thinks people talk too much and wants only peace and quiet. Two women who accompany their husbands to the Wrights' home to investigate John's mysterious murder determine, after an inspection of Minnie's dirty, messy kitchen, that the motive for the murder isn't quite as mysterious as their husbands suppose and share uniquely female experiences that help them determine their subsequent subversive course of action.

As they begin to share reminiscences about their lives, Glaspell emphasizes not only the consequences of stifled communication but also its power, as Mrs. Peters and Mrs. Hale enact the 1970s feminist slogan

"From the personal to the political." In what may be the first consciousness-raising session seen on an American stage, the women find that sharing their experiences as wives in a rural Iowa community builds their understanding of and empathy for Minnie and her isolated and silenced existence.

When Mrs. Peters tells Mrs. Hale that she is glad Mrs. Hale came along with her husband because otherwise she would have been lonely sitting in Minnie's kitchen, their thoughts then inevitably turn to how lonely Minnie must have been doing the same thing—and for a much longer period of time. "Not having children makes less work—but it makes a quiet house, and Wright out to work all day, and no company when he did come in," muses Mrs. Hale (Ben-Zvi and Gainor, 31). Mrs. Peters, too, begins to empathize with Minnie by reflecting on her personal experience: "I know what stillness is," she affirms. "When we homesteaded in Dakota, and my first baby died—after he was two years old, and me with no other then" (Ben-Zvi and Gainor, 33).

Working and talking as they put the puzzle of Minnie's disorderly kitchen together, Mrs. Peters and Mrs. Hale conclude that Minnie murdered John after he killed the canary that was her one defense against the deracinating silence with which she had to live every day. They then counter Minnie's silence with a silence of their own as they decide not to inform the sheriff and the county attorney of the dead canary, the one clue that might establish a motive for the murder. Mrs. Hale's conclusion that "I know how things can be—for women. . . . We live close together and we live far apart. We all go through the same things—it's all just a different kind of the same thing" underscores their empathy for Minnie and prepares us for their subversive act of hiding the evidence of Minnie's crime and remaining silent while the men ineffectively attempt to solve the mystery (Ben-Zvi and Gainor, 33).

The women's silence opens a space for the audience to become engaged with the issues that the play foregrounds. As Patricia L. Bryan explains, "Glaspell shapes her narrative to raise questions about the law and the legal process. The law is supposed to punish crime, but its definition of crime seems too narrow to capture moral culpability."[44] Jouve takes this analysis one step further, asserting that through the use of suspense, Glaspell involves her audience in the detection process; by discovering clues and engaging in inductive reasoning along with Mrs. Hale and Mrs. Peters, the audience is empowered to render judgment on Minnie's culpability: "Glaspell pulls off the amazing feat of turning her spectators into 'a jury of her peers.'" Furthermore, Jouve argues, the indeterminacy of the ending invites the audience "to take over from the female protagonists by taking steps in their own lives to put an end to female oppression."[45]

No reviews exist of that first production of *Trifles*, but when the play was revived by the Washington Square Players a few months later, newspaper accounts described it as "intensely moving" and "highly suspenseful" with "tension carefully sustained throughout."[46] Broun praised Glaspell's use of indirection, while Arthur Hornblow zeroed in on the gender emphasis of the play, calling it "an ingenious study in feminine ability at inductive and deductive analysis."[47]

A year and a half after the premiere of *Trifles*, Glaspell staged another one-act play for the Provincetown, a comedy called *Close the Book*. This play deals directly with the issue of free speech and centers on two characters, English professor Peyton Root and his fiancée and student, Jhansi Mason, who are writing an article on free speech for the university magazine. However, while almost every character professes to believe in free speech, its actual practice proves troublesome, as the play pokes gentle fun at people who give lip service to First Amendment freedoms as long as exercising them doesn't upset anyone's applecart.

Although Peyton's uncle George asserts that "every true American believes in free speech," Peyton's mother and grandmother have a problem with Peyton's critique of American literature, which he has likened to "a toddy with the *stick* left out" (Ben-Zvi and Gainor, 40, 39). "What business has a professor of English to say anything about society," asks Peyton's grandmother, voicing a complaint that is still heard today (Ben-Zvi and Gainor, 39). Peyton's mother agrees that "it's not what we pay our professors for," and Uncle George thinks that Jhansi is a bad influence because "she's leading our young people to criticize the society their fathers have builded up" (Ben-Zvi and Gainor, 39, 41). Peyton points out that one of his forefathers signed "a paper on free speech. It had a high falutin' name: 'The Declaration of Independence'" (Ben-Zvi and Gainor, 41). Jouve remarks that "by superimposing the revolutionary past on the present of the action and of the Roots' reproach concerning the young man's dedication to free speech, the playwright highlights the paradox of the 'untrue American' rhetoric as she draws attention to the distortion of historical principles."[48]

Enter Peyton's sister, Bessie, who has exercised her right to free intellectual inquiry and uncovered a little bad news for everybody. Bessie tells Jhansi that she is the daughter of Baptist church workers, not gypsies, thus undermining Jhansi's cherished self-constructed identity as a marginalized Other. Bessie has also learned that not all of the Root ancestors were Revolutionary War heroes; one was a grave robber, and another was convicted of selling liquor and guns to the Indians. Grandmother speaks the last words of the play, a mocking rebuke to hypocrites whose actions belie their professed beliefs: "Peyton—close that book" (Ben-Zvi and Gainor, 46).

Deceptively simple, this amusing one-act play is anything but innocuous. Sharon Friedman praises the play for its parody of university culture, "its pretensions to humanism and . . . its deviation from the original Midwestern founders' value of democracy and educational opportunity," a critique that Glaspell would make at greater length and complexity in her full-length play *Inheritors* (1921).[49] As with Glaspell's other early one-act play, *The People*, few reviewers wrote about the play. Arthur Hornblow dismissed it as "far fetched and futile," but Ralph Block found the light satire well handled.[50]

Three major plays that Glaspell staged for the Provincetown in 1921 and 1922 continue to explore the themes of free speech and expression, using a female New Woman character as the free speech advocate. *Inheritors* shares several similarities with *Close the Book*: it is set in an Iowa college town, and it features a New Woman character and a professor who are caught up in the conflict created by people who profess the importance of free speech but fail to practice it when free speech poses a threat to the power structure. Noelia Hernando-Real notes that a hallmark of Glaspell's dramaturgy is the opposing of a freedom-advocating New Woman character to a conventional True Woman character (e.g., Henrietta to Mabel in *Suppressed Desires* and Jhansi Mason to Mother and Grandmother in *Close the Book*).[51] *Inheritors* follows this pattern, pitting the New Woman Madeline Fejevary Morton, who comes of age as she learns the true cost of standing up for her belief in free speech, against her Aunt Isabel, a True Woman who urges her not to abandon the traditional values of home and family. The major conflict in the play occurs in act 2, as Madeline defends two Hindu students who have been protesting Great Britain's colonial policy toward India and is arrested for hitting a policeman with her tennis racket.

The First Amendment did little to protect free speech at the time Glaspell wrote *Inheritors*. As J. Ellen Gainor points out, "The repressive and jingoistic climate felt in the United States during the first World War, brought close to home by the trials of her friends and colleagues on *The Masses* editorial staff, accused of violating the Espionage and Sedition Acts of 1917–1918, in part prompted her to write *Inheritors*."[52] Sarah Withers agrees, arguing that Glaspell wrote the play "as a critical response to an era marked by the first Red Scare and by heightened government scrutiny of its citizenry for any hint of 'un-Americanism.'"[53]

The climate of opinion that Gainor and Withers describe as typical of the late teens and early twenties was especially chilly on college campuses. Gainor reports that professors Harold Dana and James Cattell of Columbia University were fired in 1917 because they opposed the war and that professors were similarly dismissed in Maine, Michigan, Minnesota, Washington, Missouri, Indiana, Ohio, and Virginia.[54] Glaspell's friend Sinclair Lewis represents threats to free speech and academic freedom in his eerily prescient dystopian novel, *It Can't Happen Here* (1935), in language reminiscent of that of Senator Lewis and Horace Fejevary in *Inheritors*: "Why, here, as recently as three years ago, a sickeningly big percentage of students were blatant pacifists. . . . No less than fifty-nine disloyal Red students have received their just deserts by being beaten up so severely that never again will they raise in this free country the bloodstained banner of anarchism!"[55] Withers contends that "it is precisely this culture of surveillance and censorship that is un-American, as it signals a loss of the freedom of expression that informed the founding of the nation."[56]

Tellingly, Glaspell sets the stage for this conflict in act 1, which takes place on the Fourth of July in 1879, thus emphasizing the themes of democracy and freedom that undergird the play. Madeline's grandfathers, Silas Morton and neighbor Felix Fejevary, both Civil War veterans, reflect on their military service and the freedoms that they defended. At the end of the act, Silas reveals his plans for his land: "There will one day be a college in these cornfields because long ago a great dream was fought for in Hungary," he promises his neighbor, who fought in the revolution of 1848 before immigrating to the United States (Ben-Zvi and Gainor, 193).

Fittingly, acts 2 and 3 center on three instances of the exercise of free speech that portend disastrous consequences for the practitioners. Professor Holden has protested the treatment of a former student, now imprisoned as a conscientious objector, and is therefore threatened with the loss of his job by a state legislator: "Of course this state, Mr. Fejevary, appropriates no money for radicals. Excuse me, but why do you keep this man Holden?" demands Senator Lewis (Ben-Zvi and Gainor, 195). The second instance involves the Hindu students who were posting hand-bills in support of free India, as well as those who were protesting the college's failure to fight the deportation of another Hindu student, now threatened with deportation themselves; and the third is Madeline's protest against the arrest of the Indian students, which results in her own arrest and impending incarceration. Felix Fejevary Jr., son of the Hungarian revolutionary and Civil War veteran and now president of the college that Silas Morton founded, is caught in the middle of these controversies.

In act 3, Madeline is resolute in her decision to face imprisonment rather than allow her uncle Felix to intercede with the authorities and get her off with an apology. "My grandfather gave this hill to Morton College—a place where anybody—from any land—can come and say what he believes to be true! Why, you poor simp—this is America!" she proclaims (Ben-Zvi and Gainor, 214). "For Madeline," explains Withers, "supporting the Hindu students is not only a specific defense of free speech but also a general defense of the nation's self-professed demo-cratic idealism that attracted the foreign students to America in the first place."[57]

Almost everyone in Madeline's life—not only her aunt Isabel but also her neighbor, Emil Johnson; her father, Ira Morton; and Professor Holden—tries to convince her to capitulate, but Madeline rejects all of their arguments: "There must be something pretty rotten about Morton College if you have to sell your soul to stay in it," she tells her professor (Ben-Zvi and Gainor, 222). "Madeline, like Antigone, becomes the voice that struggles for expression against the dominant discourse that con-trols nearly all modes of expression on both the level of the state and of the individual," concludes Marie Molnar.[58]

Inheritors enacts the fullest and most nuanced exploration of the free speech issue in the Glaspell canon. Although the play did attract some negative commentary, with several critics complaining that it was propagandistic and preachy, *Inheritors* nevertheless won the hearts of a number of reviewers. Ludwig Lewisohn, always a big fan of Glaspell's work, called it "the first American play in which a strong intellect and a ripe artistic nature grasped and set forth in human terms the central tradition and most burning problem of the national life quite justly and scrupulously, equally without acrimony and compromise."[59] O. W. Firkins praised the play's dialogue as well as its "keen and varied" intelligence, and Kenneth Macgowan opined that it was "beautifully and sensitively phrased."[60]

In April 1922, one of the last plays mounted by the Provincetown was Glaspell's full-length comedy, *Chains of Dew*. Cook and Glaspell had sailed for Greece before the play was mounted, and Glaspell was not present to supervise the production. Thus, heavy cuts in Glaspell's script, made without her knowledge or consent, resulted in a production script that was partly responsible for the negative reviews, although Glaspell felt that poor casting also contributed to its unappreciative reception.

Broun, usually supportive of the Provincetown's efforts, felt that the main problem with the play lay in Glaspell's construction of its protagonist, poet Seymore Standish, writing that "he is presented as an absolute prig and idiot [making it] impossible to make the audience believe that such a benighted ass can possibly be important as a poet or anything else."[61] Maida Castellun agreed, indicting Glaspell for writing caricatures rather than characters. Lewisohn, as well as Broun, faulted her use of symbolism.[62] Alison Smith felt that the play lacked focus, and the *New York Herald* reviewer thought that it lacked dramatic form and compactness.[63]

Set in New York City and Bluff City, Iowa (a fictionalized Davenport), the play explores the interrelationship of feminism, the birth control movement, and freedom of expression. At the center of the play's main plot is poet-banker Seymore Standish (a fictionalized Arthur Davison Ficke), whose conflicted identity appears to be the obstacle to a fulfilling life.[64] Seymore's identity crisis stems from his feeling of being torn between his obligations to his family and community in Bluff City and his literary aspirations, which he believes can come to fruition only when nurtured by his New York City friends in that urban environment. The Midwest and the East Coast, with their corresponding values and lifestyles, are juxtaposed when Irish poet James O'Brien; Leon Whittaker, Seymore's editor; and Nora Powers, secretary of the Birth Control League, travel from Manhattan to Bluff City to free him from his chains and shake up the Mississippi Valley with birth control activism.

Like *Inheritors*, *Chains of Dew* explores the intersection of feminism and free speech within the context of a contemporary issue. The birth control movement had been gathering steam after a hiatus during World War I. As Nora explains, "When suffrage grew so—sort of common—the really exclusive people turned to birth control" (Ben-Zvi and Gainor, 154), a remark that pokes fun at practitioners of radical chic but also indicates a shift in feminist priorities as the birth control movement moved to the fore. "Though less heralded than suffrage," writes Cathy Moran Hajo, "in many ways it was a more sweeping reform, freeing many women from uncontrolled childbearing, which in turn allowed them to pursue other goals—equal rights, careers, even the traditional roles of mother and wife."[65]

However, the birth control movement accrued additional significance because, in attacking the legality of the prohibition of circulating birth control information and instruction, its proponents were free speech activists as well as feminists. According to Stansell, "the greatest practical demonstration of the vanguard role of feminists was the birth control campaign. . . . The fight to legalize birth control was in many ways a free-speech battle—because the dissemination of contraceptive information and devices . . . fell under the obscenity provisions of the Comstock laws."[66]

By 1916, more than twenty Americans had been or would be jailed for their birth control activism.[67] Radicals such as Emma Goldman and Ben Reitman were arrested for dispensing information about contraception; Margaret Sanger herself was arrested and convicted of violating New York state's obscenity law along with her sister, Ethel Higgins Byrne, and Fania Mindell.[68] Sanger, who opened the first American birth control clinic in 1916 and founded the American Birth Control League in 1921, and Mary Ware Dennett, who cofounded the National Birth Control League, are possible models for Nora Powers, whose stated mission is to organize birth control leagues throughout the United States and who is distributing birth control pamphlets, displaying birth control propaganda posters, and preparing birth control exhibitions in violation of the Comstock Law of 1873.

This federal law and similar state laws were grounded in multiple fears. Adam Hochschild writes that "behind these laws lay a lingering Victorian prudery about sex and men's fear that giving women more control over their reproductive lives would inherently threaten male power."[69] This kind of misogynistic fear combined with nativist concerns to create a major backlash against birth control. Between 1890 and 1915, over fifteen million immigrants came to the United States, many of whom were not white Anglo-Saxon Protestants.[70]

A widespread fear of "race suicide" emerged, stoked by an awareness of modern social trends. By 1900, one out of twelve couples had been divorced, one out of five American women was employed, and the birth rate had fallen to 3.5 children per mother.[71] White supremacist books such as David Starr Jordan's *The Blood of Nations: A Study of the Death of Nations through the Survival of the Unfit* (1910), Edward Alsworth Ross's *The Old World in the New* (1914), Madison Grant's *The Passing of the Great Race* (1916), and Theodore Lothrop Stoddard's *The Rising Tide of Color against White World-Supremacy* (1920) fanned the flames of nativist fears. Tom Buchanan's remark to Jay Gatsby that "if we don't look out the white race will be—will be utterly submerged," although mocked by his wife, Daisy, was typical of the views of many at that time.[72] Authors and orators urged women to abandon career goals and social causes and focus on wifehood and motherhood to ensure the numerical superiority of whites. One of the most prominent crusaders against "race suicide" was President Theodore Roosevelt, who advised couples to have at least three and, if possible, four children; families of "better stock" were counseled to have at least six children in order to "wage the warfare of the cradle."[73]

These issues are evident in the subplot as well as the main plot of *Chains of Dew*. Seymore's wife, Dotty, a Bluff City society woman, becomes enthusiastic about the birth control movement, bobs her hair, and plans to found a chapter of Nora's organization in Bluff City, and Seymore's mother gets involved too, making dolls for Nora's birth control exhibit. However, Glaspell complicates these questions by showing that sometimes free expression works best when it isn't so free. Whittaker's belief that Seymore's ties to the Midwest are holding him back as a poet are undermined by Seymore's mother, whose insights about Seymore's poetic gift inspire the title of the play: "His soul must be the soul of an alien. It's made that way. Here—with us—longing for you, whom he cannot have. There—with you, the pull of us, to whom he must return" (Ben-Zvi and Gainor, 173–74).

Chains of Dew is replete with instances of thwarted, silenced, and ineffective communication that convey this paradox. A malfunctioning mimeograph machine, a free speech petition that Seymore balks at signing, a birth control speech that he balks at making, and birth control hymns that he balks at writing, along with meetings and exhibits that never happen, further make this point. Traditional means of free expression, such as petitions, speeches, meetings, and pamphlets, prove to be less effective here than indirect modes of persuasion, such as Nora's posters and Seymore's mother's homemade dolls.

Glaspell's comedy ultimately takes a conservative turn as Dotty realizes that Seymore needs her to be the kind of traditional woman that he can sacrifice for in order to pursue his literary endeavors successfully, and her love for him trumps her desire for liberation. However, a full-length play that Glaspell staged at the Provincetown in the spring of 1921 enacts the journey of a woman who fully explores the possibilities of a self-created identity and, through acts of free expression and invention, transcends the boundaries not only of a unitary self but of rational existence.

Aegyung Noh aptly describes Claire Archer, protagonist of *The Verge*, as "a female egoist whose Nietzschean will to break established norms of life and create a new organism through botanical experimentation is combined with sexual freedom and the complete rejection of social bonds."[74] "We need not be held in forms molded for us," asserts Claire. "There is outness—and otherness" (Ben-Zvi and Gainor, 235). As Rasha Gazzaz points out, Claire's medium of free expression is her experimentation with plants: "She experiments with nature to produce new noncompliant organisms defying the norm and this metaphorically represents her voice of rebellion."[75]

The Verge enacts Claire's rebellious journey as she seeks "outness" and "otherness," both in her botanical experiments and in herself. Relentlessly rejecting her husband, daughter, and lover as she prioritizes her project, Claire even strangles the person closest to her, Tom Edgeworthy, when she perceives that his plan to save her from herself threatens its success. The barriers to Claire's free expression are represented in act 1 by the walls and locked door of her greenhouse, designed to shut out her husband and houseguests; in act 2, a strangely bulging tower that obstructs access to Claire functions similarly. However, Glaspell takes Claire one step further in her quest for free expression than she takes Jhansi Mason, Madeline Fejevary Morton, Nora Powers, or Dotty Standish. Once her prize creation, the Breath of Life, has "gone where plants have not gone before," lab assistant Anthony tells her that its form is set, and Claire realizes that no matter how much she experiments, the only thing she will ever achieve is a new kind of form; she will never be able to transcend form itself and achieve complete "outness" and "otherness."

Gerhard Bach characterizes *The Verge* as "a play about the loss of language, the loss of the ability to communicate and relate, and consequently, the loss of self. . . . As dialogues unravel, colloquial language (Dick, Tom, Harry, Adelaide, Elizabeth) and stylized language (Claire) engage in battles of 'speaking past the other.' Increasingly in acts two and three, communication breaks down and ends in imprisoning speechlessness."[76] Hinz-Bode shows how pivotal this breakdown proves to be, explaining that "the moment that the metaphysical subject loses this faith in the process of communication and is forced to give up the idealist stance, s/he is left to a state of complete isolation without any dependable way of reaching another human being."[77]

In her determination to get beyond preestablished structures and norms, Claire experiences what Friedrich Nietzsche calls the prison house of language. She is trapped by form, as it mediates and controls everything that she knows. Of the Breath of Life, she says, "Breath of the uncaptured? / You are a novelty. / Out? / You have been brought in. / A thousand years from now, when you are but a form too long repeated, / Perhaps the madness that gave you birth will burst again, / And from the prison that is you will leap pent queernesses / To make a form that hasn't been— / To make a prison new. / And this we call creation" (Ben-Zvi and Gainor, 263). Like *Tickless Time* (the one-act comedy that Glaspell cowrote with Cook), *The Verge* functions metacritically to interrogate the modernists' futile project of formal experimentation, for whenever Claire creates a form of plant life never before seen, like the Breath of Life, she has not transcended form but merely created another form that, in time, will become as tired and timeworn as the earlier forms from which she was trying to escape.

The Verge baffled and thrilled audiences in 1921, generating extremes of opinion that persist in more recent critical appraisals. Jerry Dickey notes that Glaspell "was one of the first women playwrights in America to try to adapt a prevailing aesthetic style, expressionism, to appeal to a female sensibility."[78] The way that many of the "female sensibilit[ies]" who frequented the feminist Heterodoxy Club responded to the play supports Dickey's assertion.

Hutchins Hapgood relates a conversation with the dancer Elise Dufour, who described those Heterodoxy members: "It seemed to me, while these women were talking about *The Verge*, that I was in church, that they were worshipping at some holy shrine; their voices and their eyes were full of religious excitement."[79] Two of the female critics of that day were much of a mind with Glaspell's Heterodoxy acolytes. Ruth Hale urged playgoers to attend carefully to the nuances of the play, for Glaspell is "the painter of those wisps of shadow that cross the soul in the dead of night," and Castellun, while pointing out the play's flaws, compared Glaspell to Goethe, Strindberg, Nietzsche, and Shaw in her portrayal of Claire as superwoman, calling the play "an extraordinary study of the human mind that dares all."[80]

However, most of the newspapermen who reviewed *The Verge* were not enthusiastic, calling the play "a misdirected idea," "utter tripe," "a melodrama of neuroticism," "the pouring forth of a pathological discontent," "a thoroughly confusing display of insanity," and "a conception that lacks unity of aim and intention."[81] Some male commentators did appreciate *The Verge*. "Miss Glaspell's dramaturgic structure is clear and clean and firm," Lewisohn wrote. "The dialogue is delicately and precisely wrought." Stark Young said that "the main idea of *The Verge* provokes the imagination and sense of wonder," and Macgowan, while pointing out some of the play's weaknesses, praised "the clear and philosophic purpose of plumbing spiritual attitudes towards life" and "the flash of intense dramatic power with which, every now and then, the purpose achieves itself in terms of human character and human action." Writing insightfully sixty years later, C. W. E. Bigsby discerned that "*The Verge* is a remarkable play which takes for its structural principle its subject—the refusal to be contained by form or by language."[82]

Free speech remained a concern and a commitment for Susan Glaspell throughout her entire life. Her leadership in the Davenport censorship controversy taught her that fighting to defend First Amendment freedoms was not just individually empowering, it was the very ground on which her vocation and that of her journalistic colleagues were built, and therefore a vital safeguard of the democratic social order. Thus, she continued to emphasize that to defend free speech whenever and wherever it is threatened in order to respect and preserve expression in any form is to respect and preserve democracy. In 1929, she stated in a telegram to the publisher Covici-Friede that she was "glad to join protest against censoring [Radcliffe Hall's] Well of Loneliness have read this serious interesting novel and action against it seems preposterous to me."[83]

Nearly forty years after she led the charge against Davenport's library board, Glaspell was just as passionate when she objected to the Provincetown Library's banning of Ayn Rand's *The Fountainhead*, even though the core values of that book were very different from her own.[84] In 1946, speaking to a local women's group, she argued that "censorship by a small group violates a right that is very precious to us, and one that should be guarded at all costs. This right is the freedom of speech. We are naturally not in favor of obscene literature nor of a book that would tend to corrupt morals, but we should be very careful in our judgment in regard to these issues."[85]

Glaspell's conception of the benefits of reading matured and developed throughout her life. As World War II upended lives and nations, she spoke at the Boston Book Fair to affirm her belief that the writer's vision had a vital function: to enlighten a world menaced by the unthinking and the power mad—"The vision and fight for a better world could not have had so long a life on earth were not they of the very stuff of life itself. This is *our* great moment. Dare to dream! Be unabashed in the dream. The dreamers who fight will win!"[86] Although she reluctantly sacrificed some of her book plates for the war effort, she never lost her belief that the written word could be as powerful as guns and tanks. She reiterated that belief in an article in the *Chicago Tribune*, describing an evening when writers gathered at her home to talk of literature and World War II. Her own memories of France, heightened by Katie Dos Passos's reading of Walt Whitman's "O Star of France," made her realize anew "the companionship, the treasure we have in books" and that "books can hearten and guide us in these troubled times."[87]

Although the protagonist of her final play, *Springs Eternal*, has become disillusioned about the power of the written word to preserve democracy, the reflections of the eponymous Middle Western farmer-editor of her final novel, *Judd Rankin's Daughter*, argue otherwise: "It wasn't the Government had stopped *Out Here*; they had a look—and what did they find? Alliance with Hitler? They found an American citizen saying what he thought. Some people didn't like what he thought, but what is it you want? Do you want a man to say what he's told, or is it democracy you want? Folks who didn't like what he said blasted back as hard as they could; then it was his turn to come back at them—all the wit and drive he could muster. Such is democratic procedure—and more power to it."[88]

Here, in the novel she published three years before her death, is perhaps the most forthright (if not the most erudite) expression of Glaspell's most important legacy: her defense of free speech and expression as the lifeblood of the writer and the foundation of American democracy. For her steadfast defense of and commitment to this ideal, she was revered by her fellow writers. Lewisohn, one of her most fervent champions, describes her contribution eloquently in his review of *The Verge*: "Other American dramatists may have more obvious virtues; they may reach larger audiences and enjoy a less wavering repute. Susan Glaspell has a touch of that vision without which we perish."[89]

6

Three Midwestern Playwrights Found a Theatre Company

From 1915 to 1922 I gave up practically everything else, though I had an established position as a novelist. I wanted to do this, and I am glad I did.

—SUSAN GLASPELL TO ELEANOR FITZGERALD

For Susan Glaspell my respect and admiration grew immensely; it is a difficult position to be the wife of a man who is driven by a daemon, a position from which any mortal woman might, however great her love, shrink in dismay or turn away in weariness; but it was a position which she maintained with a sense and radiant dignity.

—FLOYD DELL

DURING THE SUMMER OF 1916, novelist Susan Glaspell found herself in a bad spot. Her husband, George Cram (Jig) Cook, had announced that their fledgling theatre company, the Provincetown Players, would be mounting one of her plays:

> "Now, Susan," he said to me, briskly, "I have announced a play of yours for the next bill."
> "But I have no play."
> "Then you will have to sit down tomorrow and begin one."[1]

Except for the one-act play, *Suppressed Desires* (1915), that Cook and Glaspell had staged during the Provincetown Players' first season,

Glaspell had no prior theatre experience. Although she was the best-selling author of three novels and over thirty short stories, she had never written a play on her own. As she related in an unpublished essay, "I started writing plays because my husband forced me to."[2]

After Cook told her that while she might not have a play, she did have a stage, she went to the Wharf Theater, a renovated fish house that had housed the Provincetown Players' first four productions during the summer of 1915. She recalled in the biography she wrote of her husband, *The Road to the Temple*, that when she sat in the theatre and looked at the stage, "after a time the stage became a kitchen. I saw just where the stove was, the table, and the steps going up. Then the door at the back opened, and people all bundled up came in—two or three men, I wasn't sure which, but sure enough about the two women" (*RTT*, 256).

Glaspell remembered such a kitchen, one that she had visited when, as a reporter for the *Des Moines Daily News*, she covered the trial of a farm wife who was accused of murdering her husband. Subsequently, Glaspell ran back and forth across the street from her house to the theatre, visualizing and remembering and writing. The play that emerged from this process was, of course, *Trifles*, her best-known and most widely produced and anthologized one-act play, which, according to Helen Deutsch and Stella Hanau, "has been translated into the language of every country where women murder their husbands."[3]

Trifles premiered at the Wharf Theater on August 8, 1916, during the Provincetown Players' second season. That summer was also noteworthy because Eugene O'Neill had joined the group and mounted his one-act sea play, *Bound East for Cardiff*, in July. One-act plays by Wilbur Daniel Steele, Louise Bryant, John (Jack) Reed, Neith Boyce, and Jig Cook, in addition to the Glaspell and O'Neill plays, rounded out the season. O'Neill would stage sixteen plays for the Provincetown and then go on to Broadway success, earning four Pulitzer Prizes for drama and the Nobel Prize for literature.

The dramaturgy of O'Neill and Glaspell, who would contribute eleven plays, sustained the Provincetown Players throughout their eight-year existence, but the genesis, driving force, and inspiration for much of their work was due to one man—Jig Cook. Cook's early grounding in Greek culture and involvement in radical activities in early twentieth-century Davenport would inform not only the plays that he wrote but also the aesthetic and theatre practice of the Provincetown Players, which emphasized experimentalism, artistic merit, collaboration, the primacy of the playwright, and the amateur spirit.

Cook conceived of a theatre collective in which all involved, including the audience, would collaborate to create plays that would enrich themselves and the culture in which they lived. This collaborative spirit was reflected in the Provincetown Players' constitution as well as the bylaw-like resolutions written by Jack Reed and adopted on September 5, 1916. Cook, who had been elected president of the company, wrote the constitution; Reed, Bryant, and Floyd Dell were named members of the Executive Committee; and Margaret Nordfeldt was elected secretary.

The constitution defined the company as a club with three classes of members: active members, associate members, and club members. The latter two groups comprised season-ticket holders and single-ticket holders, respectively. The active membership category reflected Cook's collectivist philosophy: "The active members shall be those interested and engaged in the production of plays. New Active Members may be added by a majority vote of the Active Members. Active Members who cease to be interested may be dropped by a majority vote of the Active Members." Article 5 stipulated that "the Active Members as a body shall determine what plays are to be produced."[4]

Twenty-nine persons signed up as active members that September. Besides Dell, Cook, and Glaspell, the list included Eugene O'Neill, Jack Reed and Louise Bryant, Max Eastman and Idah Rauh, Neith Boyce and Hutchins Hapgood, Margaret and Bror Nordfeldt, Margaret and Wilbur D. Steele, Marguerite and William Zorach, Edwin D. and Nancy N. Schoonmaker, Edward and Stella Ballantine, Alice and Henry Hall, Frederic Burt, Myra Carr, Charles Demuth, Mary Heaton (Vorse) O'Brian, Lucy Huffaker, David Carb, and Robert Rogers. None of these people, at that time, was a professional playwright, director, stage manager, or production designer, and only two (Burt and Edward Ballantine) were professional actors.

This amateur status was in keeping with Cook's vision of a "beloved community of life-givers," artists of various media who would come together to create an "American Renaissance of the Twentieth Century" that was grounded in communal intellectual passion (*RTT*, 224). "The arts fertilize each other; the dancer creates in space attitudes of sculpture and in time makes them flow rhythmically into each other like the successive notes of melody. Our minds are now full of the madness of painting that wants to be like music," Cook enthused (RTT, 245).

To this end, he continually reached out to artists in a variety of media to join the collective and lend their talents to the group. He urged poet Edgar Lee Masters, whose book of dramatic monologues, *Spoon River Anthology*, had caused a sensation the previous year, to try playwrighting, and he helped journalist Mike Gold revise his "very naïve one-act play" for production. Gold, at that time an assistant truck driver for the Adams Express Company, was impressed with Cook's zeal for bringing out the playwright in those he encountered: "I had never heard such talk before. He talked as though he had known me for years. He glanced through the play and I told him what I was trying to do . . . he made me feel like a god! He told me what I was trying to do. It was what he did for everyone, great, small, dumb, or literate."[5]

Cook envisioned "a whole community working together, developing unsuspected talents," a community that would "furnish the kind of audience that will cause new plays to be written" (RTT, 245, 251–52). Glaspell also stressed Cook's belief in the importance of audience involvement: "The people who had seen the plays and the people who gave them were adventurers together. The spectators were part of the Players, for how could it have been done without the feeling that came from them, without that sense of them there, waiting, ready to share, giving—finding the deep level where audience and writer and player are one" (RTT, 254).

The twenty-eight-word resolution that begins the list of seven composed by Reed comprises three central elements of the company's theatre practice that constitute the core of Cook's vision for a new theatre as articulated above: "That it is the primary object of the Provincetown Players to encourage the writing of American plays of real artistic literary and dramatic—as opposed to Broadway—merit." With this resolution, the primacy of the playwright was enshrined in the group's mission, further emphasized when, at the behest O'Neill, the actual theatre was named the Playwright's Theater.

When they adopted their resolutions, the Provincetown Players planted a contradiction within their foundational documents and thus sowed the seeds of their future demise. The first resolution further states that "the author shall produce the play without hindrance, according to his own ideas," and additional resolutions adopted by the group put the human and financial resources of the company at the playwright's disposal and required the playwright to select and rehearse the cast and direct the production. However, other resolutions enumerated the duties of the active members, duties that reflected the collaborative spirit of the company. Active members were expected "to discover and encourage new plays and playwrights." They were to attend and participate in play-reading meetings, vote on the plays that were submitted to be staged, superintend the production of their own plays, and write, stage, or act in plays at the Provincetown.[6]

A theatre collective that prioritizes group participation and yet elevates the individual playwright above all else will ultimately experience unresolvable conflict when the irresistible force meets the immovable object. This ultimately terminal conflict came to a head a few years later when O'Neill, James Light, and others pushed for taking successful Provincetown plays to Broadway while Cook, Glaspell, Edna Kenton, and others strove to preserve the original amateur and collaborative nature of the collective.

The first resolution also stipulates that native American plays would be produced. With one exception—Arthur Schnitzler's *Last Masks*, which the group mounted in 1920—the Provincetown Players adhered to this stipulation. Although companies such as the Washington Square Players and Maurice Browne's Chicago Little Theatre kept seats filled and doors open by producing well-known plays by Ibsen, Shaw, Strindberg, and Euripides, the Provincetown Players were able to survive for eight seasons by producing plays by new American playwrights. As Linda Ben-Zvi observes, this "miracle" was accomplished despite having "virtually no money, no press agent in the first years, and no advertising."[7]

The third key element in the first resolution stipulates that artistic merit rather than commercial potential would be the criterion on which production decisions would be based. Broadway is explicitly mentioned as the kind of drama that would not be done at the Provincetown, for melodramas, spectacles, romantic comedies, actor-driven vehicles, and musical revues like *Very Good Eddie* and the *Ziegfeld Follies* still dominated Broadway during the Provincetown Players' first season. As Glaspell commented about the prevalence of the formulaic in Broadway plays, "Plays, like magazine stories, were patterned. They might be pretty good within themselves, seldom did they open out to—where it surprised or thrilled your spirit to follow" (*RTT*, 248).

The Players lived up to the rebellious spirit of this resolution, mounting some plays that were so artistic that no one really knew what they meant. Louise Bryant's *The Game*, described by Deutsch and Hanau as "a simple and not particularly brilliant morality play," was one of their earliest productions.[8] Bryant's one-act play featured a postimpressionist set by Marguerite Zorach and stylized acting done to look like a series of Egyptian reliefs by players representing Life and Death gambling for the Youth and the Girl. The program states that *The Game* is "an attempt to synthesize decoration, costume, speech and action into one mood."[9]

While this attempt resulted in a visually arresting modernist work, it failed to connect with those spectators who were more interested in content than style. However, along with some of the Players' other bold stagings, it did attract media attention, which brought notice of their work to the general public. "These players are revolutionists," wrote A. J. Philpott. "They care little for stage traditions and in their work so far they have given absolutely no consideration to the great American, theatrical bugaboo, 'the tired business man,' who desires to be amused at the theatre."[10]

Reed's resolutions were complemented by a group-authored manifesto highlighting the major elements in the constitution and resolutions that was circulated to announce the Provincetown Players' first New York season (1916–17). With a successful summer season of eleven plays under their belt, they were ready to try New York City and needed to attract the city's intelligentsia and culture mavens to their shows. The manifesto stressed the company's amateur status: "The present organization is the outcome of a group of people interested in the theater, who gathered spontaneously during two summers at Provincetown, Massachusetts, for the purpose of writing, producing and acting their own plays." It also highlighted the playwright's role in the company. "The impelling desire of the group was to establish a stage where playwrights of sincere, poetic, literary and dramatic purpose could see their plays in action, and superintend their production without submitting to the commercial manager's interpretation of public taste."[11]

This freedom often resulted in plays that dealt with controversial or topical themes that the commercial theatre would not have been eager to stage, such as birth control, out-of-wedlock pregnancy, pacifism, free love, drug addiction, free speech, insanity, homelessness, and racism.

Pendleton King's *Cocaine*, produced in March 1917, is a two-hander in which a down-and-out couple commiserate and make a suicide pact that fails when neither has a quarter to feed the gas meter—not exactly the kind of evening entertainment to which *Dinner at Eight*'s Millicent Jordan would want to take her guests![12]

While reflecting the spirit of the constitution and resolutions, the manifesto also articulated a key element of the company's aesthetic—experimentalism: "Equally, it was to afford an opportunity for actors, producers, scenic and costume-designers to experiment with a stage of extremely simple resources." The manifesto went on to describe the experimental focus of the company: "The Players' theatre remains, as it began, a stage for free dramatic experiment in the true amateur spirit."[13] In practice, the Provincetown Players adhered to this experimental and amateur emphasis. Modes of theatre that were staged at the Provincetown include allegory, pastoral, commedia dell'arte, verse, symbolism, expressionism, and realism, the latter being the most frequently employed theatre style.

O'Neill was among the most enthusiastic experimentalists in the troupe. Barbara Ozieblo writes that his one-act monologue by a disgruntled wife, *Before Breakfast* (1916), was written "to test an audience's endurance when subjected to the prolonged presence of a single actor on the stage."[14] His *Where the Cross Is Made* (1918) features three scary-looking ghosts of seamen that are seen only by an insane sea captain and his son; O'Neill wanted to see if upon seeing the ghosts, the audience could be made to think that they were mad, too.[15]

By far the most successful of the Provincetown's experimental plays was O'Neill's *The Emperor Jones* (1920), which chronicled the physical and psychological deterioration of a former Pullman porter who had taken over a Caribbean island. The production featured a blue plaster dome (*kuppelhorizont*), against which Brutus Jones defiantly rose. First used in German expressionist theatre, the dome could, as Alexander Woollcott observed, allow the Players to "get such illusions of distance and the wide outdoors as few of their uptown rivals can achieve."[16]

In portraying the succeeding stages of Jones's mental disintegration, the Players also used masks, silhouettes, and a moving drum under the stage timed to the human heartbeat. Even Woollcott, a frequent critic of the company's productions, had to admit that the play was "an extraordinarily striking and dramatic study of panic fear," and Heywood Broun pronounced it "the most interesting play which has yet come from the most promising playwright in America."[17]

Not everyone was as enthusiastic about the Provincetown Players' experiments as Woollcott and Broun. Dell, who wrote four plays for the company, stated in his autobiography, *Homecoming* (1933), that Cook "fell madly in love with one toy after another—when a wind-machine was acquired, hardly a word of dialogue could be heard for months, all being drowned out by the wind-machine."[18] Dell was perhaps understandably upset because Cook's experiments adversely affected one of his own plays, *A Long Time Ago* (1917), recalling that "when I was too busy to stage-manage a play of mine, he turned it over to some new enthusiast with lunatic ideas, who put the actors on stilts, so that nothing could be heard except clump, thump, bump! Nothing was too mad or silly to do in the Provincetown Theatre, and I suffered some of the most excruciating hours of painful and exasperated boredom there as a member of the audience that I have ever experienced in my life" (*Homecoming*, 266).[19]

The company's plans for their first New York season were ambitious. Their circular announced a twenty-week season of ten bills of new plays by American authors; several of these plays were yet unwritten, and several of these authors did not yet know that they were playwrights. The theatre that would house these plays was a converted brownstone at 139 MacDougal Street with a stage that measured fourteen feet by ten feet six inches.

Despite these limitations, the troupe succeeded in mounting twenty-seven plays by O'Neill, Glaspell, Dell, Cook, Bryant, Reed, Boyce and Hapgood, Steele, and Nordfeldt, as well as new members Alfred Kreymborg, John Mosher, Saxe Commins, Kenneth MacNichol, David Pinski, Rita Wellman, Harry Kemp, Pendleton King, and Irwin Granich (Mike Gold). An audience was assured when Reed sold associate memberships (season tickets) to the four-hundred-member New York Stage Society.

Although critics were not offered free tickets, some of them came anyway. Perhaps the newspaper reviewer who was most keen on the troupe was Broun; this excerpt from a January 1917 piece he wrote could have been used in one of their promotional circulars: "As we understand it, an experiment is something which turns cinders into gold dust or explodes with a fearful crash and odor. In this sense the Provincetown Players have established a most efficient experimental theatre. Some of the explosions can be heard even when the plays are read miles away from Macdougal Street."[20]

Kenton, who joined the company during the fall of 1916 as a play reader and Executive Committee member, recalled that the struggle to live up to the group ideal set forth in the constitution, resolutions, and manifesto was already beginning: "But a great theory fell by the wayside. Direction, you see, according to the fine idea of 'group synthesis,' would come not from one, but spontaneously from the group acting as one. Perhaps in some millennium on some Hyperborean isle! But never in Macdougal Street. . . . Surrendering this group ideal would have been [a] more severe wrench than it was if we had not been so weary. As it was, fatigue did not wait on commonsense; we succumbed to directorship wholeheartedly."[21] During that season a professional director, Nina Moise, was hired, and as the production values of the company waxed, their allegiance to the amateur spirit and collaborative aesthetic waned.

This aesthetic was articulated and promulgated primarily by Cook, who aspired to develop a theatre company modeled on what he understood to be the Greek ideal of ritualized theatre springing from Dionysian ecstasy that would enrich American culture. According to Ben-Zvi, Cook believed that "what marked the Golden Age of Pericles was a community of like-minded people who could, through their shared commitment to ideals of beauty, harmony and art, shape the society as a whole."[22] A circular from the 1917–18 season reflects these influences: "That a closely knit group of creative and critical minds is capable of calling forth from the individuals who compose it richer work than they can produce in isolation is the basic faith of the founder of our playhouse."

The circular went on to assert that "the art of the theatre cannot be pure, in fact can not be an art at all, unless its various elements— playwrighting, acting, setting, costuming, lighting—are by some means fused into unity." The origin of drama in ancient Greece was then invoked as an aspirational ideal for the Provincetown Players: "Primitive drama, the expression of the communal or religious life of the organic human group, the tribe, had spontaneously the unity of pure art. . . . Unity is not imposed on them by the will of one of their number but comes from that deep level in the spirit of each where all their spirits are one."[23]

Cook's obsession with all things Greek began early in life when his mother, Ellen Dodge Cook, taught him to revere Greek art and literature.

He grew up with Plato and Plotinus, studied Greek art at Harvard, and, as a college student, planned to travel to Greece with his friend John Alden, a trip he reluctantly postponed due to a family financial exigency. Glaspell wrote to Kenton that for Cook, "Greece begins in Iowa," and so the Provincetown begins there, too.[24] "One man cannot produce drama," Cook wrote, articulating his foundational principles for the company. "True drama is born of one feeling animating all members of a clan—a spirit shared by all and expressed by the few for the all. If there is nothing to take the place of the common religious purpose and passion of the primitive group, out of which the Dionysian dance was born, no new vital drama can arise in any people" (*RTT*, 252–53).

Frederick Coppleston writes of Friedrich Nietzsche that "one cannot question his vast reputation and the power of his ideas to act like a potent wine in the minds of a good many people."[25] Cook was definitely one of those people; he had been a Nietzsche enthusiast since he encountered the philosopher's work as an instructor at the University of Iowa. *The Road to the Temple* includes many notes and observations that Cook made on Nietzsche's work. "Great moving new ideas, but it is the passion with which he thinks them and stamps them into words that sets the reader's soul on fire," Cook wrote in his German edition of Nietzsche's works. "His works pass through the soul like music—the soul of the whole moving on entire through every part" (*RTT*, 138).

Cook's allusion to Dionysian dance resulting from group passion in the passage quoted above reflects his understanding of Nietzsche's theory of Apollonian and Dionysian drama. For Nietzsche, art is born when the opposing forces of the Apollonian (representing restraint, order, rationality, and individuation) and the Dionysian (encompassing freedom, vitality, emotion, and chaos) come together in aesthetic synthesis: "The origin and essence of Greek tragedy [is] the expression of two interwoven artistic impulses, the Apollinian [sic] and the Dionysian," writes Nietzsche in *The Birth of Tragedy* (Kaufmann, 81).

In this book, Nietzsche sounds very much like Cook when he writes of "a community of unconscious actors who consider themselves and one another transformed," such transformation constituting "the presupposition of all dramatic art."[26] For Nietzsche, explains Coppleston, "true culture is a unity of the forces of life, the Dionysian element, with the love of form and beauty, which is characteristic of the Apollinian [sic] attitude."[27]

Cook, however, appeared to discount the Apollonian part of the equation and take Nietzsche's analogy of Dionysian intoxication quite literally. Moreover, despite his later conversion to Socialism, he never completely abandoned his enchantment with the Nietzschean concept of the Übermensch (Superman) that he had embraced as a young man. Cook's internal conflict between the Nietzschean ideal that privileged individualism and the Socialist ideal that prioritized communitarianism would be reflected a few years later in the larger conflict between warring Provincetown factions that would end in the demise of the Provincetown Players.

Undergirding Nietzsche's theory was a Monistic premise—that "mystic feeling of oneness" that the artist attains when the Apollonian and Dionysian impulses come together in art.[28] This concept resonated deeply with Cook, who had embraced Monism with Dell in Davenport in 1907, having likely encountered the work of Ernst Haeckel while living and studying in Germany in the mid-1890s. Haeckel, an evolutionary biologist who promulgated a theory of the essential oneness of the universe, was hugely influential for Cook and Dell.

Haeckel based his Monistic theory on the fact that any natural force can be converted into any other. In *The Riddle of the Universe at the Close of the Nineteenth Century* (1900), he argues that the unity of nature follows from this premise and offers Monism as an alternative to Christianity, substituting the trinity of the true, the good, and the beautiful to guide humans in their ethical endeavors. "Just as the infinite universe is one great whole in the light of our monistic teaching, so the spiritual and moral life of man is a part of this cosmos. . . . There are not two different, separate worlds—the one physical and material, and the other moral and immaterial," argues Haeckel, echoing Nietzsche's description of "the mystery of union" that results from the Apollonian-Dionysian synthesis in art.[29]

Perhaps the strongest element in the Provincetown aesthetic derived from Cook's Socialist activism in Davenport. In *The Road to the Temple*, Glaspell writes of Cook hosting Socialist picnics at the Cabin and using his experience as a truck farmer to argue for the labor theory of value; this Socialist activism culminated in his 1910 run for Congress. Campaigning as a Socialist in early twentieth-century Davenport was a losing proposition, as Cook must have known, but it's likely that he took it on because it offered the opportunity to travel throughout Iowa's

Second Congressional District and explain the principles of Socialism to farmers and factory workers.

For Cook, Socialism, with its emphasis on collectivism and communitarianism, was a perfect complement to his view of the Greek ideal of art as the expression of members of a community. The conjoining of these two beliefs, inflected by Haeckel's Monism and Nietzsche's theory of Apollonian and Dionysian synthesis, resulted in a collectivist aesthetic that governed the theatre practice of the Provincetown Players for the better part of eight years. As C. W. E. Bigsby notes, "He wished to provoke a renaissance in American writing, a resurgence, socialist in spirit and poetic in its ability to generate dramatic images of human unity. The model and inspiration was always the Greek theatre, which dominated his imagination and which led him to stress the correspondence of the arts."[30]

Cook's vision was still intact during the Provincetown Players' second New York season (1917–18), which featured nineteen plays by O'Neill, Glaspell, Dell, Cook, Granich, Kreymborg, and Wellman, as well as plays by newcomers James Oppenheim, Maxwell Bodenheim, Mary Caroline Davies, Grace Potter, Alice Woods, Edna St. Vincent Millay, and F. B. Kugelman (Frederick Kaye). This season was notable in that the Provincetown Players mounted their first full-length production, Cook's *The Athenian Women* (1918), and for the company's move to a converted stable at 133 MacDougal Street that gave them a much-needed expanded playing space—a stage that measured twelve feet by twenty-six feet—as well as more room for the audience and an area for a restaurant on the second floor.

The 1918–19 season featured twenty one-act plays, but only seven of these were by new playwrights: Mary F. Barber, Bosworth Crocker, Robert A. Parker, Alice L. Rostetter, Otto K. Liveright, Florence Kiper Frank, and Rita C. Smith. The group was losing members, partly due to a 1917 purge in which B. J. O. Nordfeldt was asked to resign, and his wife, Margaret, who until that time had been serving as the Provincetown's secretary, was not reelected. Dell, Eastman, and Hapgood, who had resigned earlier, were taken off the membership rolls. Another factor in the Provincetown's loss of talent was World War I. Their spring 1918 circular noted the change: "Seven of the Provincetown Players are in France, and more are going." The circular went on to assert that in time of war, theatre is more important than ever:

One faculty, we know, is going to be of vast importance to the half-destroyed world—indispensable for its rebuilding—the faculty of creative imagination. That spark of it which has given this group of ours such life and meaning as we have is not so insignificant that we should now let it die. The social justification which we feel to be valid now for makers and players of plays is that they shall help keep alive in the world the light of imagination. Without it the wreck of the world that was cannot be cleared away and the new world shaped. (*RTT*, 267)

The 1919–20 season saw no plays by Dell, Cook, or Glaspell. Dell had left the players because he thought that his own antiwar play, *A Long Time Ago*, had been mishandled, although Deutsch and Hanau list him as a member of the cast of the previous season's *The Athenian Women*. Cook and Glaspell had taken a sabbatical to concentrate on writing plays for the 1920–21 season. Only fourteen new plays were mounted, seven by first-timers Harold Chapin, Winthrop Parkhurst, Lewis Beach, Lawrence Langner, Edna Ferber, Djuna Barnes, and Wallace Stevens. Of the returning playwrights, Edna St. Vincent Millay was a standout. Millay, primarily known as a poet and later as one of the Provincetown's best actresses, had seen her *The Princess Marries the Page* produced by the company during the previous season and would triumph with her antiwar play *Aria da Capo*, mounted on December 5, 1919. A little gem of a theatre classic, *Aria da Capo* was produced as recently as August 2020 by the Shakespeare Theater of New Jersey.

Only eight new plays were mounted during the 1920–21 season, and only four new playwrights contributed plays: Lawrence Vail, Evelyn Scott, Gustave Wied, and Cloyd Head. Cook and Glaspell launched their full-length plays, *The Spring* and *Inheritors*, in January and March 1921, respectively. Both were overshadowed, however, by O'Neill's *The Emperor Jones*, staged the previous fall, which Bigsby lauds as "a brilliant exposition of physical and psychological collapse."[31] Kenneth Macgowan rhapsodized, "The moment when [Brutus Jones] raises his naked body against the moonlit sky beyond the edge of the jungle and prays, is such a dark lyric of the flesh, such a cry of the primitive being, as I have never seen in the theatre."[32] *The Emperor Jones* proved to be both a critical and a popular success, such a big hit that it would later move to Broadway and then go on tour, sorely taxing the resources of the small theatre company.

The Provincetown Players' final season was that of 1921–22; seven plays were staged, and four new playwrights were introduced: Theodore

Dreiser, Norman C. Lindau, Donald Corley, and Pierre Loving. This season was memorable for two plays that employed expressionist techniques: O'Neill's *The Hairy Ape* (1921) and Glaspell's *The Verge* (1921). Glaspell's full-length comedy *Chains of Dew*, the last play to be mounted by the Provincetown, was produced in April 1922 after she and Cook had left for Greece. Cook, feeling betrayed because O'Neill had sought another director for *The Hairy Ape*, which he had championed, decided that his old dream was dead and it was time to move on.

By 1922, it had become clear that the Provincetown Players had not produced Jig Cook's "beloved community of life-givers." Instead, it had produced two factions: the Old Guard (Cook, Glaspell, Kenton, and others) that wanted to stay true to Cook's ideal of an experimental theatre collective and the Young Turks (O'Neill, James Light, and others) who, ambitious for their own careers, saw the Provincetown Players primarily as a tryout stage for Broadway. A way to understand this schism is to see it as deriving from the conflict between process and product. For Cook, as Robert Karoly Sarlos explains, "the group was not a means of creating theatre, but instead theatre became the ideal means of creating a group":

> Consequently of paramount importance was the organic relationship *between* process and product: resulting [sic] works of art he considered significant only as momentarily surviving agents of communal health. As such, under optimum conditions a work might enable its creators to engender in an audience the duplicate of the very healing process that benefited them. Here lies the seminal value of Jig's ideas and the Provincetown Players' attempt at putting them into practice. Group dynamics, social regeneration through art, and emphasis on process has [sic] proven a durable potion, which, injected into the veins of American theatre, released its active substance gradually, delivering a cumulative effect.[33]

When the Young Turks showed little interest in revitalizing American society through collaborative theatre and much interest in developing productions that would succeed on Broadway, Cook felt that the Provincetown Players had fallen short of their aspirations and should say so and end things. In 1922, he wrote to Kenton that "our individual gifts and talents have sought their private perfection. We have not, as we had hoped, created the community of life-givers. . . . Since we have failed spiritually in the elemental things . . . and since the result is mediocrity, we keep our promise: we give this theater we love good death; the Provincetown Players end their story here" (*RTT*, 309–10).

However, that was not quite the end of the Provincetown Players' story. After seven key members, including O'Neill, Cook, Glaspell, and Kenton, incorporated to preserve their company, the group announced a one-year hiatus. Cook and Glaspell immigrated to Delphi, Greece, in March 1922, partly in response to the tensions that had been building between the two factions. By the time the group reorganized in 1924, Cook was dead, and Glaspell had returned from Greece and was seeing to her ailing mother in Davenport. She then spent a month with her college friend Lucy Huffaker and her husband, Edward Goodman, in New York before settling in Provincetown.

On May 28, 1924, Kenneth Macgowan, along with O'Neill and production designer Robert Edmond Jones, took over the Provincetown Players with a reconstituted group that they called the Experimental Theatre.[34] This Triumvirate, as the three were called, wanted to retain the name "Provincetown Playhouse" for the theatre building in Greenwich Village. However, Glaspell objected to that plan, as well as to the reorganization, as Kenton had been pushed out of the new company.

She wrote to Eleanor Fitzgerald, the group's manager, that the Triumvirate's continuing to call the theatre building the Provincetown Playhouse was an effort to trade on the Provincetown Players' name by an entirely different group: "There was a man named Jig Cook. He gave some eight years of his life to creating the Provincetown Playhouse. If it had not been for him, there would not be that place in which you now put on your plays. He worked until he had worked himself out, and then he went away, and he died. You are profiting from what he did, and you have forgotten him."[35] At O'Neill's behest, a brass plaque honoring Cook's work was installed in the theatre, but Glaspell was not mollified, resigning from the group and writing to Fitzgerald that "Fitzie, and all of you, for this letter is for all of you, from very deep down, I am through."[36]

Was the Provincetown Players a success or a failure? "When the Provincetown Players had succeeded, Jig felt they had failed," concluded Glaspell (*RTT*, 298). Macgowan put the case similarly: "The secret of their success was that they gave no thought to success. The secret of their failure—or rather their fulfillment—was again their success."[37] Macgowan's comment suggests that, in his view, the Provincetown Players had succeeded in their goal of developing new plays by American playwrights; they had done their job and should therefore cease to exist.

Others, such as Kenton, who clung to Jig Cook's old dream of a drama developed collectively out of Dionysian ecstasy, saw things differently. Kenton's had been the single vote against moving *The Emperor Jones* to Broadway, and she saw this decision as the beginning of the end: "Face to face with the lure of 'expansion,' and without a treasury to aid us, we had taken the hand of the subtle enemy to experiment as if it were the hand of a friend. We had sent 'The Emperor' up-town, had depleted our own actor-group, had enlarged the group, were for the first time paying 'salaries,' and were, for the first time, paying in spirit. Values had shifted overnight, astonishingly. To go up-town with our first success was higher honor than to stay down-town with our experiments . . . and we lost our balance and fell."[38]

For Cook, Kenton, and like-minded others, the Provincetown Players had failed. Assuming this premise, the roots of their failure lay in the contradictions inherent in their aesthetic. One of these contradictions, discussed above, was the prioritizing of both the development of the individual playwright and the collaborative production of authentic drama. Although F. Scott Fitzgerald would maintain in "The Crack-Up" that the test of maturity was the ability to hold two contradictory ideas in mind simultaneously, his maxim did not seem to hold true in this case. In a country like the United States, where individual desires and needs almost always trump the common good, the dominance of the individual playwright was pretty much inevitable if a gifted playwright ever came on the scene. Two did—O'Neill and Glaspell—so the demise of the collective was foreordained from the get-go. Only a delusional dreamer like Cook could think otherwise.

The second contradiction that doomed the Provincetown Players lay in the group's establishment via constitution and resolutions as a theatre collective that was undermined in actual practice by the dominance of Cook.[39] Dell remembers that Cook couldn't delegate authority: "He thought that nothing could get done without his doing it himself, and he ran hastily from one thing to another, and nobody was allowed to drive a nail if George were there to do it" (*Homecoming*, 266). Although the constitution and resolutions required that production decisions be made by majority vote of the group, Cook made two major decisions unilaterally—once in 1916 when he spent most of the company's treasury to put a steel girder in the 139 MacDougal Street theatre and again in 1920 when, contrary to majority opinion, he again depleted the group's finances to put in the blue plaster dome for *The Emperor Jones*. In this instance, Kenton, usually a supporter of Jig and Susan, was forced to face facts: "Here I had come suddenly face to face with 'dictatorship,' a deliberate 'going against the group,' a reversal of an executive decision, with no warning—and an outstanding example of fine dictatorship as to purpose and, as fate would have it, to result as well."[40]

Accounts of the Provincetown Players may differ regarding their success or failure, but all agree that Cook was the dominant member of the group. Dell described Cook's modus operandi as that of generating chaos to facilitate creativity: "Drunk and sober, he whipped and hell-raised and praised and prayed it into something that—though this was not what he was aiming at—did impress Broadway. Many fine talents got their chance in that maelstrom" (*Homecoming*, 266). O'Neill's take on Cook seems to have varied according to whether his words were for public consumption. He praised Cook in Barrett Clark's *Eugene O'Neill: The Man and His Plays* but wrote to Eleanor Fitzgerald that Cook "drove all our best talent that we had developed away from the theatre for daring to disagree with him. This is a supposed group democracy! Then he beat it to Greece, leaving a hollow shell as a monument to his egotism."[41]

Eastman called Cook a dynamo and explained that his dynamism was a result of "his abstract wish to be a genius combined with an inability to retire into a lonely corner and get down to concrete work."[42] Another eyewitness to Cook's management style was his wife. "It was his intensity that held the thing together," she wrote in *The Road to the Temple*, although she was less tactful a few pages later: "Sometimes Jig was about as true as a hurricane to the group ideal" (*RTT*, 262, 277). Kenton highlighted the irony inherent in Cook's methods when she characterized him as "a dictatorial god risen from a group 'animated by the group spirit.'"[43]

Perhaps the best way to determine the relative success or failure of the Provincetown Players is to examine the scholarly assessments of their legacy. According to William Warren Vilhauer (whose two-part dissertation, "A History and Evaluation of the Provincetown Players," was an early and meticulously thorough study of the company), their legacy was extensive, although Vilhauer, unlike Sarlos and later scholars, considers the Provincetown Players to include the Experimental Theatre run by the Triumvirate of Macgowan, O'Neill, and Jones. Vilhauer credits the Provincetown with providing a stage for new American playwrights to experiment, see their first plays produced, and develop as artists, as well as with producing three Pulitzer Prize–winning American dramatists— O'Neill, Glaspell, and Paul Green—and fourteen other authors whose work with the Provincetown advanced their careers.

Vilhauer also observes that the Provincetown provided the first American stage for new modes of theatre, such as O'Neill's sea plays and expressionistic dramas, Glaspell's satirical and psychologically realistic comedies, Kreymborg's poetic plays, and Green's and Hatcher Hughes's folk plays. In addition, the Provincetown Players used African American actors instead of white actors in blackface in three O'Neill plays—*The Dreamy Kid*, *The Emperor Jones*, and *All God's Chillun Got Wings*—and in Green's *In Abraham's Bosom*, thus helping integrate the American theatre and leading the fight against censorship in the theatre as well as the effort to rid it of prejudice.[44]

Vilhauer also notes that the Provincetown Players led the way in the development of new stagecraft. To this list of contributions should be added the Provincetown's pioneering efforts as the country's first theatre collective, efforts that paved the way for future collaborative endeavors, such as the Group Theater. Finally, Vilhauer points out that the Provincetown Players helped fill the void created by the breakup of two theatrical trusts and the decline of road productions due to rising railroad rates and the growing popularity of the movies:

> America needed a new type of theatre. . . . A number of insurgent groups sprang up across the country attempting to supply this demand. The Provincetown Players must be recognized as one of the prime forces in this movement. Their experimental work with new American play-wrights and the new stagecraft in the intimate surroundings of the small Provincetown Playhouse not only helped in establishing new trends in the types of plays presented in America but also aided in the development of the little theatre movement in America. Because of their influence, the Provincetown Players will remain as one of the im-portant theatrical groups in the establishment of our modern American theatre practices.[45]

In 1982, Sarlos published his dissertation as *Jig Cook and the Province-town Players: Theatre in Ferment*. Sarlos broke with the 1915–29 concep-tualization of the Provincetown Players established by Vilhauer and earlier by Deutsch and Hanau, the press agents for the Experimental Theatre. Sarlos makes a clear distinction between the original group that functioned from 1915 until 1922 and the reconstituted Experimental Theatre, calling the original company "the single most fruitful theatre company prior to the Second World War."[46]

To the list of contributions that Vilhauer compiled, Sarlos adds that the Players "encouraged and accelerated a general transformation of American playwriting from mere craft into art"[47] and lists the Players who went on to careers in theatre: actors Mary Blair, Charles Ellis, Ann Harding, Luther Adler, Harrison Dowd, and Ida Rauh; directors Helen Westley, James Light, and Jasper Deeter; producer Theron Bamberger; production designer Cleon Throckmorton; and drama professor Samuel Eliot. Sarlos also records the Provincetown Players who went on to found or work in future theatres: Rauh, Deeter, and Mike Gold became part of the Workers' Drama League in 1926, and Deeter founded the Hedgerow Theatre in 1923, where Glaspell's *Inheritors* was staged annually for many years. Throckmorton later worked for the Theatre Guild, and he, Light, Gold, Kreymborg, Fitzgerald, and Glaspell went to work for the Federal Theatre Project during the Great Depression.

Sarlos also examines the theoretical underpinnings of the Provincetown aesthetic and the ways in which these concepts helped fertilize the aesthetics of later theatres. "The activity of the Workers' Drama League and the New Playwrights' Theatre both nurtured seeds of political radicalism that had sprouted at The Playwrights' Theatre," he argues. He adds that the Theatre Union carried on the Provincetown tradition of providing a stage for new dramatists, and the Federal Theatre Project continued their emphasis on developing native talent and producing plays that dealt with social issues, as did the Playwrights' Producing Company. Sarlos notes that theatre collectives that arose in the 1960s, such as the Living Theatre and the San Francisco Mime Troupe, reflected in their theatre practice the collectivist spirit first in evidence over forty years earlier at the Provincetown. "Ultimately, the greatest tribute to Jig Cook and his Provincetown Players is that their impact is too pervasive to be documented conclusively," he opines.[48]

Also in 1982, Bigsby published the first volume of *A Critical Introduction to Twentieth-Century American Drama*; his first chapter discusses the Provincetown Players' role in the transition from a Broadway-based American theatre to one that nurtured serious plays. "The accomplishment of the Provincetown was considerable," Bigsby concludes, emphasizing that its contributions went far beyond producing over ninety

American plays and discovering Glaspell and O'Neill: "It established the theatre for the first time in America as a serious focus of artistic activity. Its ensemble acting and its emphasis on the central importance of a group working together and integrating all elements of performance established a model later embraced by other groups. Together with the Washington Square Players, it laid the foundations for the modern American theatre."[49]

In 2004, J. Ellen Gainor assessed the role of the Provincetown Players in the transformation of American theatre in *Susan Glaspell in Context: American Theater, Culture, and Politics, 1915–48*. Gainor emphasizes the Provincetown's development of the one-act play form as key in this respect. Calling the one-act play "the dramatic mode par excellence for experimentation, innovations, and ultimately the foundation of a national theatrical culture," Gainor highlights Glaspell's staging one-act plays at the Provincetown as "striving to make the drama and theater part of the development of a national literature and performance culture."[50]

Before the rise of the little theatre movement in the early twentieth century, the one-act play was little respected; however, the Provincetown Players, as well as the Chicago Little Theatre and Boston's Toy Theatre, among others, was instrumental in changing this situation, as were the visits in 1911, 1912, and 1914 of the Irish Players, whose repertoire included thirty-four one-act plays. Between 1915 and 1922, the Provincetown Players mounted nearly eighty one-act plays and, in so doing, helped develop the kind of theatre audience that would support challenging drama. Of that number, Glaspell contributed seven (including the two she wrote with Cook), Dell contributed four, and Cook contributed three (including the two he wrote with Glaspell). "Glaspell's one-acts explore and expand the parameters of the form, exemplifying the idea of a theater in dialogue with evolving critical and social discourses," argues Gainor.[51]

In 2005, Brenda Murphy published her comprehensive study *The Provincetown Players and the Culture of Modernity*, which examines the impact of the Provincetown project on the development of modernism in the United States. In her final chapter, "The Legacy," Murphy focuses on the Provincetown's impact on theatres such as the Theatre Guild. "The success of the Provincetown's experimental productions, particularly *The Emperor Jones* and *The Hairy Ape*, had a clear influence on the Guild," she argues, noting that after these triumphs, the Theatre Guild made a concerted effort to include more expressionist plays in their repertoire and thus worked to move expressionism into the mainstream of American culture.[52]

Murphy also examines the work of three authors whose plays were produced by the Provincetown: Edmund Wilson, Stark Young, and e. e. cummings. Each eschewed realism for a more presentational model of drama, and, although none of them went on to have a career in the theatre, Murphy believes that as a result of their work with the Provincetown, each writer ultimately contributed significantly to the development of American modernism. Collaboration with members of the Provincetown informed the criticism of Wilson and Young and the poetry of cummings as well as the art of Provincetown Players William and Marguerite Zorach, Charles Demuth, and Bror Nordfeldt. Other Provincetown playwrights, too, developed their modernist aesthetics in part due to their work with the company. Alfred Kreymborg developed his puppet theatre after putting on *Vote the New Moon* with its marionette-like actors at the Provincetown, and Djuna Barnes went on to write an avant-garde novel, *Nightwood*, as well as several modernist one-act plays, as a result of her staging three plays there.

In 2007, Jeff Kennedy completed a two-part dissertation, "The Artistic Life of the Provincetown Playhouse, 1918–1922." Extremely valuable for its detailed and deeply contextualized account of the lives, performances, and works of the Provincetown playwrights, Kennedy's dissertation concludes with a brief section on the major contributions of the company: plays that used the American vernacular, emphasized social movements, employed psychological realism, developed innovations in stagecraft, furthered the cause of the Little Theatre and future Off-Broadway movements, and, most significantly, prioritized the staging of new American works.[53]

Neither Glaspell and Cook's Provincetown Players nor Macgowan, O'Neill, and Jones's Experimental Theatre exists today. A group called the Provincetown Theatre now puts on plays in Provincetown, Massachusetts. Glaspell's strong feeling that "a quite other thing should have a quite other name" was ignored in 1924 by the Triumvirate, who insisted—over her strong objections—on calling their theatre building the Provincetown Playhouse; when, in 1946, a New York company came to town calling themselves the Provincetown Players, Glaspell was roused again to protest, writing a stern letter to the *Provincetown Advocate* that ended in a question: "If haddock began calling themselves mackerel, would the fish-minded be fooled?"[54] Although it might not be the legacy that Glaspell and Cook had envisioned, perhaps the persistence of the association between Provincetown and the development of noncommercial theatre, in Provincetown and elsewhere, has proved to be the most eloquent testimony to the significance of the Provincetown Players in American theatre history.

Arthur Davison Ficke, Harvard freshman. *Courtesy of the Beinecke Rare Book and Manuscript Library, Yale University.*

ABOVE, Arthur Davison Ficke (*center*), president of the *Harvard Advocate*, 1903–04. *Courtesy of the Beinecke Rare Book and Manuscript Library, Yale University.*

FACING, *Left to right*: Arthur Davison Ficke, Edna St. Vincent Millay, and Eugen Boissevain, 1923. *Courtesy of the University of Michigan Library.*

Floyd Dell, young journalist. *Courtesy of the Newberry Library, Chicago.*

Floyd Dell, age twenty-one. *Courtesy of the Newberry Library, Chicago.*

ABOVE, George Cram Cook in midlife. *Courtesy Quad-City Times.*

FACING, George Cram Cook and Susan Glaspell, ca. 1913. *Courtesy of the Berg Collection, New York Public Library.*

George Cram Cook (*left*) and Susan Glaspell (*right*) in Delphi, Greece, ca. 1922.
Courtesy of the Berg Collection, New York Public Library.

Susan Glaspell, ca. 1913.
Courtesy of the Berg Collection, New York Public Library.

Left, Mollie Price Cook with daughter Nilla. *Right*, George Cram Cook with daughter Nilla, ca. 1908–9. *Courtesy of the Newberry Library, Chicago.*

Edna St. Vincent Millay and Arthur Davison Ficke, 1926, Santa Fe,
New Mexico, photographed by Millay's husband, Eugen Boissevain.
Courtesy of the Seiffent Papers Special Collection, University of Colorado, Boulder.

William L'Engel's portrait of Susan Glaspell, 1920.
Courtesy of the Berg Collection, New York Public Library.

Susan Glaspell, ca. 1894. *From collection of the author.*

Conclusion

Three Midwestern Playwrights Venture beyond P-Town

I'm an American. We've translated democracy and brotherhood and
equality into enterprise and opportunity and success—and that's
getting Americanised.

—SUSAN GLASPELL

ALTHOUGH THE CURTAIN WENT down on the Provincetown Players' last production in 1922, Floyd Dell, George Cram Cook, and Susan
Glaspell continued to work in theatre, although in different ways than
they might have imagined during that first golden Provincetown summer of 1915. After he and his wife immigrated to Delphi, Greece, Cook
kept alive his old dream of a beloved community of life-givers creating
Dionysian drama. He envisioned an autochthonous theatre developed
by the villagers of Delphi, the Delphic Players, and had sketched out a
three-part drama that told the story of Delphi, beginning in biblical
times and moving through Greece's Golden Age before ending in 1893.
Cook envisioned his project as "another Oberammergau" and had begun
working with the villagers on the play. However, before his plans could
come to fruition, he died of glanders on January 11, 1924, a little less
than two years after he and Glaspell first arrived in Greece.[1]

In 1919, Floyd Dell began his second act, wedding suffragist Berta
(B. Marie) Gage, a fellow Socialist to whom he was married for fifty
years. The Dells moved to Croton-on-Hudson, where they raised two

sons, Anthony and Christopher, and later relocated to a New Hampshire farm. When Dell took a job with the Works Progress Administration in 1935, the family moved to Washington, DC; later, Floyd and B. Marie made a home in Bethesda, Maryland, where they enjoyed visits from Christopher's daughters, Jerri and Katie.[2]

Between 1920 and 1934, Dell published eleven novels, the best known of which is *Moon-Calf*. Focused on his Davenport years, this autobiographical coming-of-age novel garnered excellent reviews and was discussed favorably in Carl Van Doren's review essay, "The Revolt from the Village: 1920," along with F. Scott Fitzgerald's *This Side of Paradise*, Sinclair Lewis's *Main Street*, Edgar Lee Master's *Spoon River Anthology*, and Sherwood Anderson's *Winesburg, Ohio*.[3]

Another of Dell's novels, *An Unmarried Father*, was adapted in 1928 as a hit Broadway play, cowritten by and starring Thomas Mitchell. *Little Accident* ran for 289 performances and was later adapted twice for feature films. In 1931, another Dell-Mitchell collaboration, *Cloudy with Showers*, ran for seventy Broadway performances. After twelve years with the federal government, Dell retired in 1947. He did not become conservative in his later years like Max Eastman and John Dos Passos; Mike Gold notwithstanding, he remained a Socialist and a feminist until he died on July 23, 1969, in Bethesda.[4]

Susan Glaspell's later theatre work was sporadic but notable. Although she had gone back to her first love, fiction, after she returned from Greece (publishing six more novels and several short stories, as well as a biography of Cook, *The Road to the Temple*, and a collection of his poems, *Greek Coins*), she did not abandon drama. In 1926, she wrote a full-length play, *The Comic Artist*, with Norman Matson, a novelist with whom she lived in Provincetown and Truro for eight years.

After they broke up, Matson took the play to Broadway, where it encountered numerous production difficulties and mixed reviews, running for only thirty-six performances in 1933, a few years after Dell had his Broadway hit. Two years earlier, Glaspell's *Alison's House*, set in Buffalo, Iowa, where the Cook Cabin once stood, had won the Pulitzer Prize for drama. Her *Springs Eternal*, a World War II comedy, was rejected by the Theatre Guild and remains unproduced. Drafts of unpublished and unproduced plays, such as "Wings" and "The Good Bozo," can be found among her papers in the Berg Collection of the New York Public Library.[5]

Glaspell's contributions to American theatre did not end with play-wrighting. In 1936, she moved to Chicago to head the Midwest Play Bureau of the Federal Theatre Project, where, very much in the spirit of the Provincetown Players, she helped fledgling midwestern playwrights develop and produce their plays. Arnold Sundgaard's Living Newspaper production, *Spirochete*, and Theodore Ward's *Big White Fog* were two standouts that Glaspell shepherded to production. Glaspell served as the director of the Midwest Play Bureau until May 1938.

After her year and a half of government service in Chicago, she lived mainly in Provincetown and Truro, where she provided a home for step-grandson Sirius Cook and enjoyed visits from stepson Harl Cook, god-daughter Susan Meyer, and Karl Meyer, Susan's brother. She continued to write and to socialize with friends such as Ernie and Dorothy Meyer, Eben Given and Phyllis Duganne, and John and Katie Dos Passos until her death on July 27, 1948.[6]

And what of that romantic and miraculous city, aka Port Royal, Free-port, the Red City of Iowa, Fairport, Baghdad-on-the-Mississippi? Time took the cultural riches of the city that had enchanted Dell, radicalized Cook, and acclaimed and then ostracized Glaspell as it took their youth and naivete. During the ensuing decades, Davenport suffered and sur-vived through two world wars and the Great Depression; the farm crisis of 1980 and the collapse of the agricultural implements industry; reces-sions, floods, and pandemics.

Today, as Davenporters (like many other Americans) prefer to educate and entertain themselves in front of screens in their homes rather than in public venues, international celebrities like Mark Twain no longer lecture there to hundreds, nor do superstars like Sarah Bernhardt travel to Davenport to appear in plays. Only one liberal arts college and one daily newspaper remain. Bookstores and newsstands are in short sup-ply; you can search in vain for a place to buy a *New York Times* or a *Wall Street Journal*, let alone an *Atlantic Monthly* or an *Economist*. More than twice as many people live in Davenport today than when Dell, Cook, and Glaspell arrived in 1903, yet the cultural infrastructure is not twice as rich as it was then, when popular culture and high culture were not as differentiated and people of all social classes attended public lectures, concerts, and plays together.[7]

Although not as vibrant as that of the early 1900s, the cultural life of Iowa's third-largest city has seen its center of gravity shift from literature, theatre, and lectures to music and the visual arts. The Adler Theater is home to the Quad-City Symphony and Broadway at the Adler, and hosts performances by Ballet Quad-Cities. On the Mississippi riverfront, the Figge Art Museum, inaugurated in 1925 as the Davenport Municipal Art Gallery with a collection of 334 works donated by former mayor C. A. Ficke, now has over 4,000 holdings and is home to the Grant Wood archive. The River Music Experience offers performance venues for musicians, music lessons, and music education programs, while the annual Bix Beiderbecke Jazz Festival and the Mississippi Valley Blues Festival draw many fans to the city. The attractive German American Heritage Center and Museum greets motorists driving into Davenport from the Centennial Bridge.

Some of the city's cultural resources from Dell, Cook, and Glaspell's day survive. The Putnam Museum, the lifework of Mary Louisa Duncan Putnam, now holds 160,000 artifacts and boasts an interactive science center and a big-screen theatre. The Davenport Public Library, where Marilla Freeman mentored Dell, still sustains and inspires readers while promoting community literacy. Temple Emanuel, once the first pulpit of the dynamic Rabbi William H. Fineshriber, remains the spiritual home of Davenport's Reform Jews. Black Hawk's Watch Tower is no more, but a young man can still treat his sweetheart to a Green River at Lagomarcino's Confectionary, now with an East Davenport as well as a Moline location, where Mary Beth, Lisa, and Tom Lagomarcino Jr. have introduced a fourth generation to the family business. The 130-year-old Tuesday Club, which Glaspell was thrilled to be asked to join in 1906, continues to meet at Davenport's historic Outing Club, as does the 126-year-old Contemporary Club, where, in 1910, Cook read his paper on Socialism and warned Davenport's business and professional men that they had only twelve more years before the revolution would overtake them.

Dell, Cook, and Glaspell did more than write groundbreaking plays; they dreamed big dreams, and they asked big questions. What is the relationship between art and life? Can art change the world? Can remaking our lives remake society? Their dreams and their questions were informed by the institutions, social movements, publications, and progressive organizations that shaped their intellectual and political development in early twentieth-century Davenport: the Monist Society, Temple Emanuel, Turner Hall, the Davenport Public Library, the

Unitarian Church, the Ethical Society, the Political Refugees Defense League, the Socialist local, *Trident*, and the *Tri-City Workers Magazine*.

Although their contributions to American drama were significant, their contributions to American life were even more so. As they matured and began to realize that they couldn't, as they once had envisioned, change the world "with pens, paintbrushes, and new publications," they gave us, through their writings, a belief in new possibilities and new goals.[8] In Cook's *The Athenian Women*, Aspasia offers us a vision of the Athenian ideal as a model for his new "American Renaissance of the Twentieth Century." Dell spent his career exploring the relation between life and literature and professing the belief that literature can help us put things in perspective, make us more empathetic, and give us a new understanding of our lives, our fellow humans, and our world. In *Intellectual Vagabondage*, he expresses the hope that the younger generation would embrace a literature that "will help them to love generously, to work honestly, to think clearly, to fight bravely, to live nobly."[9] Glaspell, too, put her faith in literature and literacy, declaring that "the best books take us a little farther into understanding, into tolerance, to a keener amusement and to warmer sympathies."[10] Through their lives and works, Dell, Cook, and Glaspell challenge us to be our best selves. As Glaspell advises in her most inspiring play, *Inheritors*, "Then—be the most you can be, so that life will be more because you were."[11]

ACKNOWLEDGMENTS

I thank many people for their help, inspiration, patience, understanding, and support. Among them are David Hulsey, Anna Francis, Rachel Erin Rosolina, and Darja Malcolm-Clarke of Indiana University Press, Carol McGillivray of Amnet, and Denise Carlson of North Coast Indexing Services. I also thank Kathryn Kuntz and her staff at the Davenport Public Library, Kay Runge and Mary Ann Linden of Davenport's Tuesday Club, Kelly Lao of Davenport's German American Heritage Center and Museum, Andrea L. Beckendorf and Hayley Jackson of the Luther College Library, and Lester E. Barber, professor emeritus of English at Bowling Green State University. I am especially grateful to Al Salatka, who helped me access microfilm and hard-to-locate sources; to my interns, Tyler Preston, Meredith Maxwell, Bryanna Jones, and Keeley Osbrink; and to my husband, Robert Lloyd Marlowe.

My colleagues in Glaspell studies have built an essential foundation on which this book rests; the scholarship of Gerhard Bach, Linda Ben-Zvi, Patricia L. Bryan, Martha Carpentier, Sharon Friedman, J. Ellen Gainor, Rasha Gazzaz, Noelia Hernando-Real, Emeline Jouve, Mary Papke, Cheryl Black, Veronica Makowsky, Kristina Hinz-Bode, Lucia V. Sander, Drew Eisenhauer, Brenda Murphy, Judith Barlow, and Barbara Ozieblo has informed my work here. My heartfelt thanks to G. Thomas Tanselle; Jeff Kennedy; Susan C. Kemper Walsh; Rasha Gazzaz; and Deanne Watts Hay, acting for the estate of William Warren Vilhauer, for permission to quote from their dissertations. Special thanks to Jerri Dell for her generous assistance and for permission to quote from the unpublished papers of her grandfather, Floyd Dell. Thanks also to Samuel Lourie for permission to quote from the unpublished papers of his great-great-grandfather, George Cram Cook, and his step-great-great-grandmother, Susan Glaspell, and to Jeffrey Moskin for permission to quote from the unpublished papers of his grandfather, W. H. Fineshriber. Most of all, I am grateful to Jon K. Lauck, without whose help and encouragement this book would never have been published.

ABBREVIATIONS

DDT   *Davenport Daily Times*
DDL   *Davenport Democrat and Leader*
DMD   *Davenport Morning Democrat*
QCT   *Quad-City Times*
RTT   *The Road to the Temple*

NOTES

INTRODUCTION: THREE MIDWESTERN PLAYWRIGHTS AND THE PROVINCETOWN PLAYERS

1. Dorothy Chansky, *Composing Ourselves: The Little Theatre Movement and the American Audience* (Carbondale: Southern Illinois University Press, 2004), 5.

2. A word here about the "founders" of the Provincetown Players. Of the twenty-nine charter members, George Cram Cook was clearly the guiding light. Elected president of the company in 1916, he functioned as the de facto artistic director until the troupe disbanded in 1922 and was usually acknowledged by theatre scholars as the group's founder until the surge of feminist recovery work in the 1970s and 1980s, when some scholars (including me) began to claim that Cook cofounded the Provincetown Players with his wife, Susan Glaspell, the second most prolific playwright in the group and, by many accounts, an inspirational actress. A case could be made that Jack Reed, who wrote the resolutions for the company when it was established as a theatre club in 1916 and also wrote and acted in several of its early productions, was also a cofounder. In his biography of another charter member, Max Eastman, Christoph Irmscher claims that Ida Rauh (Eastman's wife at the time, one of the twenty-nine charter members, and one of the group's finest actresses) cofounded the Provincetown Players (*Max Eastman: A Life* [New Haven, CT: Yale University Press, 2017], 108). Dell, also a charter member and a member of the company's first executive committee, mounted four of his plays with the Provincetown and also did some set designing and acting, but he was less involved on a day-to-day basis than Glaspell, who, in turn, was less involved than Cook. In the early years of its existence, the Provincetown

Players functioned much as Cook had envisioned, with many charter members actively involved in all aspects of production, so, arguably, there were a number of charter cofounders. Calling Dell, Cook, and Glaspell founders is not intended to equate their respective contributions but rather to emphasize the progressive beliefs and values that they shared that shaped not only the plays they wrote but also the theatre practice of the Provincetown Players.

3. In 1922, Cook and Glaspell immigrated to Greece; Dell had resigned earlier. After a yearlong hiatus, Eugene O'Neill, Kenneth Macgowan, Robert Edmond Jones, and several people from the original company formed the Experimental Theatre, which became a victim of the Great Depression in 1929.

1. THREE MIDWESTERN PLAYWRIGHTS DISCOVER THE NEW

1. Floyd Dell, *Homecoming: An Autobiography* (New York: Farrar and Rinehart, 1933), 216–17.

2. Adam Hochschild, *Rebel Cinderella: From Rags to Riches to Radical, the Epic Journey of Rose Pastor Stokes* (Boston: Houghton Mifflin Harcourt, 2020), 6.

3. Susan C. Kemper, "The Novels, Plays, and Poetry of George Cram Cook, Founder of the Provincetown Players" (PhD diss., Bowling Green State University, 1982), 3.

4. Henry F. May, *The End of American Innocence: A Study of the First Years of Our Own Time, 1912–1917* (New York: Alfred A. Knopf, 1959).

5. Floyd Dell, *Janet March* (New York: Alfred A. Knopf, 1923), 198.

6. Christine Stansell, *American Moderns: Bohemian New York and the Creation of a New Century* (Princeton, NJ: Princeton University Press, 2010), 1–2.

7. Stansell, 151.

8. Veronica Makowsky, "Susan Glaspell and Modernism," in *The Cambridge Companion to American Women Playwrights*, ed. Brenda Murphy (Cambridge: Cambridge University Press, 1999), 50.

9. I am indebted to the work of Adele Heller and Lois Rudnick; the articles they gathered in *1915, the Cultural Moment: The New Politics, the New Woman, the New Psychology, the New Art, and the New Theatre in America* (New Brunswick, NJ: Rutgers University Press, 1991) inform much of this introduction.

10. Sarah Grand, "The New Aspect of the Woman Question," *North American Review*, March 1894, 270–76. For good sources on the cult of true womanhood, see Nancy Cott, *The Bonds of Womanhood: Women's Sphere in New England, 1780–1835* (New Haven, CT: Yale University Press, 1977); Barbara Welter, "The Cult of True Womanhood: 1820–1860," *American Quarterly* 18, no. 2 (1966): 151–74. For a more recent examination of the New Woman, see Martha H. Patterson, *Beyond the Gibson Girl: Reimagining the American New Woman, 1895–1915* (Urbana: University of Illinois Press, 2008).

11. See June Sochen, *The New Woman in Greenwich Village, 1910–1920* (New York: Quadrangle Books, 1972); June Sochen, *Movers and Shakers: American Women Thinkers and Activists, 1900–1970* (New York: Random House, 1974); Hochschild, *Rebel Cinderella*; Elizabeth Gurley Flynn, *Rebel Girl: An Autobiography, My First Life (1906–1926)* (New York: International Publishing Company, 1973); Ida B. Wells, *Crusade for Justice: The Autobiography of Ida B. Wells,*

ed. Eve L. Ewing et al., 2nd ed., Negro American Biographies and Autobiographies (Chicago: University of Chicago Press, 2020). The novels cited in this paragraph are Willa Cather's *The Song of the Lark* (1915), Frances E. W. Harper's *Iola Leroy* (1892), Elia W. Peattie's *The Precipice* (1914), and Edna Ferber's *Emma McChesney and Co.* (1915).

12. Patterson, *Beyond the Gibson Girl*, 3–4.

13. Mabel Dodge, quoted in Judith Schwartz, *Radical Feminists of Heterodoxy: Greenwich Village, 1912–1940* (Norwich, VT: New Victoria, 1986), 1.

14. Ellen Kay Trimberger, "The New Woman and the New Sexuality: Conflict and Contradiction in the Writings and Lives of Mabel Dodge and Neith Boyce," in Heller and Rudnick, *1915, the Cultural Moment*, 98.

15. Leona Rust Egan, *Provincetown as a Stage: Provincetown, the Provincetown Players, and the Discovery of Eugene O'Neill* (Orleans, MA: Parnassus Imprints, 1994), 164, 165–67.

16. Martin Green, "The New Art," in Heller and Rudnick, *1915, the Cultural Moment*, 158.

17. Green, 160.

18. Quoted in Edward Abrahams, "Alfred Stieglitz's Faith and Vision," in Heller and Rudnick, *1915, the Cultural Moment*, 185.

19. John C. Burnham, "The New Psychology," in Heller and Rudnick, *1915, the Cultural Moment*, 117.

20. Susan Glaspell, *The Road to the Temple* (New York: Frederick A. Stokes, 1927), 250.

21. Dell, *Homecoming*, 291.

22. Sanford Gifford, "The American Reception of Psychoanalysis, 1908–1922," in Heller and Rudnick, *1915, the Cultural Moment*, 142.

23. Glaspell, *Road to the Temple*, 225.

24. Douglas Clayton, *Floyd Dell: The Life and Times of an American Rebel* (Chicago: Ivan R. Dee, 1994), xiii.

25. Quoted in Eugene E. Leach, "The Radicals of the Masses," in Heller and Rudnick, *1915, the Cultural Moment*, 28.

26. I am indebted to my physicist husband, Dr. Robert Lloyd Marlowe, who helped write this section on the New Science.

27. Stuart Kauffman, *At Home in the Universe: The Search for the Laws of Self-Organization and Complexity* (New York: Oxford University Press, 1995), 4.

28. Quoted in John Horgan, *The End of Science* (New York: Broadway Books, 1996, 1997), 149.

29. Helen Deutsch and Stella Hanau, *The Provincetown: A Story of the Theatre* (New York: Farrar and Rinehart, 1931), 5.

30. Robert L. Dorman, *Revolt of the Provinces: The Regionalist Movement in America, 1920–1945* (Chapel Hill: University of North Carolina Press, 1993), 22.

31. Cheryl Black, *The Women of Provincetown, 1915–1922* (Tuscaloosa: University of Alabama Press, 2002), 3.

32. William Archer, "The Great Contribution of 'Little Theaters' to Our Drama's Future," *New York Post*, February 24, 1921, quoted in Louis Sheaffer, *O'Neill: Son and Playwright* (Boston: Little, Brown, 1968), 342.

33. Carl Van Doren and Mark Van Doren, *American and British Literature since 1890* (New York: Chautauqua, 1926), 99.

34. Harry Hansen, *Midwest Portraits* (New York: Harcourt, Brace, 1923), 209.

35. Three great biographical sources on Dell are G. Thomas Tanselle, "Faun at the Barricades: The Life and Work of Floyd Dell, Parts 1 and 2" (PhD diss., Northwestern University, 1959); Clayton, *Floyd Dell*, which emphasizes Dell's internal conflict between aesthetic and political goals as the impetus for his writing; and John E. Hart, *Floyd Dell* (Boston: Twayne, 1971), which contains a very useful chronology.

36. Brenda Murphy, *The Provincetown Players and the Culture of Modernity* (Cambridge: Cambridge University Press, 2005), xiii.

37. Three great biographical sources on Cook are Glaspell, *Road to the Temple*; Robert Karoly Sarlos, *Jig Cook and the Provincetown Players: Theatre in Ferment* (Amherst: University of Massachusetts Press, 1982); and Kemper, "Novels, Plays, and Poetry."

38. Three critical biographies of Glaspell are Marcia Noe, *Susan Glaspell: Voice from the Heartland* (Macomb: Western Illinois University, 1983); Barbara Ozieblo, *Susan Glaspell: A Critical Biography* (Chapel Hill: University of North Carolina Press, 2000); and Linda Ben-Zvi, *Susan Glaspell: Her Life and Times* (Oxford: Oxford University Press, 2005).

39. John Galsworthy, *A Modern Comedy*, bk. 2, *The Silver Spoon* (New York: Charles Scribner's Sons, 1926), 536.

40. See Robert Humphrey, *Children of Fantasy: The First Rebels of Greenwich Village* (New York: John Wiley and Sons, 1978), for this view of the World War I–era Greenwich Villagers as playing at revolution. For additional sources on Greenwich Village radicals and bohemians, see Albert Parry, *A History of Bohemianism in America, 1885–1915* (New York: Covici-Friede, 1933); Allen Churchill, *The Improper Bohemians: A Re-creation of Greenwich Village in Its Heyday* (New York: E. P. Dutton, 1959); Emily Hahn, *Romantic Rebels: An Informal History of Bohemianism in America* (New York: Houghton Mifflin, 1967); Leslie Fishbein, *Rebels in Bohemia: The Radicals of the Masses, 1911–1917* (Chapel Hill: University of North Carolina Press, 1982); Rick Beard and Leslie Cohen Berlowitz, eds., *Greenwich Village Culture and Counterculture* (New Brunswick, NJ: Rutgers University Press, 1993); Ross Wetzsteon, *Republic of Dreams: Greenwich Village—the American Bohemia, 1910–1960* (New York: Simon and Schuster, 2002).

2. THREE MIDWESTERN PLAYWRIGHTS ARRIVE IN A ROMANTIC AND MIRACULOUS CITY

1. See the *Davenport Daily Times*, August 15, 22, 28, and 29 and September 2, 1903. Hereafter this source is abbreviated as *DDT*. The "western town" in Alice French's *Stories of a Western Town* (1893) is based on Davenport, renamed "Fairport." Readers interested in Alice French should start with *Stories of a Western Town*, her best work.

2. "Davenport in Brief," *DDT*, April 24, 1903, 5; "Davenport in Brief," *DDT*, June 2, 1903, 5; "Davenport in Brief," *DDT*, September 4, 1903, 5. Glaspell had actually returned to Davenport from Des Moines the previous year to reside with her parents and write fiction, so a bit of poetic license is taken here, although she did literally "return" to Davenport from Chicago during the summer of 1903, as she would several times during that decade.

3. "Davenport a Kicking Town," *DDT*, November 23, 1903, 6.

4. *Davenport Morning Democrat*, Centennial ed., October 11, 1955, sec. 6, n.p. Hereafter this source is abbreviated as *DMD*.

5. Quoted in Bill Roba, *The River and the Prairie* (Quad Cities: Hesperian, 1986), 103.

6. J. M. D. Burrows, *Fifty Years in Iowa, 1838–1888* (Davenport, IA: Davenport Glass, 1888), 107.

7. Bill Roba, "Davenport," in *Joined by a River: Quad Cities* (Davenport, IA: Lee Enterprises, 1982), 69; Marlys A. Svendsen, *Davenport: A Pictorial History* ([Davenport, IA?]: G. Bradley, 1985), 122.

8. Roba, "Davenport," 78; William J. Petersen, *The Story of Iowa: The Progress of an American State*, vol. 2 (New York: Lewis Historical, 1952), 918.

9. Timothy R. Mahoney, *River Towns in the Great West: The Structure of Provincial Urbanization in the American Midwest, 1820–1970* (Cambridge: Cambridge University Press, 1990), 265. See also Timothy R. Mahoney, "Down in Davenport: The Social Response of Antebellum Elites to Regional Urbanization," *Annals of Iowa* 50, no. 6 (1990): 593–622.

10. Mahoney, *River Towns*, 265–66; Timothy R. Mahoney, "Down in Davenport: A Regional Perspective on Antebellum Town Economic Development," *Annals of Iowa* 50, no. 5 (1990): 473.

11. Mahoney, *River Towns*, 266–67.

12. Marlys A. Svendsen and Martha H. Bowers, *Davenport, Where the Mississippi Runs West: A Survey of Davenport History and Architecture* (Davenport, IA: City of Davenport, 1982), 4–1; Mahoney, "Regional Perspective," 466;"Points of View," *Davenport Weekly Outlook*, March 20, 1897, 1.

13. William L. Bowers, "Davenport, Iowa, 1906–1907: A Glimpse into a City's Past," *Annals of Iowa* 38, no. 5 (1966): 364. Bowers also notes that early twentieth-century Davenport was not without its problems. Roads and streets needed improvement, and public health and sanitation were below par, leading to the diphtheria epidemic that Floyd Dell wrote about in the *Tri-City Workers Magazine*. Davenport also had more saloons at this time than any other city in Iowa, and the citizens of the "Free and Independent State of Scott," as some of them liked to call their city, were not inclined to enforce the mulct law that regulated them or to obey the state law that prohibited prize fights (Bowers, "Davenport, Iowa," 375–87). Davenport's wide-open entertainment district, Bucktown (where Al Jolson once worked as a singing waiter) attracted its share of crime, especially prostitution. By 1900, there were more prostitutes in Davenport than barbers, bartenders, or butchers, comprising 4 percent of the female workforce in the city. See Sharon E. Wood,

The Freedom of the Streets: Work, Citizenship, and Sexuality in a Gilded Age City (Chapel Hill: University of North Carolina Press, 2005), 217; Jonathan Turner, *A Brief History of Bucktown: Davenport's Infamous District Transformed* (Charleston, SC: History Press, 2016), 48.

14. Petersen, *Story of Iowa*, 956.

15. Hildegard Binder Johnson, *German Forty-Eighters in Davenport* (Davenport, IA: Davenport Schuetzenpark Gilde, 1998), 49; Svendsen, *Davenport*, 24; Svendsen and Bowers, *Davenport*, 14–1, 14–2.

16. Rick L. Woten, "Benjamin F. Gue," in *The Biographical Dictionary of Iowa*, ed. David Hudson, Marvin Bergman, and Loren F. Horton (Iowa City, IA: University of Iowa Press, 2008), 202–3.

17. G. Galin Berrier, "The Negro Suffrage Issue in Iowa, 1865–1868," *Annals of Iowa* 39, no. 4 (1968): 259.

18. Johnson, *German Forty-Eighters*, 54–60; Svendsen, *Davenport*, 23. See also Svendsen and Bowers, *Davenport*, 7–2.

19. Quoted in Wood, *Freedom of the Streets*, 49.

20. Wood, 49, 264n3.

21. Scott Roller, "Mary Louisa Duncan Putnam," in Hudson, Bergman, and Horton, *Biographical Dictionary of Iowa*, 415–16; Wood, *Freedom of the Streets*, 109.

22. "Reviews the Life of Mrs. M. P. Peck," *DDT*, December 6, 1909, 10.

23. "Reviews the Life of Mrs. M. P. Peck," 10.

24. Francesca Morgan, "'Regions Remote from Revolutionary Scenes': Regionalism, Nationalism, and the Iowa Daughters of the American Revolution, 1890–1930," *Annals of Iowa* 56, no. 1 (1997): 46–47; "Some Leaders of Women's Clubs," *DDT*, October 1911, New Home ed., n.p.

25. "Maria Purdy Peck," *Annals of Iowa* 11, no. 7 (1914): 560; "Reviews the Life of Mrs. M.P. Peck," *DDT*, December 6, 1909, 10; Wood, *Freedom of the Streets*, 247, 248.

26. Robert F. Martin, "Sarah Ann 'Annie' Turner Wittenmyer," in Hudson, Bergman, and Horton, *Biographical Dictionary of Iowa*, 565–66; Jim Arpy, "Remarkable Annie Wittenmyer," in *Legends of Our Land: A Unique History of the Mississippi Valley* (Davenport, IA: Times-Democrat, 1968), 23–24.

27. "Scholarships for Girls Is Discussed," *DDT*, November 30, 1910, 10; "Women Confer at Iowa City," *DDT*, November 9, 1909, 1.

28. *Trident*, March 26, 1904; clipping, *Davenport Democrat and Leader* (hereafter cited as *DDL*), August 14, 1910.

29. *Trident*, January 2, 1904, 10.

30. Kathy Penningroth, "Phebe W. Sudlow," in Hudson, Bergman, and Horton, *Biographical Dictionary of Iowa*, 501–3.

31. "Women's Organizations Develop with Growth of Davenport," *DDT*, 50th Anniversary ed., July 11, 1936, n.p.; "Ladies Industrial Relief Society," *Davenport Weekly Outlook*, June 24, 1897, 1; Harry Downer, *History of Davenport and Scott County, Iowa* (Chicago: S. J. Clarke, 1910), 790.

32. *Trident*, March 19, 1904, 13; *Trident*, April 23, 1904, 15; clipping, *Quad-City Times*, August 4, 1975. Hereafter this source is cited as *QCT*.

33. Sharon E. Wood, "Jennie C. McCowen," in Hudson, Bergman, and Horton, *Biographical Dictionary of Iowa*, 351–52; Downer, *History of Davenport*, 1026–29; Sharon E. Wood, "Jennie McCowen," *Iowa Heritage Illustrated* 89, nos. 1 and 2 (2008), 50–51; "Women in Iowa," *Annals of Iowa* 1884, no. 4 (1884): 95–113.

34. Wood, "Jennie McCowen," 50–51.

35. August P. Richter, "A True History of Scott County," *DDL*, August 13, 1922, 2; Wood, *Freedom of the Streets*, 49–54; "Women's Organizations Develop with Growth of Davenport," n.p.

36. Bill Wundrum, *A Time We Remember: Celebrating a Century in Our Quad-Cities* (Davenport, IA: Quad-City Times, 1999), 131; "Working Girls Find Places to Rest," *DMD*, October 11, 1955, Centennial ed., sec. 5, n.p.; "Women's Clubs as Factors in Tri-City Development," *DDT*, October 1911, New Home ed., n.p.

37. Quoted in Julie Jensen, "Davenport—Rich, Robust History," *QCT*, July 4, 1976, 3E.

38. Wundrum, *Time We Remember*, 124.

39. Jensen, "Davenport," 3E.

40. Wood, *Freedom of the Streets*, 54.

41. Roba, *River and the Prairie*, 105; "Issues Police Report," *DDT*, August 2, 1904, 4.

42. W. L. Purcell, "Along the Bucktown Rialto," in *Them Was the Good Old Days in Davenport, Scott County, Iowa* ([Davenport, IA?]: Purcell Printing, 1922), 171.

43. Wood, *Freedom of the Streets*, 117.

44. Quoted in Wood, *Freedom of the Streets*, 160.

45. Wood, *Freedom of the Streets*, 182; Turner, *Brief History of Bucktown*, 13, 39, 41.

46. Wood, *Freedom of the Streets*, 110.

47. Quoted in Wood, *Freedom of the Streets*, 120.

48. Wood notes that although Davenport did establish the position of police matron, by the time of Mayor Vollmer's regulated prostitution program, her role was largely that of registering prostitutes. See *Freedom of the Streets*, 166.

49. Roba, "Davenport," 79; "Trade Unions Help in City Development," *DDT*, 50th Anniversary ed., July 11, 1936, n.p.; "What's This? Workers Want Sundays Off," *DMD*, Centennial ed., October 5, 1955, n.p.

50. Quoted in Petersen, *Story of Iowa*, 997.

51. Petersen, 998.

52. *Trident*, May 7, 1904, 19; "Labor News of Iowa for March," *DDT*, July 12, 1910, 10; *Trident*, April 6, 1907, n.p.; *Trident*, July 20, 1907, n.p.; Downer, *History of Davenport*, 1003; "Carpenters Refuse to Continue Work," *DDT*, February 1, 1910, 6; "Men Make a Statement," *DDT*, April 14, 1920, 6.

53. "Cradle of Trade Unionism in Tri-Cities Where Local Chapters of I. A. M. Organized," *DDL*, September 17, 1911, 4; "Angry Men Attack Foreman," *DDL*, November 26, 1905, 11.

54. "Labor Trouble Threatens to Close Rock Island Arsenal," *DMD*, October 8, 1905, 5; "100 Men Have Been Laid Off," *DDL*, November 26, 1905, 11. A few years later, Blunt would become Arthur Davison Ficke's father-in-law when Ficke married his daughter Evelyn.

55. "Labor Trouble Threatens to Close Rock Island Arsenal," 5.

56. "Davenport in Brief," *DDT*, April 26, 1905, 5; "Carpenters Will Picnic June 25," *DDT*, May 5, 1905, 6.

57. Clipping, *DDL*, February 15, 1903, 3, Special Collections, Davenport Public Library; "Davenport in Brief," *DDT*, April 2, 1904, 5; *Trident*, May 7, 1904, 13; clipping, *DDL*, November 26, 1905, 10, Special Collections, Davenport Public Library; "Davenport in Brief," *DDT*, June 29, 1904, 5; "Hundred Typos at Celebration," *DDT*, May 5, 1910, 14.

58. Clipping, *DDL*, November 5, 1904, 1, Special Collections, Davenport Public Library; Downer, *History of Davenport*, 1003; "Big Parade of Labor Unions of Tri-Cities," *DDT*, September 4, 1904, 1; "Unionists Gather at Suburban Park," *DDT*, September 5, 1904, 2; "Arranging for Labor Revival," *DDT*, February 9, 1910, 7; "Men to Speak at Big Labor Revival," *DDT*, March 25, 1910, 14.

59. Johnson, *German Forty-Eighters*, 4–6, 51.

60. Downer, *History of Davenport*, 813–37, esp. 821–22; Harry Hansen, "A Davenport Boyhood," *Palimpsest* 37, no. 4 (1956): 193–94; Dorothy Schwieder, Thomas Moran, and Lynn Nielsen, eds., *Iowa Past to Present: The People and the Prairie*, rev. 3rd ed. (Iowa City: University of Iowa Press, 2011), 121.

61. Christine Stansell, *American Moderns: Bohemian New York and the Creation of a New Century* (Princeton, NJ: Princeton University Press, 2000), 47.

62. Quoted in Johnson, *German Forty-Eighters*, 24.

63. Johnson, 24.

64. Quoted in Johnson, 18.

65. Johnson, 21–24, 25–28, 54–60.

66. Hansen, "Davenport Boyhood," 183; quoted in Johnson, *German Forty-Eighters*, 3.

67. Petersen, *Story of Iowa*, 927.

68. Roba, *River and the Prairie*, 105.

69. Floyd Dell, *Moon-Calf* (New York: Alfred A. Knopf, 1920), 254.

70. Quoted in Kory Darnall, *Schuetzenpark: Davenport's Lost Playland, 1870–1923*, 2nd ed. (Davenport, IA: Davenport Schuetzenpark Gilde, 2000), 2.

71. Hansen, "Davenport Boyhood," 187.

72. Darnall, *Schuetzenpark*, 12–15, 34; Downer, *History of Davenport*, 830.

73. Gerhard Bach, "Susan Glaspell: Mapping the Domains of Critical Revision," in *Susan Glaspell: Essays on Her Theater and Fiction*, ed. Linda Ben-Zvi (Ann Arbor: University of Michigan Press, 1995), 242.

74. Johnson, *German Forty-Eighters*, 16.

75. Richter, "True History of Scott County," 4.

76. "Socialists at Dubuque," *Davenport Morning Republican*, April 10, 1902, 5.

77. Bowers, "Davenport, Iowa," 374–75.

78. *Tri-City Workers Magazine*, November 1905, 3.

79. *Tri-City Workers Magazine*, December 1905.

80. *Tri-City Workers Magazine*, February 1906.

81. *Tri-City Workers Magazine*, February 1906, 2; "Socialists Fling Defiance to Teacher," *DDL*, October 13, 1907, Davenport Public Library.

82. Bartholow V. Crawford, "Susan Glaspell," *Palimpsest* 2, no. 12 (1930): 520.

83. Susan Glaspell, "Here Is the Piece. . . . ," Susan Glaspell Papers, Henry and Albert Berg Collection, New York Public Library, New York, NY.

84. Dell, *Moon-Calf*, 394.

85. Floyd Dell, *Homecoming: An Autobiography* (New York: Farrar and Rinehart, 1933), 361.

3. FLOYD DELL EMBRACES FEMINISM IN PORT ROYAL

1. Floyd Dell, *Homecoming: An Autobiography* (New York: Farrar and Rinehart, 1933), 85. Hereafter, this source is cited parenthetically in the text. Biographical facts and information, when not cited specifically, were obtained from *Homecoming*; *Moon-Calf*, Dell's first novel; G. Thomas Tanselle, "Faun at the Barricades: The Life and Work of Floyd Dell, Parts 1 and 2" (PhD diss., Northwestern University, 1959); Dale Kramer, *Chicago Renaissance: The Literary Life in the Midwest, 1900–1930* (New York: Appleton Century, 1966); John E. Hart, *Floyd Dell* (Boston: Twayne, 1971); Douglas Clayton, *Floyd Dell: The Life and Times of an American Rebel* (Chicago: Ivan R. Dee, 1994); and Timothy B. Spears, *Chicago Dreaming: Midwesterners in the City, 1871–1919* (Chicago: University of Chicago Press, 2005). Tanselle's dissertation includes an extremely useful comprehensive checklist of Dell's publications from 1905 to 1958.

2. Feutcher was an important mentor and intellectual resource for Dell in many ways. When Dell was reviewing German-language plays for the *Davenport Daily Times*, his inability to speak German was mitigated by assistance from Feuchter, who attended the plays with him. Dell remembered Feuchter affectionately throughout his life; his third novel, *Janet March* (1923), is dedicated to "Frederick Feuchter, guide, philosopher, and friend." Feuchter also makes a cameo appearance in Dell's ninth novel, *Souvenir* (1929). In 1920, when the Socialists took over the Davenport City Council, Feuchter was one of the Socialist aldermen who were elected.

3. "Socialists Hold Mass Convention," *Davenport Daily Times*, December 15, 1905, 8. Hereafter this source is cited as *DDT*. This story says Dell was elected recording secretary; however, in *Homecoming*, Dell says that he was elected financial secretary, remarking that "it is doubtful if they ever did get the books straightened out afterward" (119). Possibly he held both offices at different times. See also "Many Socialists at Claus Groth," *DDT*, May 3, 1905; "Addresses Socialists," *DDT*, May 6, 1905, 5; "Socialists Go to Convention," *DDT*, July 2, 1906, 4; "Sample Ballot," *DDT*, October 29, 1906, 8.

4. See Tanselle, "Faun at the Barricades." In the checklist at the end of part 2, Tanselle identifies Dell's Thersites articles in the *Tri-City Workers Magazine* as "Diphtheria in Davenport," December 1905, 5–6; "Socialists and Their Critics," December 1905, 11–13; "The Only Original Socialist," January 1906, 10–11; "The Children vs. the Library Board," February 1906, 16–17; and "Why People Go to Brick Munro's," September 1096, 1–4. Tanselle also attributes to Dell the following articles: "The Autocratic School Board," May 1906, 13–14, signed "Vesuvius"; "A Candy Factory from the Inside," January 1906, 17–20, signed "Sally Thompson"; "The Davenport Public Schools," January 1906, 11–14, signed "John Smith"; "Socialists and Kindergarten," February 1906, 7–11, unsigned; "The Salvation of the Working Class," July 1906, 8–10, unsigned; "Editorial Comments," August 1906, 10–13, unsigned; "A Municipal Crime! Moline's Antiquated Garbage Dump," August 1906, 1–5, unsigned; and "Socialism and Backbone," September 1906, 10–12. In *Homecoming*, Dell explicitly claims credit for "A Municipal Crime! Moline's Antiquated Garbage Dump," "The Children vs. the Library Board," and "Why People Go to Brick Munro's."

5. Daniel Bell, "The Background and Development of Marxian Socialism in the United States," in *Socialism and American Life*, vol. 1, ed. Donald Drew Egbert and Stow Persons (Princeton, NJ: Princeton University Press, 1952), 265–66; Jack Ross, *The Socialist Party of America: A Complete History* (Lincoln, NE: Potomac Books, 2015), 73, 103.

6. Ross, 159–60; Harold W. Currie, *Eugene V. Debs* (Boston: Twayne, 1976), 104–6.

7. Sally M. Miller, "Casting a Wide Net: The Milwaukee Movement to 1920," in *Socialism in the Heartland: The Midwestern Experience, 1900–1925*, ed. Donald R. Critchlow (Notre Dame, IN: Notre Dame University Press, 1986), 27.

8. Floyd Dell, *Moon-Calf* (New York: Alfred A. Knopf, 1920), 255. Hereafter this source is cited parenthetically in the text. See also Sharon E. Wood, *The Freedom of the Streets: Work, Citizenship, and Sexuality in a Gilded Age City* (Chapel Hill: University of North Carolina Press, 2005), for a thorough discussion of lawlessness in Davenport during the late nineteenth century. Wood reports that while Iowa had prohibited the manufacture or sale of alcoholic beverages since 1884, by 1890, over two hundred saloons were operating in the city by license.

9. "Girls Frequent Dance Halls," *DDT*, August 12, 1904, 4; "Issues Police Report," *DDT*, August 2, 1904, 4.

10. "Thersites," "Why People Go to Brick Munro's," *Tri-City Workers Magazine*, September 1906, 1–4. Munro's response to Dell's article is illuminating; he asserted that if he thought there were any decent girls in his establishment, he would have sent them home! See *Homecoming*, 132.

11. Harry Hansen, *Midwest Portraits* (New York: Harcourt, Brace, 1923), 212. Hansen is referring to Vander Veer Park, which was called Central Park at the time that he and Dell would walk there.

12. Floyd Dell, *Looking at Life* (New York: Alfred A. Knopf, 1924), 302. Dell didn't despise him for long. Arthur Davison Ficke and Floyd Dell became life-long friends and correspondents. The character of George Weatherby in Dell's novel *Runaway* (1925) is an affectionate portrait of Ficke, to whom the novel is dedicated; three years earlier, Ficke had dedicated *Sonnets of a Portrait-Painter, and Other Sonnets* (1922) to Dell.

13. Edward Bellamy, *Looking Backward* (Mineola, NY: Dover, 1996), 27. Here-after this source is cited parenthetically in the text.

14. William Morris, *News from Nowhere* (Boston: Harper Brothers, 1891), 50, 68–69.

15. Clipping, *DDT*, November 25, 1905, pt. 4, 20, Special Collections, Daven-port Public Library.

16. Robert Sklar, "Chicago Renaissance," *Commonweal*, vol. 6, January 6, 1967, 377.

17. H. L. Mencken, "The Literary Capital of the United States," *Nation*, April 17, 1920, 10, 92.

18. Clayton, *Floyd Dell*, 54.

19. Tanselle, "Faun at the Barricades," 176, quoting Sinclair in *Money Writes* (New York: Albert and Charles Boni, 1927), 185; G. Thomas Tanselle, "Ezra Pound and a Story of Floyd Dell's," *Notes and Queries*, n.s., 8, no. 9 (1961): 350–52.

20. Eunice Tietjens, *The World at My Shoulder* (New York: Macmillan, 1938), 19, 58. Cook had been working on a dictionary in Chicago but became associ-ate editor of the *Friday Literary Review* when Dell was promoted to editor. Dell wrote to John T. Flanagan that he liked to think of himself, Cook, and Hal-linan as the Three Musketeers, always ready to adjourn to a nearby watering hole for liquid refreshment and literary and political discussions. See John T. Flanagan, "A Letter from Floyd Dell," *American Literature* 45, no. 3 (1973): 449. For his part, Ficke was a frequent guest of Dell and Currey, seeking the kind of intellectual stimulation that he felt he could not find in Davenport since Dell, Cook, Glaspell, and Banks had already departed.

21. Clayton, *Floyd Dell*, 57. Some great sources on Dell's role in the Chicago Renaissance are Bernard Duffey, *The Chicago Renaissance in American Letters: A Critical History* (East Lansing: Michigan State University Press, 1956); Dale Kramer, *Chicago Renaissance: The Literary Life in the Midwest, 1900–1930* (New York: Appleton-Century, 1966); and Timothy B. Spears, *Chicago Dreaming: Midwesterners and the City, 1871–1919* (Chicago: University of Chicago Press, 2005).

22. R. Craig Sautter, ed., *Floyd Dell: Essays from the* Friday Literary Review, *1909–1913* (Highland Park, IL: December Press, 1995), 5. Sautter's book histor-icizes the *Friday Literary Review* in a very helpful introduction.

23. Clayton, *Floyd Dell*, 75.

24. Floyd Dell, *Women as World Builders: Studies in Modern Feminism* (Chi-cago: Forbes, 1913), 8.

25. Dell, 28, 32.

26. Dell, 14.

27. Dell, 17.

28. Dell, 23–24.

29. Dell, 35–40, 43, 55.

30. Floyd Dell, *The Outline of Marriage*, Pamphlets on Birth Control, no. 12 (New York: American Birth Control League, 1926), 6.

31. Dell, 10.

32. Kathleen Kennedy, "Meridel LeSueur: A Voice for Working-Class Women," in *The Human Tradition in America between the Wars, 1920–1945*, ed. Donald W. Whisenhunt (Wilmington, DE: Scholarly Resources, 2002), 140.

33. Floyd Dell, "Feminism for Men," in *Looking at Life*, 14. This essay was originally published in the *Masses*, as were the other essays in this collection.

34. Dell, 14.

35. Dell, 15.

36. Dell, 15.

37. Dell, 16.

38. Dell, 22.

39. Dell, 22.

40. Floyd Dell, *Intellectual Vagabondage*, with an introduction by Douglas Clayton (Chicago: Ivan R. Dee, 1990), 139.

41. Dell, "Feminism for Men," 23–24.

42. Floyd Dell, "Dolls and Abraham Lincoln," in *Looking at Life*, 234.

43. Ludwig Lewisohn, *Expression in America* (New York: Harper and Brothers, 1932), 412.

44. Max Eastman, *Love and Revolution: My Journey through an Epoch* (New York: Random House, 1956), 17. Dell was actually listed as "Managing Editor" on the magazine's masthead.

45. Christoph Irmscher, *Max Eastman: A Life* (New Haven, CT: Yale University Press, 2017), 94–97.

46. Max Eastman, *The Enjoyment of Living* (New York: Harper and Brothers, 1948), 443–44.

47. Clayton, *Floyd Dell*, 133.

48. Helen Deutsch and Stella Hanau, *The Provincetown: A Story of the Theatre* (New York: Farrar and Rinehart, 1931), 29; Tanselle, "Faun at the Barricades," 190.

49. Clayton, *Floyd Dell*, 144.

50. Christine Stansell, *American Moderns: Bohemian New York and the Creation of a New Century* (Princeton, NJ: Princeton University Press, 2000), 276.

51. Floyd Dell, *King Arthur's Socks*, in *King Arthur's Socks and Other Village Plays* (New York: Alfred A. Knopf, 1922), 149–74, 152.

52. Dell, 169.

53. Clayton, *Floyd Dell*, 147.

54. Floyd Dell, *The Angel Intrudes*, in *King Arthur's Socks and Other Village Plays*, 49.

55. Dell, 46.

56. William Shakespeare, *Twelfth Night*, in *The Complete Plays of William Shakespeare*, ed. William Allan Neilson and Charles Jarvis Hill (Cambridge, MA: Riverside Press, Houghton Mifflin, 1942), act 2, scene 3, 51–52.

57. Floyd Dell, *Sweet and Twenty*, in *King Arthur's Socks and Other Village Plays*, 90. Hereafter this source is cited parenthetically in the text.

58. Floyd Dell, *A Long Time Ago*, in *King Arthur's Socks and Other Village Plays*, 104.

59. Dell, 125.

60. See Irmscher, *Max Eastman*, 130–33; Eastman, *Love and Revolution*, 85–91; Floyd Dell, "Not without Dust and Heat," in *Looking at Life*, 151–68. Three others were indicted along with Dell, Eastman, Rogers, and Young. The indictment against Josephine Bell was dismissed at the outset of the trial, Jack Reed was in Russia, and H. J. Glintenkamp was in Mexico.

61. Dell, "Not without Dust and Heat," 153.

62. Dell, 153–54.

63. Dell, 158.

64. Dell, 160.

65. Stansell, *American Moderns*, 316.

66. Clayton, *Floyd Dell*, 4.

67. Spears, *Chicago Dreaming*, 216.

68. Floyd Dell to Ralph Cram, January 14, 1924, Floyd Dell Papers, Newberry Library, Chicago, IL.

4. GEORGE CRAM COOK RUNS FOR CONGRESS IN THE RED CITY OF IOWA

1. Floyd Dell, *Homecoming: An Autobiography* (New York: Farrar and Rinehart, 1933), 177–79. Hereafter, this source is cited parenthetically in the text.

2. E. E. Cook, unpublished diary, October 1, 1908, Cook Family Papers, manuscript 109, box 1, Special Collections, University of Iowa Library, Iowa City, IA.

3. "Contemporary Club in First Meeting," *Davenport Daily Times*, October 2, 1908, 10. Hereafter this source is cited as *DDT*.

4. Susan Glaspell, *The Road to the Temple* (New York: Frederick A. Stokes, 1927), 192. Hereafter this source is cited parenthetically in the text as *RTT*. Biographical facts and information about Cook's life were taken from this source and from G. Thomas Tanselle, "George Cram Cook and the Poetry of Living, with a Checklist," *Books at Iowa* 24 (1976), 3–37; Susan C. Kemper, "The Novels, Plays, and Poetry of George Cram Cook, Founder of the Provincetown Players" (PhD diss., Bowling Green State University, 1982); and Robert Karoly Sarlos, *Jig Cook and the Provincetown Players: Theatre in Ferment* (Amherst: University of Massachusetts Press, 1982).

5. "On Christian Rudowitz," *DDT*, December 10, 1908, 6.

6. "Urge Action on Rudowitz Case," *DDT*, December 16, 1908, 11.

7. "Resolutions in Rudowitz Matter," *DDT*, December 21, 1908, 7.

8. "Rudowitz Wins against Russia," *DDT*, January 26, 1909, 1.

9. George Cram Cook, "Some Modest Remarks on Socialism," in *Papers of the Contemporary Club* 15 (1910–1911) (Davenport, IA: Mossman and Vollmer, 1911), 9.

10. Cook, 3.

11. George Cram Cook, "Socialism the Issue in 1912," *Masses*, July 1912, 7.

12. Cook, "Some Modest Remarks," 15.

13. "Grilk Favorite through District," *DDT*, October 21, 1910, 14.

14. "TR Arrives at 3:00 AM," *DDT*, November 4, 1910, 1.

15. "Pepper Carries Every County," *DDT*, November 9, 1910, 1. See also "Vote for Members of Congress—1902–1910," *Iowa Official Register, 1909–1910*, no. 23, (Des Moines, IA: Emory H. English, State Printer, 1910), 459.

16. Christine Stansell, *American Moderns: Bohemian New York and the Creation of a New Century* (Princeton, NJ: Princeton University Press, 2000), 48.

17. Kemper, "Novels, Plays, and Poetry," 83.

18. Kemper, 80.

19. Unsigned review of *The Chasm*, by George Cram Cook, *Literary Digest*, April 22, 1911, 794.

20. George Cram Cook, *The Chasm: A Novel* (New York: Frederick A. Stokes, 1911), 40–41.

21. Walter B. Rideout, *The Radical Novel in the United States, 1900–1954: Some Interrelations of Literature and Society* (Cambridge, MA: Harvard University Press, 1956), 54.

22. E. D., "The Visioning Placed on Sale at the Davenport Book Stores," *DDT*, May 3, 1911, 4.

23. *Book Review Digest, Seventh Annual Cumulation*, edited by Justina Leavitt Wilson and Clara Elizabeth Fanning (Minneapolis: H. W. Wilson, 1911).

24. Tanselle, "George Cram Cook," lists three reviews of *The Chasm*: Francis Hackett, *Friday Literary Review, Chicago Evening Post*, February 17, 1911, 1; *American Review of Reviews* 43 (1911): 761; and J. Fuchs, *International*, July 1911.

25. Dale Kramer, *Chicago Renaissance: The Literary Life in the Midwest, 1900–1930* (New York: Appleton-Century, 1966), 112. Anecdotal evidence suggests that Sinclair Lewis and Susan Glaspell were romantically involved at some point between 1911 and 1913. Certainly there is proof that they were acquainted. Susan and Jig's copy of *Our Mr. Wrenn* is inscribed, "To Susan Glaspell, but for whose encouragement and understanding this book never would have been finished, and to George Cram Cook—prince—from the author." See Marcia Noe, *Susan Glaspell: Voice from the Heartland* (Macomb: Western Illinois University, 1983), 35. Lewis also goes out of his way to give Glaspell a shout-out in *Main Street* when Erik Valborg says, "I'd like to stage 'Suppressed Desires' by Cook and Miss Glaspell." His description of the set he would design for the play indicates that Lewis had attended some of the Provincetown Players' productions. Part of his projected set design includes

"a cyclorama of a blue that would simply hit you in the eye," suggesting his acquaintance with the blue dome that Cook used to stage *The Emperor Jones*, and his inclusion of "just one tree-branch, to suggest a park below" is most likely an allusion to the set Floyd Dell designed for his *Sweet and Twenty* that featured one large blossoming cherry branch painted on a screen (Sinclair Lewis, *Main Street* [New York: Harcourt, Brace and Howe, 1920], 340). Apparently, Lewis and Glaspell maintained contact through the years. Dorothy Meyer reports that Glaspell organized a party at her house for Lewis in the 1940s so that her journalist husband Ernie and fellow journalist Ted Robinson could write about Lewis's acting in a production of *Ah, Wilderness!* in Provincetown. However, Lewis showed up drunk, entering through a window with a young actress (possibly Marcella Powers), and was so obnoxious that Ernie and Ted abandoned their plans to help publicize his theatre venture. See Noe, *Susan Glaspell*, 71. Further evidence of Lewis's involvement with Glaspell appears in Richard Lingeman's biography of Lewis, in which appears a photograph of a woman who is identified there as Lewis's first wife, Grace Hegger; however, this photograph is actually one of Susan Glaspell, apparently found among the Lewis papers and mistakenly identified. In 1975, a cousin of Glaspell, Margaret Hudson, gave me an 8" × 10" glossy of this very photograph and mentioned Glaspell and Lewis's romantic connection when I interviewed her.

26. Tanselle, "George Cram Cook," 9–10.

27. W. H. Fineshriber to Floyd Dell, October 11, 1910, Floyd Dell Papers, Newberry Library, Chicago, IL; Susan Glaspell to Floyd Dell, May 11, 1911, Floyd Dell Papers, Newberry Library, Chicago, IL.

28. George Cram Cook to Floyd Dell, April 13, 1913, Floyd Dell Papers, Newberry Library, Chicago, IL.

29. Leona Rust Egan, *Provincetown as a Stage: Provincetown, the Provincetown Players, and the Discovery of Eugene O'Neill* (Orleans, MA: Parnassus Imprints, 1994), 125.

30. Egan, x–xi.

31. C. W. E. Bigsby, *A Critical Introduction to Twentieth-Century American Drama, 1900–1940*, vol. 1 (Cambridge: Cambridge University Press, 1982), 11; Tanselle, "George Cram Cook," 14.

32. Sarlos, *Jig Cook*, 15.

33. J. Ellen Gainor, *Susan Glaspell in Context: American Theater, Culture, and Politics, 1915–48* (Ann Arbor: University of Michigan Press, 2004), 20–21.

34. Brenda Murphy, *The Provincetown Players and the Culture of Modernity* (Cambridge: Cambridge University Press, 2005), 69–70.

35. Egan, *Provincetown as a Stage*, 131.

36. Helen Deutsch and Stella Hanau, *The Provincetown: A Story of the Theatre* (Farrar and Rinehart, 1931), 8.

37. Edna Kenton, *The Provincetown Players and the Playwrights' Theatre, 1915–1922*, ed. Travis Bogard and Jackson R. Bryer (Jefferson, NC: McFarland, 2004), 15.

38. Susan Glaspell, *Suppressed Desires*, with George Cram Cook, in *Susan Glaspell: The Complete Plays*, ed. Linda Ben-Zvi and J. Ellen Gainor (Jefferson, NC: McFarland, 2010), 15. Hereafter this source is cited parenthetically as Ben-Zvi and Gainor.

39. Deutsch and Hanau, *Provincetown*, 10.

40. George Cram Cook, *Change Your Style*, in *1915, the Cultural Moment: The New Politics, the New Woman, the New Psychology, the New Art, and the New Theatre in America*, ed. Adele Heller and Lois Rudnick (New Brunswick, NJ: Rutgers University Press, 1991), 296.

41. Cook, 297.

42. Cook, 299; *Some Like It Hot*, dir. Billy Wilder, screenplay by Billy Wilder and A. I. Diamond (Metro-Goldwyn-Mayer, 1959).

43. Sarlos, *Jig Cook*, 18.

44. Murphy, *Provincetown Players*, 75.

45. Bigsby, *Critical Introduction*, 26.

46. Heywood Broun, "Drama: Susan Glaspell and George Cook Have Bright One-Act Play," *New York Tribune*, December 23, 1918, 9.

47. Tanselle, "George Cram Cook," 17; Dorothy Chansky, "Kitchen Sink Realism: American Drama, Dining and Domestic Labor Come of Age in Little Theatre," *Journal of American Drama and Theatre* 16, no. 2 (2004): 42.

48. *Dinner at Eight*, dir. George Cukor, adaptation by Frances Marion and Herman J. Mankiewicz (Metro-Golden-Mayer, 1933).Adapted from the play *Dinner at Eight* by George S. Kaufman and Edna Ferber.

49. Floyd Dell, *Love in the Machine Age* (New York: Farrar and Rinehart, 1930), 6.

50. Egan, *Provincetown as a Stage*, 94.

51. Bergson, quoted in Gainor, *Susan Glaspell in Context*, 87.

52. Kristina Hinz-Bode, *Susan Glaspell and the Anxieties of Expression: Language and Isolation in the Plays* (Jefferson, NC: McFarland, 2006), 236.

53. Linda Ben-Zvi, *Susan Glaspell: Her Life and Times* (Oxford: Oxford University Press, 2005), 207.

54. Aegyung Noh, "Historiographies of Modernity: Susan Glaspell and 'Jig' Cook," *Feminist Studies in English Literature* 21, no. 1 (2013): 152.

55. Noh, 153, 151–52.

56. Hinz-Bode, *Susan Glaspell*, 237; Gainor, *Susan Glaspell in Context*, 91.

57. Noh, "Historiographies of Modernity," 155.

58. Deutsch and Hanau, *Provincetown*, 29.

59. Quoted in Kenton, *Provincetown Players*, 71.

60. George Cram Cook, *The Athenian Women: A Play*, with the original text and a modern Greek translation made by the author and revised by C. Carthaio (Athens: Estia, 1926), 62, 172. Hereafter this source is cited parenthetically in the text.

61. Kemper, "Novels, Plays, and Poetry," 124.

62. Tanselle, "George Cram Cook," 16.

63. Barbara Ozieblo, *Susan Glaspell: A Critical Biography* (Chapel Hill: University of North Carolina Press, 2000), 118.

64. Heywood Broun, *New York Tribune*, March 4, 1918, 9.

65. Kenton, *Provincetown Players*, 133.

66. Sarlos, *Jig Cook*, 56.

67. George Cram Cook, *The Spring: A Play* (New York: Frank Shay, 1921), 59. Hereafter, this source is cited parenthetically in the text.

68. Quoted in William Warren Vilhauer, "A History and Evaluation of the Provincetown Players," pt. 1 (PhD diss., University of Iowa, 1965), 159, 160.

69. Kenneth Macgowan, "Broadway Bows to By-Way," *Theatre Arts Magazine*, July 1921, 175–83.

70. Alexander Woollcott, "Second Thoughts on First Nights," *New York Times*, November 6, 1921, 6:2; *Homecoming*, 266.

71. Deutsch and Hanau, *Provincetown*, 41.

72. Ozieblo, *Susan Glaspell*, 174; Gainor, *Susan Glaspell in Context*, 116.

73. Kemper, "Novels, Plays, and Poetry," 166.

74. Tanselle, "George Cram Cook," 18.

75. Quoted in Ozieblo, *Susan Glaspell*, 174.

76. Sarlos, *Jig Cook*, 137.

77. Hutchins Hapgood, *A Victorian in the Modern World* (New York: Harcourt, Brace, 1939), 174–75.

78. Quoted in Gladys Denny Schultz, "Susan Glaspell," in *A Book of Iowa Authors*, ed. Johnson Brigham (Des Moines: Iowa State Teachers Association, 1930), 121.

79. Tanselle, "George Cram Cook," 3.

80. Arthur Waterman, "From Iowa to Greece: The Achievement of George Cram Cook," *Quarterly Journal of Speech* 45, no. 1 (1959): 50.

81. Bigsby, *Critical Introduction*, 11.

82. Sarlos, *Jig Cook*, 53

83. Quoted in Barrett Clark, *Eugene O'Neill: The Man and His Plays* (New York: Robert M. McBride, 1929), 43.

84. Floyd Dell, "A Living and Inexplicable Man," *New York Herald Tribune Books*, March 13, 1927, 1–2.

5. SUSAN GLASPELL FIGHTS FOR FREE SPEECH IN FREEPORT

1. "On Religious Liberty," *Davenport Daily Times*, February 14, 1910, 6. Hereafter this source is cited as *DDT*.

2. "Buy Books That the People Want," *Davenport Democrat and Leader*, February 16, 1910, 10. Hereafter this source is cited as *DDL*.

3. "Geo. C. Cook Answers Sharon," *DDL*, February 16, 1910, 10.

4. "Issues Challenge to E. M. Sharon" and "J. F. Bredow in Reply to Sharon," *DDL*, February 17, 1910, 8.

5. "Denies That He Is Book Censor," *DDL*, February 18, 1910, 9.

6. "Bishop Morrison on Library Board" and "America Is a Christian Nation," *DDL*, February 20, 1910, 8.

7. "Monsignor Ryan Gives His Views," *DDL*, February 27, 1910, 14.

8. "'Let Truth and Falsehood Grapple; Who Fears,' He Asks," *DDL*, February 23, 1910, 2.

9. "Well! Well! Well! See What's Here!," *DDL*, February 24, 1910, 2. Could Floyd Dell have written this article? The reference to Cook as a "market gardner" evokes Dell's job as Cook's hired man a few years earlier.

10. "Should Buy the Book," *DDT*, February 22, 1910, 2; "Prof. Foster's Book Reviewed," *DDL*, March 7, 1910, 8; "Again Turn Down Foster's Book," *DDL*, March 11, 1910, 13.

11. "Socialists Take Shot at Library Board," *DDT*, February 26, 1910, 7.

12. "Religious Crisis Marks Present Day," *DDT*, March 18, 1910, 14.

13. Susan Glaspell, *The Road to the Temple* (New York: Frederick A. Stokes, 1927), 193. Hereafter this source is cited parenthetically in the text as *RTT*.

14. Floyd Dell, *Homecoming: An Autobiography* (New York: Farrar and Rinehart, 1933), 237.

15. "Democrats Adopt Their Resolutions," *DDT*, March 29, 1910, 12; "Mayor Scott's Financial Policy Handicaps the City," *DDT*, March 31, 1910, 4.

16. "Alfred Mueller Elected Next Mayor of Davenport," *DDL*, April 3, 1910, 2.

17. Susan Glaspell, "Social Life," *Weekly Outlook*, October 10, 1896, 6; February 6, 1897, 6; February 27, 1897, 6.

18. Marcia Noe, *Susan Glaspell: Voice from the Heartland* (Macomb: Western Illinois University, 1983), 16. Biographical information about Susan Glaspell is taken from this source and from Barbara Ozieblo, *Susan Glaspell: A Critical Biography* (Chapel Hill: University of North Carolina Press, 2000), and Linda Ben-Zvi, *Susan Glaspell: Her Life and Times* (Oxford: Oxford University Press, 2005).

19. "Amateur Club Discusses Great Passion Play," *DDT*, November 13, 1905, 5.

20. Noe, *Susan Glaspell*, 16.

21. "Miss French Talks of the Short Story," *DDT*, June 16, 1909, 2.

22. *Trident*, July 30, 1904, 17; February 4, 1905, 17. The *Trident* archive is located at Davenport's Putnam Museum.

23. "Davenport People Are on Program," *DDT*, June 29, 1904, 4; "Miss Glaspell Given Office in Western Writers Association," *DDT*, July 14, 1905, 7.

24. "Charles Eugene Banks Speaks at Mothers' Club," *DDT*, October 27, 1904, 5.

25. Bettye Adler, "'The Glory of the Conquered': Miss Glaspell's First Novel," *DDT*, March 12, 1909, 9.

26. "How to Get Things Done through Newspapers: Susan Glaspell Reads 'The Influence of the Press' at the Tuesday Club Today," *DDT*, April 2, 1907, 4.

27. Both Arthur Waterman and Gerhard Bach, who wrote the first two dissertations on Glaspell's work, told me that their wives became jealous of Susan. "Miss Blanche Campbell, Miss Ada Drechsler: Winners of the Democrat's Free Trip to Europe Contest," *DDL*, February 15, 1903, 6. If only Susan

had sold a few more subscriptions to the *Democrat and Leader*, she might have gone to Europe with my grandmother, Ada Drechsler!

28. "In the Social World," February 25, 1908, 7. Was Susan Glaspell a card-carrying, dues-paying Socialist? The facts are inconclusive. The last words in her entry in *Woman's Who's Who in America* (1914–1915) are "Socialist. Favors woman suffrage." However, Jig Cook was almost certainly referring to Susan when, in refuting charges that the censorship protest was a Socialist project, he noted that "a non-Socialist writer of national reputation present in the audience raised the question whether the spirit of religious liberty was not violated by what amounts to a censorship of religious books." See note 3 above. The fact that Glaspell declined to run when asked by the Davenport Socialists to be one of their candidates for the school board in the spring of 1910 could indicate either that she was a party member and thus eligible to be nominated as a Socialist candidate or that she was not a party member and therefore did not wish to run on their ticket. The *Democrat and Leader* article states that she declined because she was nominated without being consulted, which suggests that, not being a Socialist, she had no reason to attend the nominating meeting. See "Socialists for the School Board," *DDL*, March 13, 1910, 16. Among the Ludwig Lewisohn papers is an undated inscription from Glaspell, written on Election Day, 1944, urging him to "vote for [Socialist presidential candidate Norman] Thomas, because too many are hungry," but these Depression-era feelings seem to have subsided by the mid-1940s. In her last novel, *Judd Rankin's Daughter* (New York: J. B. Lippincott, 1945), Frances Rankin Mitchell reflects on her youthful enthusiasm for leftist politics: "Long ago she had been a Socialist who knew very little about the Marxian philosophy but thought too many people weren't getting enough fun out of life" (105). Granted, this is a fictional character speaking but one whose life and values parallel those of Susan Glaspell.

29. E. E. Cook, unpublished diary, Cook Family Papers, MS 109, box 1, Special Collections, University of Iowa Library, Iowa City, IA.

30. George Cram Cook to Floyd Dell, n.d., Floyd Dell Papers, Newberry Library, Chicago, IL.

31. "Praises Miss Glaspell," *DDT*, July 14, 1911, 14.

32. George Cram Cook to Floyd Dell, September 12, 1910, Floyd Dell Papers, Newberry Library, Chicago, IL. Perhaps the extent to which Glaspell and Cook became pariahs in Davenport has been a bit overplayed by some scholars, myself included. On May 29, 1911, well after the news that Cook and Glaspell were a couple had broken, she spoke on "Social Consciousness in Fiction" for the Study Department of the Davenport Women's Club. Would such a mainstream organization have invited her to speak if they considered her to be an immoral woman? See "Fiction Awakens Social Conscience," *DDT*, May 30, 1911, 5.

33. Laura Stein, *Speech Rights in America: The First Amendment, Democracy, and the Media* (Urbana: University of Illinois Press, 2006), 3.

34. Christine Stansell, *American Moderns: Bohemian New York and the Creation of a New Century* (Princeton, NJ: Princeton University Press, 2000), 74.

35. Stansell, 74–76.

36. Stansell, 316.

37. Stansell, 366.

38. Heywood Broun, "Looking Up and Down and Around with the Province-town Players," *New York Tribune*, March 18, 1917, sec. 4, 3.

39. Susan Glaspell, *The People*, in *Susan Glaspell: The Complete Plays*, ed. Linda Ben-Zvi and J. Ellen Gainor (Jefferson, NC: McFarland, 2010), 55–56. Hereafter, plays from this source are cited parenthetically in the text as Ben-Zvi and Gainor.

40. Kristina Hinz-Bode, *Susan Glaspell and the Anxieties of Expression: Language and Isolation in the Plays* (Jefferson, NC: McFarland, 2006), 82.

41. Hinz-Bode, 23.

42. Martha C. Carpentier and Emeline Jouve, eds., introduction to *On Susan Glaspell's* Trifles *and "A Jury of Her Peers": Centennial Essays, Interviews, and Adaptations* (Jefferson, NC: McFarland, 2015), 3.

43. Emeline Jouve, *Susan Glaspell's Poetics and Politics of Rebellion* (Iowa City: University of Iowa Press, 2017), 25.

44. Patricia L. Bryan, "Foreshadowing 'A Jury of Her Peers': Susan Glaspell's 'The Plea' and the Case of John Wesley Elkins," in *Susan Glaspell: New Directions in Critical Inquiry*, ed. Martha Carpentier (Newcastle-upon-Tyne: Cambridge Scholars Publishing, 2006), 46.

45. Jouve, *Susan Glaspell's Poetics*, 45–46, 176.

46. "Bushido the Climax of the Washington Square Players' Finest Program," *New York Times*, November 14, 1916, 8; "New Attractions for New York Playgoers: Washington Square Players," *New York Dramatic Mirror*, November 25, 1916, 7.

47. Heywood Broun, "Best Bill Seen at the Comedy: Washington Square Players Set New Mark in Skill," *New York Tribune*, November 14, 1916, 7; Arthur Hornblow, "Mr. Hornblow Goes to the Play: The Washington Square Players," *Theatre Magazine*, January 1917, 21–24.

48. Jouve, *Susan Glaspell's Poetics*, 71.

49. Sharon Friedman, "'What There Is Behind Us': Susan Glaspell's Challenge to Nativist Discourse in Stage Adaptations of Her *Harper's Monthly* Fiction," in *Intertextuality in American Drama: Critical Essays on Eugene O'Neill, Susan Glaspell, Thornton Wilder, Arthur Miller and Other Playwrights*, ed. Drew Eisenhauer and Brenda Murphy (Jefferson, NC: McFarland, 2013), 241.

50. Arthur Hornblow, "Mr. Hornblow Goes to the Play," *Theatre Magazine*, June 1918, 355–58; Ralph Block, "Drama: The Provincetown Players Reopen in Macdougal Street," *New York Tribune*, November 3, 1917, 13.

51. Noelia Hernando-Real, *Self and Space in the Theater of Susan Glaspell* (Jefferson, NC: McFarland, 2011), 105–6.

52. J. Ellen Gainor, "*Woman's Honor* and the Critique of Slander Per Se," in Carpentier, *Susan Glaspell*, 67.

53. Sarah Withers, "Intertextuality on the Frontier in Susan Glaspell's *Inheritors*," in Eisenhauer and Murphy, *Intertextuality in American Drama*, 127.

54. J. Ellen Gainor, *Susan Glaspell in Context: American Theater, Culture, and Politics, 1915–48* (Ann Arbor: University of Michigan Press, 2004), 125–26.

55. Sinclair Lewis, *It Can't Happen Here* (New York: Signet Classics, 1970), 21. Could Glaspell's *Inheritors* (1921) have been a source for *It Can't Happen Here* (1935)? It would not have been the first time that Glaspell had come to Lewis's aid. In an inscription in the Cooks' copy of *Our Mr. Wrenn* (1914), Lewis credits Glaspell's "encouragement and understanding" that buoyed him as he wrote the book.

56. Withers, "Intertextuality on the Frontier," 127.

57. Withers, 137.

58. Marie Molnar, "Antigone Redux: Female Voice and the State in Susan Glaspell's Inheritors," in Carpentier, *Susan Glaspell*, 38.

59. Ludwig Lewisohn, "Drama: Inheritors," *Nation*, April 6, 1921, 515.

60. O. W. Firkins, "Inheritors—Drama at Provincetown and Nice People on Broadway," *Weekly Review*, April 13, 1921, 344–46; Kenneth Macgowan, "The New Play: Susan Glaspell Attacks Reaction in Inheritors," *Globe and Commercial Advertiser*, March 24, 1921, 12.

61. Heywood Broun, "Drama," *New York World*, April 28, 1922, 11.

62. Maida Castellun, "The Plays That Pass," *New York Call*, April 30, 1922, 4; Ludwig Lewisohn, "Aftermath," *Nation*, May 24, 1922, 627.

63. Alison Smith, "The New Play," *New York Evening Globe*, April 28, 1922, n.p., clipping, Provincetown Players Collection, New York Public Library, New York, NY; "Susan Glaspell's *Chains of Dew* Is Sharp Satire: Provincetown Players' Production Attacks Bobbed Hair and Birth Control," *New York Herald*, April 28, 1922, 10.

64. Unlike Dell, Ficke hated Davenport, where he felt constrained to practice law with his father and socialize with his wife's friends. A poet and a connoisseur of Japanese prints, he made frequent trips to Chicago, where Dell and his wife, Margery Currey, maintained a salon frequented by the journalists, artists, and writers of the Chicago Renaissance. Unlike Seymore Standish, Ficke broke his Iowa chains. After serving in World War I, he left Davenport, his socialite wife, and his law practice behind, relocating to upstate New York, where he remarried and continued to write poetry.

65. Cathy Moran Hajo, *Birth Control on Main Street: Organizing Clinics in the United States, 1916–1939* (Urbana: University of Illinois Press, 2010), 1.

66. Stansell, *American Moderns*, 234.

67. Adam Hochschild, *Rebel Cinderella: From Rags to Riches to Radical, the Epic Journey of Rose Pastor Stokes* (Boston: Houghton Mifflin Harcourt, 2020), 3.

68. Hajo, *Birth Control*, 12.

69. Hochschild, *Rebel Cinderella*, 159.

70. Adele Heller and Lois Rudnick, eds., introduction to *1915, the Cultural Moment: The New Politics, the New Woman, the New Psychology, the New Art, and the New Theatre in America* (New Brunswick, NJ: Rutgers University Press, 1991), 2.

71. Martha H. Patterson, *Beyond the Gibson Girl: Reimagining the American New Woman, 1895–1915* (Urbana: University of Illinois Press, 2008), 6, 8.

72. F. Scott Fitzgerald, *The Great Gatsby* (New York: Charles Scribner's Sons, 1925), 17.

73. Quoted in Hochschild, *Rebel Cinderella*, 160.

74. Aegyung Noh, "'The Critical Entangled in the Creative': Modernist Credos and Female Egoism in Susan Glaspell's The Verge," *Journal of English Language and Literature* 60, no. 2 (2014): 271.

75. Rasha Asim Hussein Gazzaz, "Women and Class in the Fiction of Susan Glaspell" (PhD diss., University of Leicester, 2015), 188.

76. Gerhard Bach, "Susan Glaspell: Mapping the Domains of Critical Revision," in *Susan Glaspell: Essays on Her Theater and Fiction*, ed. Linda Bez-Zvi (Ann Arbor: University of Michigan Press, 1995), 252–53.

77. Hinz-Bode, *Susan Glaspell*, 26.

78. Jerry Dickey, "Sophie Treadwell: The Expressionist Moment," in *The Cambridge Companion to American Women Playwrights*, ed. Brenda Murphy (Cambridge: Cambridge University Press, 1999), 76.

79. Quoted in Hutchins Hapgood, *A Victorian in the Modern World* (New York: Harcourt, Brace, 1939), 377.

80. Ruth Hale, "Concerning *The Verge*," *New York Times*, November 20, 1921, sec. 6, 1; Maida Castellun, "*The Verge*, Daring Venture in Drama by Susan Glaspell—Margaret Wycherly Transcends Herself," *New York Call*, November 16, 1921, 4.

81. See Weed Dickinson, "*The Verge*—Bad Insanity Clinic," *New York Evening Telegraph*, November 15, 1921, n.p., clipping, Provincetown Players Collection, New York Public Library, New York, NY; "Philosophers Wrestle with *The Verge* While Bread Burns," *Greenwich Villager*, November 23, 1921, 1; J. Ranken Towse, "The Play," *New York Evening Post*, November 15, 1921, 10; Robert A. Parker, "Plays—Domestic and Imported," *Independent*, December 17, 1921, 296, respectively.

82. See Ludwig Lewisohn, "Drama: *The Verge*," *Nation*, December 14, 1921, 708–9; Stark Young, "Susan Glaspell's *The Verge*," *New Republic*, December 7, 1921, 47; Kenneth Macgowan, "Seen on the Stage," *Vogue*, January 15, 1922, 48–49; C. W. E. Bigsby, *A Critical Introduction to Twentieth-Century American Drama, 1900–1940*, vol. 1 (Cambridge: Cambridge University Press, 1982), 29, respectively.

83. Susan Glaspell to Covici-Friede, January 19, 1929, Susan Glaspell Papers, Henry and Albert Berg Collection, New York Public Library, New York, NY.

84. Noe, *Susan Glaspell*, 80.

85. "Author Describes Work of Writing," *Provincetown Advocate*, March 28, 1946, 1.

86. Susan Glaspell, "The Huntsmen Are up in America," October 21, 1942, Susan Glaspell Papers, Henry and Albert Berg Collection, New York Public Library, New York, NY.

87. "Susan Glaspell Says We Need Books Today as Never Before," *Chicago Tribune*, December 6, 1942, clipping, Susan Glaspell Papers, Henry and Albert Berg Collection, New York Public Library, New York, NY.

88. Glaspell, *Judd Rankin's Daughter*, 83.

89. Lewisohn, "Drama: *The Verge.*"

6. THREE MIDWESTERN PLAYWRIGHTS FOUND A THEATRE COMPANY

1. Susan Glaspell, *The Road to the Temple* (New York: Frederick A. Stokes, 1927), 255. Hereafter this source is cited parenthetically in the text as *RTT*.

2. Susan Glaspell, "Here is the piece . . . ," unpublished essay, Susan Glaspell Papers, Henry and Albert Berg Collection, New York Public Library, New York, NY.

3. Helen Deutsch and Stella Hanau, *The Provincetown: A Story of the Theatre* (New York: Farrar and Rinehart, 1931), 14. Information about the Provincetown Players, when not specifically cited, has been taken from Deutsch and Hanau and also from these sources: William Warren Vilhauer, "A History and Evaluation of the Provincetown Players," pts. 1 and 2 (PhD diss., University of Iowa, 1965); Robert Karoly Sarlos, *Jig Cook and the Provincetown Players: Theatre in Ferment* (Amherst: University of Massachusetts Press, 1982); Leona Rust Egan, *Provincetown as a Stage: Provincetown, the Provincetown Players, and the Discovery of Eugene O'Neill* (Orleans, MA: Parnassus Imprints, 1994); Brenda Murphy, *The Provincetown Players and the Culture of Modernity* (Cambridge: Cambridge University Press, 2005).

4. Vilhauer, "History and Evaluation," pt. 2, 57, 773, 774. Vilhauer's two-part dissertation is an excellent source for its detailed account of the Provincetown Players' history and for the interviews he conducted with Idah Rauh and other living members of the Provincetown Players. Part 2 includes several appendices that reprint the group's charter membership roll, constitution, resolutions, season-by-season roster of plays, and other documents.

5. Quoted in Deutsch and Hanau, *Provincetown*, 41–42. Italics in original.

6. Vilhauer, "History and Evaluation," pt. 2, 777, 775, 777.

7. Linda Ben-Zvi, "George Cram Cook's *Road to the Temple*," in *Americans and the Experience of Delphi*, ed. Paul Lorenz and David Roessel (Boston: Somerset Hall, 2013), 105.

8. Deutsch and Hanau, *Provincetown*, 13.

9. Quoted in Murphy, *Provincetown Players*, 95.

10. A. J. Philpott, "Laboratory of the Drama on Cape Cod's Farthest Wharf," *Boston Sunday Globe*, August 13, 1916, reprinted in Edna Kenton, *The Provincetown Players and the Playwrights' Theatre, 1915–1922*, ed. Travis Bogard and Jackson R. Bryer (Jefferson, NC: McFarland, 2004), 185–88, 186.

11. Kenton, *Provincetown Players*, 32.

12. George S. Kaufman and Edna Ferber, *Dinner at Eight*, in *Kaufman and Company: Comedies*, ed. Lawrence Maslon (New York: Library of America, 2014), 469–590.

13. Kenton, *Provincetown Players*, 32, 33.

14. Barbara Ozieblo, *Susan Glaspell: A Critical Biography* (Chapel Hill: University of North Carolina Press, 2000), 101–2.

15. Sarlos, *Jig Cook*, 98.

16. Alexander Woollcott, "The New O'Neill Play," *New York Times*, November 7, 1920, 8.

17. Woollcott, 8; Heywood Broun, "The Emperor Jones by O'Neill Gives Chance for Cheers," *New York Tribune*, November 4, 1920.

18. Floyd Dell, *Homecoming: An Autobiography* (New York: Farrar and Rinehart, 1933), 266. Hereafter this source is cited parenthetically in the text.

19. Dell exaggerates here; the actors were not actually on stilts but on high-heeled boots made to resemble the buskins used in classical Greek theatre, probably another of Jig Cook's innovations intended to bring his theatre closer to that of his ideal: ancient Greece.

20. Heywood Broun, "Down an Alley on Drama Trail: Gold Dust and Foreign Substances in Plays of Provincetown," *New York Herald Tribune*, January 30, 1917, 9.

21. Kenton, *Provincetown Players*, 52.

22. Ben-Zvi, "George Cram Cook's *Road to the Temple*," 90.

23. C. W. E. Bigsby, *A Critical Introduction to Twentieth-Century American Drama, 1900–1940*, vol. 1 (Cambridge: Cambridge University Press, 1982), 13.

24. Susan Glaspell to Edna Kenton, October 1924, Edna Kenton Papers, Butler Library, Columbia University, New York, NY.

25. Frederick Coppleston, *A History of Philosophy*, vol. 7 (Garden City, NY: Image Books, 1965), 164.

26. Friedrich Nietzsche, *The Birth of Tragedy*, in *Basic Writings of Nietzsche*, ed. and trans. Walter Kaufmann (New York: Modern Library, 1968), 81, 64. Italics in original.

27. Coppleston, *History of Philosophy*, 172.

28. Nietzsche, *Birth of Tragedy*, 380.

29. Ernst Haeckel, *The Riddle of the Universe at the Close of the Nineteenth Century*, trans. Joseph McCabe (New York: Harper and Brothers, 1900), 254, 336, 347; Nietzsche, *Birth of Tragedy*, 48.

30. Bigsby, *Critical Introduction*, 10.

31. Bigsby, 19.

32. Quoted in Ozieblo, *Susan Glaspell*, 170.

33. Sarlos, *Jig Cook*, 55.

34. See Vilhauer, "History and Evaluation," apps. C and D, 779–91.

35. Susan Glaspell to Eleanor Fitzgerald, May 25, 1924, Houghton Library, Harvard University, Cambridge, MA.

36. Susan Glaspell to Eleanor Fitzgerald, May 31, 1924, Houghton Library, Harvard University, Cambridge, MA.

37. Quoted in Deutsch and Hanau, *Provincetown*, x.

38. Edna Kenton, "Provincetown and MacDougal Street," in *Greek Coins: Poems by George Cram Cook, with Memorabilia by Floyd Dell, Edna Kenton, and Susan Glaspell* (New York: George H. Doran, 1925), 28.

39. Although Sarlos claims that the Provincetown Players was a theatre collective, for an alternate perspective, see Seth Baumrin, "Jig Cook: Stage

Manager for an American Renaissance," *Journal of American Drama and Theatre* 12 (2000): 55–74.

40. Kenton, "Provincetown and MacDougal Street," 26.

41. Quoted in Barrett Clark, *Eugene O'Neill: The Man and His Plays* (New York: Robert M. McBride, 1929), 43; quoted in Vilhauer, "History and Evaluation," 307.

42. Max Eastman, *The Enjoyment of Living* (New York: Harper and Brothers, 1948), 366.

43. Kenton, *Provincetown Players*, 125.

44. Although Vilhauer is correct on the whole, white actors did black their bodies to appear in *The Emperor Jones*. See Glaspell, *Road to the Temple*, 291, when she quotes Jig regarding "the discomfort of blacking bodies" for that play.

45. Vilhauer, "History and Evaluation," 769.

46. Sarlos, *Jig Cook*, 160.

47. Sarlos, 161.

48. Sarlos, 166–67.

49. Bigsby, *Critical Introduction*, 20.

50. J. Ellen Gainor, *Susan Glaspell in Context: American Theater, Culture, and Politics, 1915–48* (Ann Arbor: University of Michigan Press, 2004), 10–11.

51. Gainor, 17.

52. Murphy, *Provincetown Players*, 224.

53. Jeff Kennedy, "The Artistic Life of the Provincetown Playhouse, 1918–1922" (PhD diss., New York University, 2007), 895.

54. Susan Glaspell to Edna Kenton, October 23, 1923, Houghton Library, Harvard University, Cambridge, MA; Susan Glaspell, letter to the editor, *Provincetown Advocate*, July 11, 1946, 5.

CONCLUSION: THREE MIDWESTERN PLAYWRIGHTS VENTURE BEYOND P-TOWN

1. Susan Glaspell, *The Road to the Temple* (New York: Frederick A. Stokes, 1927), 403–6.

2. Telephone interview with Jerri Dell, April 29, 2020.

3. Carl Van Doren, "The Revolt from the Village: 1920," *Nation*, October 21, 1921, 407–12. See also Harlan Hatcher, *Creating the Modern American Novel* (New York: Farrar and Rinehart, 1935), which contains a chapter, "The Younger Generation," that compares Dell and F. Scott Fitzgerald.

4. Douglas Clayton, *Floyd Dell: The Life and Times of an American Rebel* (Chicago: Ivan R. Dee, 1994), 273–87; telephone interview with Jerri Dell, April 29, 2020. Mike Gold, one of the editors of the *New Masses*, had accused Dell of selling out when he resigned his editorship of that publication in 1929.

5. Marcia Noe, *Susan Glaspell: Voice from the Heartland* (Macomb: Western Illinois University, 1983), 47–64.

6. Noe, 65–81.

7. The census of 2020 records Davenport's population as 100,934.

8. Edward Abrahams, "Alfred Stieglitz's Faith and Vision," in *1915, the Cultural Moment: The New Politics, the New Woman, the New Psychology, the New Art, and the New Theatre in America*, ed. Adele Heller and Lois Rudnick (New Brunswick, NJ: Rutgers University Press, 1991), 186.

9. Floyd Dell, *Intellectual Vagabondage*, with an introduction by Douglas Clayton (Chicago: Ivan R. Dee, 1990), 260–61. Over the years, Dell's thinking about literature evolved. He wrote to Miriam Gurko in 1963 that "literature became more cultish, more irresponsible and to a considerable extent it encourages the younger generation to love selfishly, work dishonestly, think stupidly, fight foolishly if at all and live ignobly." See Jerri Dell, *Blood Too Bright: Floyd Dell Remembers Edna St. Vincent Millay* (Warwick, NY: Glenmere, 2017), 208.

10. Susan Glaspell, "On the Subject of Writing," unpublished typescript, 1–2, Susan Glaspell Papers, Henry and Albert Berg Collection, New York Public Library, New York, NY.

11. Susan Glaspell, *Inheritors* (Boston: Small, Maynard, 1921), 154.

MANUSCRIPT COLLECTIONS CONSULTED

Beinecke Rare Book and Manuscript Library, Yale University, New Haven, CT
Butler Library, Columbia University, New York, NY
Henry and Albert Berg Collection, New York Public Library, New York, NY
Houghton Library, Harvard University, Cambridge, MA
Newberry Library, Chicago, IL
Provincetown Players Collection, New York Public Library, New York, NY
Special Collections, Davenport Public Library, Davenport, IA
Special Collections, University of Iowa Library, Iowa City, IA

SOURCES FOR
CHAPTER EPIGRAPHS

Chapter 1

"Bliss was it in that dawn to be alive . . ." William Wordsworth, *The Prelude*, bk. 11, lines 108–9.

Chapter 2

"In those days . . ." Arthur Davison Ficke, journal entry, June 14, 1936, Arthur Davison Ficke Papers, Beinecke Rare Book and Manuscript Library, Yale University, New Haven, CT.

"Davenport as a Literary Center . . ." Susan Glaspell to Floyd Dell, September 17, 1910, Floyd Dell Papers, Newberry Library, Chicago, IL.

"But Davenport was in many ways a romantic and miraculous city . . ." Floyd Dell, "A Living and Inexplicable Man," review of *The Road to the Temple*, by Susan Glaspell, *New York Herald Tribune Books*, March 13, 1927, 1–2.

Chapter 3

"Floyd Dell was in high school when I first heard of him . . ." Harry Hansen, *Midwest Portraits* (New York: Harcourt, Brace, 1923), 209.

Chapter 4

"It is difficult to write even a review . . ." Arthur Davison Ficke, review of *The Road to the Temple*, by Susan Glaspell, *Saturday Review of Literature*, March 26, 1927, 1150.

"George Cram Cook had always been temperamentally at odds . . ." Floyd Dell, *Homecoming* (New York: Farrar and Rinehart, 1933), 150.

Chapter 5

"Saw Susie Glaspell last night . . ." George Cram Cook to Mollie Price, November 26, 1907, George Cram Cook Papers, Henry W. and Albert A. Berg Collection of English and American Literature, New York Public Library, New York, NY.

"For the thunder of my anger rolls mostly for Susan . . ." W. H. Fineshriber to Floyd Dell, October 11, 1910, Floyd Dell Papers, Newberry Library, Chicago, IL.

Chapter 6

"From 1915 to 1922 I gave up practically everything else . . ." Susan Glaspell to Eleanor Fitzgerald, May 7, 1929, Eleanor Fitzgerald Papers, Houghton Library, Harvard University, Cambridge, MA.

"For Susan Glaspell my respect and admiration grew immensely . . ." Floyd Dell, *Homecoming* (New York: Farrar and Rinehart, 1933), 268.

Conclusion

"I'm an American . . ." Susan Glaspell, "His America," in *Lifted Masks* (New York: Frederick A. Stokes, 1912), 201.

WORKS CITED AND CONSULTED

Abrahams, Edward. "Alfred Stieglitz's Faith and Vision." In Heller and Rudnick, *1915, the Cultural Moment*, 185–95.

Arpy, Jim. "Remarkable Annie Wittenmyer." In *Legends of Our Land: A Unique
History of the Mississippi Valley*, 23–24. Davenport, IA: Times-Democrat,
1968.

Bach, Gerhard. "Susan Glaspell: Mapping the Domains of Critical Revision."
In Ben-Zvi, *Susan Glaspell*, 235–58.

Baumrin, Seth. "George Cram Cook: Stage Manager for an American Renaissance." *Journal of American Drama and Theatre* 12 (2000): 55–74.

Beard, Rick, and Leslie Cohen Berlowitz, eds. *Greenwich Village Culture and
Counterculture*. New Brunswick, NJ: Rutgers University Press, 1993.

Bell, Daniel. "The Background and Development of Marxian Socialism in
the United States." In *Socialism and American Life*, vol. 1, edited by Donald
Drew Egbert and Stowe Persons, 213–405. Princeton, NJ: Princeton University Press, 1952.

Bellamy, Edward. *Looking Backward*. Mineola, NY: Dover, 1996. First published 1888.

Ben-Zvi, Linda. "George Cram Cook's *Road to the Temple*." In *Americans and
the Experience of Delphi*, edited by Paul Lorenz and David Roessel, 89–117.
Boston: Somerset Hall, 2013.

———. *Susan Glaspell: Essays on Her Theater and Fiction*. Ann Arbor: University of Michigan Press, 1995.

———. *Susan Glaspell: Her Life and Times*. Oxford: Oxford University Press,
2005.

Ben-Zvi, Linda, and J. Ellen Gainor, eds. *Susan Glaspell: The Complete Plays.* Jefferson, NC: McFarland, 2010.

Berrier, G. Galen. "The Negro Suffrage Issue in Iowa, 1865–1868." *Annals of Iowa* 39, no. 4 (1968): 248–61.

Bigsby, C. W. E. *A Critical Introduction to Twentieth-Century American Drama, 1900–1940.* Vol 1. Cambridge: Cambridge University Press, 1982.

Black, Cheryl. *The Women of Provincetown, 1915–1922.* Tuscaloosa: University of Alabama Press, 2002.

Bowers, William L. "Davenport, Iowa, 1906–1907: A Glimpse into a City's Past." *Annals of Iowa* 38, no. 5 (1966): 363–87.

Bryan, Patricia L. "Foreshadowing 'A Jury of Her Peers': Susan Glaspell's 'The Plea' and the Case of John Wesley Elkins." In Carpentier, *Susan Glaspell,* 45–65.

Burnham, John C. "The New Psychology." In Heller and Rudnick, *1915, the Cultural Moment,* 117–27.

Burrows, J. M. D. *Fifty Years in Iowa, 1838–1888.* Davenport, IA: Davenport Glass, 1888.

Carpentier, Martha, ed. *Susan Glaspell: New Directions in Critical Inquiry.* Newcastle-upon-Tyne: Cambridge Scholars Publishing, 2006.

Carpentier, Martha, and Emeline Jouve, eds. Introduction to *On Susan Glaspell's* Trifles *and "A Jury of Her Peers": Centennial Essays, Interviews, and Adaptations,* 1–10. Jefferson, NC: McFarland, 2015.

Chansky, Dorothy. *Composing Ourselves: The Little Theatre Movement and the American Audience.* Carbondale: Southern Illinois University Press, 2004.

———. "Kitchen Sink Realism: American Drama, Dining and Domestic Labor Come of Age in Little Theatre." *Journal of American Drama and Theatre* 16, no. 2 (Spring 2004): 37–56.

Churchill, Allen. *The Improper Bohemians: A Re-creation of Greenwich Village in Its Heyday.* New York: E. P. Dutton, 1959.

Clark, Barrett. *Eugene O'Neill: The Man and His Plays.* New York: Robert M. McBride, 1929.

Clayton, Douglas. *Floyd Dell: The Life and Times of an American Rebel.* Chicago: Ivan R. Dee, 1994.

Coppleston, Frederick. *A History of Philosophy.* Vol. 7. Garden City: NY: Image Books, 1965.

Cott, Nancy. *The Bonds of Womanhood: Women's Sphere in New England, 1780–1835.* New Haven, CT: Yale University Press, 1977.

Crawford, Bartholow V. "Susan Glaspell." *Palimpsest* 2, no. 12 (December 1930): 517–21.

Currie, Harold W. *Eugene V. Debs.* Boston: Twayne, 1976.

Darnall, Kory. *Schuetzenpark: Davenport's Lost Playland, 1870–1923.* 2nd ed. Davenport, IA: Davenport Schuetzenpark Gilde, 2000.

Dell, Jerri. *Blood Too Bright: Floyd Dell Remembers Edna St. Vincent Millay.* Warwick, NY: Glenmere, 2017.

Deutsch, Helen, and Stella Hanau. *The Provincetown: A Story of the Theatre.* New York: Farrar and Rinehart, 1931.

Dickey, Jerry. "Sophie Treadwell: The Expressionist Moment." In Murphy, *Cambridge Companion*, 66–81.

Donnelly, Ignatius [Edmund Boisgilbert]. *Caesar's Column: A Story of the Twentieth Century*. Chicago: L. J. Schulte, 1890.

Dorman, Robert L. *The Revolt of the Provinces: The Regionalist Movement in America, 1920–1945*. Chapel Hill: University of North Carolina Press, 1993.

Downer, Harry. *History of Davenport and Scott County, Iowa*. Chicago: S. J. Clarke, 1910.

Duffey, Bernard. *The Chicago Renaissance in American Letters: A Critical History*. East Lansing: Michigan State University Press, 1956.

Eastman, Max. *The Enjoyment of Living*. New York: Harper and Brothers, 1948.

———. *Love and Revolution: My Journey through an Epoch*. New York: Random House, 1956.

Egan, Leona Rust. *Provincetown as a Stage: Provincetown, the Provincetown Players, and the Discovery of Eugene O'Neill*. Orleans, MA: Parnassus Imprints, 1994.

Fishbein, Leslie. *Rebels in Bohemia: The Radicals of the Masses, 1911–1917*. Chapel Hill: University of North Carolina Press, 1982.

Fitzgerald, F. Scott. *The Great Gatsby*. New York: Charles Scribner's Sons, 1925.

Flanagan, John T. "A Letter from Floyd Dell." *American Literature* 45, no. 3 (1973): 441–52.

Flynn, Elizabeth Gurley. *Rebel Girl: An Autobiography, My First Life (1906–1926)*. New York: International Publishing Company, 1973.

Friedman, Sharon. "'What There Is Behind Us': Susan Glaspell's Challenge to Nativist Discourse in Stage Adaptations of Her *Harper's Monthly* Fiction." In *Intertextuality in American Drama: Critical Essays on Eugene O'Neill, Susan Glaspell, Thornton Wilder, Arthur Miller, and Other Playwrights*, edited by Drew Eisenhauer and Brenda Murphy, 232–52. Jefferson, NC: McFarland, 2013.

Gainor, J. Ellen. *Susan Glaspell in Context: American Theater, Culture, and Politics, 1915–48*. Ann Arbor: University of Michigan Press, 2004.

———. "*Woman's Honor* and the Critique of Slander Per Se." In Carpentier, *Susan Glaspell*, 66–79.

Galsworthy, John. *A Modern Comedy*. Bk. 2, *The Silver Spoon*. New York: Charles Scribner's Sons, 1926.

Gazzaz, Rasha Asim Hussein. "Women and Class in the Fiction of Susan Glaspell." PhD diss., University of Leicester, 2015.

Gifford, Sanford. "The American Reception of Psychoanalysis, 1908–1922." In Heller and Rudnick, *1915, the Cultural Moment*, 128–45.

Grand, Sarah. "The New Aspect of the Woman Question." *North American Review* 158 (March 1894): 270–76.

Green, Martin. "The New Art." In Heller and Rudnick, *1915, the Cultural Moment*, 157–63.

Haeckel, Ernst. *The Riddle of the Universe at the Close of the Nineteenth Century*. Translated by Joseph McCabe. New York: Harper and Brothers, 1900.

Hahn, Emily. *Romantic Rebels: An Informal History of Bohemianism in America*. New York: Houghton Mifflin, 1967.

Hajo, Cathy Moran. *Birth Control on Main Street: Organizing Clinics in the United States, 1916–1939*. Urbana: University of Illinois Press, 2010.

Hansen, Harry. "A Davenport Boyhood." *Palimpsest* 37, no. 4 (1956): 161–221.

———. *Midwest Portraits*. New York: Harcourt, Brace, 1923.

Hapgood, Hutchins. *A Victorian in the Modern World*. New York: Harcourt, Brace, 1939.

Hart, John E. *Floyd Dell*. Boston: Twayne, 1974.

Hatcher, Harlan. *Creating the Modern American Novel*. New York: Farrar and Rinehart, 1935.

Heller, Adele, and Lois Rudnick, eds. *1915, the Cultural Moment: The New Politics, the New Woman, the New Psychology, the New Art, and the New Theatre in America*. New Brunswick, NJ: Rutgers University Press, 1991.

Hernando-Real, Noelia. *Self and Space in the Theatre of Susan Glaspell*. Jefferson, NC: McFarland, 2011.

Hinz-Bode, Kristina. *Susan Glaspell and the Anxieties of Expression: Language and Isolation in the Plays*. Jefferson, NC: McFarland, 2006.

Hochschild, Adam. *Rebel Cinderella: From Rags to Riches to Radical, the Epic Journey of Rose Pastor Stokes*. Boston: Houghton Mifflin Harcourt, 2020.

Horgan, John. *The End of Science*. New York: Broadway Books, 1996, 1997.

Hudson, David, Marvin Bergman, and Loren F. Horton, eds. *The Biographical Dictionary of Iowa*. Iowa City: University of Iowa Press, 2008.

Humphrey, Robert. *Children of Fantasy: The First Rebels of Greenwich Village*. New York: John Wiley and Sons, 1978.

Irmscher, Christoph. *Max Eastman: A Life*. New Haven, CT: Yale University Press, 2017.

Johnson, Hildegard Binder. *German Forty-Eighters in Davenport*. Davenport, IA: Davenport Schuetzenpark Gilde, 1998.

Jouve, Emeline. *Susan Glaspell's Poetics and Politics of Rebellion*. Iowa City: University of Iowa Press, 2017.

Kauffman, Stuart. *At Home in the Universe: The Search for the Laws of Self-Organization and Complexity*. New York: Oxford University Press, 1995.

Kaufman, George S., and Edna Ferber. *Dinner at Eight*. In *Kaufman and Company: Comedies*, edited by Lawrence Maslon, 469–590. New York: Library of America, 2014.

Kemper, Susan C. "The Novels, Plays, and Poetry of George Cram Cook, Founder of the Provincetown Players." PhD diss., Bowling Green State University, 1982.

Kennedy, Jeff. "The Artistic Life of the Provincetown Playhouse, 1918–1922." PhD diss., New York University, 2007.

Kennedy, Kathleen. "Meridel LeSueur: A Voice for Working-Class Women." In *The Human Tradition in America between the Wars, 1920–1945*, edited by Donald W. Wisenhunt, 137–52. Wilmington, DE: Scholarly Resources, 2002.

Kenton, Edna. "Provincetown and MacDougal Street." In *Greek Coins: Poems by George Cram Cook, with Memorabilia by Floyd Dell, Edna Kenton, and Susan Glaspell*, 17–30. New York: George H. Doran, 1925.

————. *The Provincetown Players and the Playwrights' Theatre, 1915–1922.* Edited by Travis Bogard and Jackson R. Bryer. Jefferson, NC: McFarland, 2004.

Kramer, Dale. *Chicago Renaissance: The Literary Life in the Midwest, 1900–1930.* New York: Appleton-Century, 1966.

Leach, Eugene E. "The Radicals of the Masses." In Heller and Rudnick, *1915, the Cultural Moment*, 27–47.

Lewis, Sinclair. *It Can't Happen Here.* New York: Signet Classics, 1970. First published 1935.

————. *Main Street.* New York: Harcourt, Brace and Howe, 1920.

Lewisohn, Ludwig. *Expression in America.* New York: Harper and Brothers, 1932.

Mahoney, Timothy R. "Down in Davenport: A Regional Perspective on Antebellum Town Economic Development." *Annals of Iowa* 50, no. 5 (Summer 1990): 451–74.

————. "Down in Davenport: The Social Response of Antebellum Elites to Regional Urbanization." *Annals of Iowa* 50, no. 6 (Fall 1990): 593–622.

————. *River Towns in the Great West: The Structure of Provincial Urbanization in the American Midwest, 1820–1970.* Cambridge: Cambridge University Press, 1990.

Makowsky, Veronica. "Susan Glaspell and Modernism." In Murphy, *Cambridge Companion*, 49–65.

Martin, Robert F. "Sarah Ann 'Annie' Turner Wittenmyer." In Hudson, Bergman, and Horton, *Biographical Dictionary of Iowa*, 565–66.

May, Henry F. *The End of American Innocence: A Study of the First Years of Our Own Time, 1912–1917.* New York: Alfred A. Knopf, 1959.

Mencken, H. L. "The Literary Capital of the United States." *Nation*, April 17, 1920, 10, 92.

Miller, Sallie M. "Casting a Wide Net: The Milwaukee Movement to 1920." In *Socialism in the Heartland: The Midwestern Experience, 1900–1925*, edited by Donald T. Chritchlow, 18–45. Notre Dame, IN: University of Notre Dame Press, 1986.

Molnar, Marie. "Antigone Redux: Female Voice and the State in Susan Glaspell's *Inheritors*." In Carpentier, *Susan Glaspell*, 37–44.

Morgan, Francesca. "'Regions Remote from Revolutionary Scenes': Regionalism, Nationalism, and the Iowa Daughters of the American Revolution, 1890–1930." *Annals of Iowa* 56, no. 1 (1997): 46–79.

Morris, William. *News from Nowhere.* Boston: Harper Brothers, 1891.

Murphy, Brenda, ed. *The Cambridge Companion to American Women Playwrights.* Cambridge: Cambridge University Press, 1999.

————. *The Provincetown Players and the Culture of Modernity.* Cambridge: Cambridge University Press, 2005.

Nietzsche, Friedrich. *The Birth of Tragedy.* In *Basic Writings of Nietzsche*, edited and translated by Walter Kaufmann, 17–144. New York: Modern Library, 1968.

Noe, Marcia. *Susan Glaspell: Voice from the Heartland*. Macomb: Western Illinois University, 1983.

Noh, Aegyung. "'The Critical Entangled in the Creative': Modernist Credos and Female Egoism in Susan Glaspell's *The Verge*." *Journal of English Language and Literature* 60, no. 2 (June 2014): 269–93.

———. "Historiographies of Modernity: Susan Glaspell and 'Jig' Cook." *Feminist Studies in English Literature* 21, no. 1 (2013): 141–76.

Ozieblo, Barbara. *Susan Glaspell: A Critical Biography*. Chapel Hill: University of North Carolina Press, 2000.

Parry, Albert. *A History of Bohemianism in America, 1885–1915*. New York: Covici-Friede, 1933.

Patterson, Martha H. *Beyond the Gibson Girl: Reimagining the American New Woman, 1895–1915*. Urbana: University of Illinois Press, 2008.

Penningroth, Kathy. "Phebe W. Sudlow." In Hudson, Bergman, and Horton, *Biographical Dictionary of Iowa*, 501–3.

Petersen, William J. *The Story of Iowa: The Progress of an American State*. Vol. 2. New York: Lewis Historical, 1952.

Purcell, W. L. *Them Was the Good Old Days in Davenport, Scott County, Iowa*. [Davenport, IA?]: Purcell Printing, 1922.

Rideout, Walter B. *The Radical Novel in the United States, 1900–1954: Some Interrelations of Literature and Society*. Cambridge, MA: Harvard University Press, 1956.

Roba, Bill. "Davenport." In *Joined by a River: Quad Cities*, 66–85. Davenport, IA: Lee Enterprises, 1982.

———. *The River and the Prairie*. Quad Cities: Hesperian, 1986.

Roller, Scott. "Mary Louisa Duncan Putnam." In Hudson, Bergman, and Horton, *Biographical Dictionary of Iowa*, 415–16.

Ross, Jack. *The Socialist Party of America: A Complete History*. Lincoln, NE: Potomac Books, 2015.

Sarlos, Robert Karoly. *Jig Cook and the Provincetown Players: Theatre in Ferment*. Amherst: University of Massachusetts Press, 1982.

Sautter, R. Craig, ed. *Floyd Dell: Essays from the Friday Literary Review, 1909–1913*. Highland Park, IL: December Press, 1995.

Schultz, Gladys Denny. "Susan Glaspell." In *A Book of Iowa Authors*, edited by Johnson Brigham, 109–22. Des Moines: Iowa State Teachers Association, 1930.

Schwartz, Judith. *Radical Feminists of Heterodoxy: Greenwich Village, 1912–1940*. Norwich, VT: New Victoria, 1986.

Schwieder, Dorothy, Thomas Moran, and Lynn Nielsen, eds. *Iowa Past to Present: The People and the Prairie*. Rev. 3rd ed. Iowa City: University of Iowa Press, 2011.

Shakespeare, William. *Twelfth Night*. In *The Complete Plays of William Shakespeare*, edited by William Allan Neilson and Charles Jarvis Hill. Cambridge, MA: Riverside Press, Houghton Mifflin, 1942.

Sheaffer, Louis. *O'Neill: Son and Playwright*. Boston: Little, Brown, 1968.

Sklar, Robert. "Chicago Renaissance." *Commonweal*, vol. 6, January 6, 1967, 377.

Sochen, June. *Movers and Shakers: American Women Thinkers and Activists, 1900–1970*. New York: Random House, 1974.

———. *The New Woman in Greenwich Village, 1910–1920*. New York: Quadrangle Books, 1972.

Spears, Timothy B. *Chicago Dreaming: Midwesterners and the City, 1871–1919*. Chicago: University of Chicago Press, 2005.

Stansell, Christine. *American Moderns: Bohemian New York and the Creation of a New Century*. Princeton, NJ: Princeton University Press, 2000.

Stein, Laura. *Speech Rights in America: The First Amendment, Democracy, and the Media*. Urbana: University of Illinois Press, 2006.

Svendsen, Marlys A. *Davenport: A Pictorial History*. [Davenport, IA?]: G. Bradley, 1985.

Svendsen, Marlys A., and Martha H. Bowers. *Davenport, Where the Mississippi Runs West: A Survey of Davenport History and Architecture*. Davenport, IA: City of Davenport, 1982.

Tanselle, G. Thomas. *American Publishing History: The Tanselle Collection*. New Haven, CT: Beinecke Rare Book and Manuscript Library, 2020.

———. "Ezra Pound and a Story of Floyd Dell's." *Notes and Queries*, n.s., 8, no. 9 (1961): 350–52.

———. "Faun at the Barricades: The Life and Work of Floyd Dell, Parts 1 and 2." PhD diss., Northwestern University, 1959.

———. "Floyd Dell." In *Portraits and Reviews*, 3–12. Charlottesville, VA: Bibliographical Society of the University of Virginia, 2015.

———. "George Cram Cook and the Poetry of Living, with a Checklist." *Books at Iowa* 24 (1976): 3–37.

Tietjens, Eunice. *The World at My Shoulder*. New York: Macmillan, 1938.

Trimberger, Ellen Kay. "The New Woman and the New Sexuality: Conflict and Contradiction in the Writings and Lives of Mabel Dodge and Neith Boyce." In Heller and Rudnick, *1915, the Cultural Moment*, 98–115.

Turner, Jonathan. *A Brief History of Bucktown: Davenport's Infamous District Transformed*. Charleston, SC: History Press, 2016.

Van Doren, Carl. "The Revolt from the Village: 1920." *Nation*, October 21, 1921, 307–12.

Van Doren, Carl, and Mark Van Doren. *American and British Literature since 1890*. New York: Chautauqua, 1926.

Vilhauer, William Warren. "A History and Evaluation of the Provincetown Players." Pts. 1 and 2. PhD diss., University of Iowa, 1965.

"Vote for Members of Congress—1902–1910," *Iowa Official Register*, 1909–1910, no. 23. Des Moines, IA: Emory H. English, State Printer, 1911.

Waterman, Arthur. "From Iowa to Greece: The Achievement of George Cram Cook." *Quarterly Journal of Speech* 45, no. 1 (1959): 46–50.

Wells, Ida B. *Crusade for Justice: The Autobiography of Ida B. Wells*. Edited by
Eve L. Ewing et al. 2nd ed. Negro American Biographies and
Autobiographies. Chicago: University of Chicago Press, 2020.

Welter, Barbara. "The Cult of True Womanhood: 1820–1860." *American
Quarterly* 18, no. 2 (1966): 151–74.

Wetzsteon, Ross. *Republic of Dreams: Greenwich Village—the American
Bohemia, 1910–1960*. New York: Simon and Schuster, 2002.

Wilson, Justina Leavitt, and Clara Elizabeth Fanning, eds. *Book Review Digest*.
Seventh Annual Compilation. Minneapolis, MN: H. W. Wilson, 1911.

Withers, Sarah. "Intertextuality on the Frontier in Susan Glaspell's *Inheritors*."
In *Intertextuality in American Drama: Critical Essays on Eugene O'Neill, Susan
Glaspell, Thornton Wilder, Arthur Miller, and Other Playwrights*, edited by
Drew Eisenhauer and Brenda Murphy, 126–41. Jefferson, NC: McFarland,
2013.

Wood, Sharon E. *The Freedom of the Streets: Work, Citizenship, and Sexuality in a
Gilded Age City*. Chapel Hill: University of North Carolina Press, 2005.

———. "Jennie C. McCowen." In Hudson, Bergman, and Horton, *Biographical
Dictionary of Iowa*, 351–52.

———. "Jennie McCowen." *Iowa Heritage Illustrated* 89, nos. 1 and 2 (2008):
50–52.

Woten, Rick L. "Benjamin F. Gue." In Hudson, Bergman, and Horton,
Biographical Dictionary of Iowa, 202–3.

Wundrum, Bill. *Sweet Memories: The Lagomarcino Story*. Davenport, IA:
Lagomarcino's, 2008.

———. *A Time We Remember: Celebrating a Century in Our Quad-Cities*.
Davenport, IA: Quad-City Times, 1999.

GEORGE CRAM COOK

A Classified Primary Source Bibliography

Compiled by Tyler Preston

FICTION

Novels

Banks, Charles Eugene, and George Cram Cook. *In Hampton Roads: A Dramatic Romance*. Chicago: Rand McNally, 1899.

Roderick Taliaferro: A Story of Maximilian's Empire. Illustrated by Seymour M. Stone. New York: Macmillan, 1903.

The Chasm: A Novel. New York: Frederick A. Stokes, 1911.

Short Stories

"An American Hero." *Metropolitan* 308, no. 4 (February 1913): 28.

Drama

Cook, George Cram, and Susan Glaspell. *Suppressed Desires*. In *Provincetown Plays, Second Series*. New York: Frank Shay, 1917, 113–44.

Glaspell, Susan, and George Cram Cook. *Tickless Time: A Comedy in One Act*. In *Plays*, by Susan Glaspell, 231–71. New York: Dodd, Mead, 1920.

The Spring: A Play. New York: Frank Shay, 1921.

The Athenian Women: A Play. With the original text and a modern Greek translation made by the author and revised by C. Carthaio. Athens: Estia, 1926.

Change Your Style. In *1915, the Cultural Moment: The New Politics, the New Woman, the New Psychology, the New Art, and the New Theatre in America*, edited by Adele Heller and Lois Rudnick, 292–99. New Brunswick, NJ: Rutgers University Press, 1991.

Poetry

"Sonnet: On the Evening of October 16th, 1891." *The Hawkeye: Junior Annual of the Class of '93, State University of Iowa* 2 (1892): 176.
"Frolic Elves in Eyes of Blue." *Century* 67 (January 1904): 480.
"Battle Hymn of the Workers." *Progressive Woman*, October 1912, 9.

Poetry Collection

Greek Coins: Poems by George Cram Cook. New York: George H. Doran, 1925.

NONFICTION

Book-Length Nonfiction

Banks, Charles Eugene, George Cram Cook, and Marshall Everett. *Beautiful Homes and Social Customs of America: A Complete Guide to Correct Social Forms and Artistic Living*. Chicago: Bible House (Henry Neil), 1902.

Essays

"The Primary Condition of Understanding Whitman and the Secondary Condition of Understanding Anybody." *Dial*, February 1, 1897, 77–78.
"The Prose and Verse of Kipling." *Papers of the Contemporary Club* 3 (1898–1899), 61–85.
"Evolution." *Papers of the Contemporary Club* 11 (1906–1907), 57–86.
"Some Modest Remarks on Socialism." In *Papers of the Contemporary Club* 15 (1910–1911), 1–17. Davenport, IA: Mossman and Vollmer, 1911.
"Frank Norris' Chicago—Chicago in Fiction: The Seventh Paper." *Friday Literary Review*, March 8, 1912, 1.
"More Authors of National Reputation Than Any Other City in State." *Davenport Democrat and Leader*, March 10, 1912, 17.
"Susan Glaspell's Chicago—Chicago in Fiction: The Eighth Paper." *Friday Literary Review*, March 15, 1912, 1.
"Frank Harris' Chicago—Chicago in Fiction: The Ninth Paper." *Friday Literary Review*, March 22, 1912, 1.
"Answer to Harriet Monroe on Musical Notation of Verse." *Friday Literary Review*, April 26, 1912, 8.
"Socialism the Issue in 1912." *Masses*, July 1912, 7.
"The Third American Sex." *Forum*, October 1913, 445–63.
"The C.T.U." *Forum*, October 1914, 543–61.

Autobiography/Memoir

Company B of Davenport. Davenport, IA: Democrat Company, 1899.

Biography

Banks, Charles Eugene, George Cram Cook, and Marshall Everett. *Authorized and Authentic Life and Works of T. DeWitt Talmage*. Chicago: Bible House, 1902.

Book Reviews

"Two Views of Walt Whitman." Review of *Whitman: A Study and Thomas Donaldson's Walt Whitman the Man*, by John Burroughs. *Dial*, January 1, 1897, 15–17.

"Art and Politics." Review of *Little Cities of Italy*, by Andre Maurel. *Friday Literary Review*, May 26, 1911, 7.

"Fifty Years After." Review of *The World of Life*, by Alfred Russel Wallace. *Friday Literary Review*, August 11, 1911, 1.

"The Will to Fly." Review of *Forse che si forse che no*, by Gabriele d'Annunzio. *Friday Literary Review*, September 1, 1911, 1.

"Ruskin Today." Review of *Ruskin: A Study in Personality*, by Arthur Christopher Benson. *Friday Literary Review*, September 8, 1911, 1.

"A New Yankee at Court." Review of *Pandora's Box*, by J. A. Mitchell. *Friday Literary Review*, September 15, 1911, 1.

"A University of Books." Review of the *Home University Library of Modern Knowledge*. *Friday Literary Review*, September 22, 1911, 6.

"An American Satirist" Review of *Black Beetles in Amber*, by Ambrose Bierce. *Friday Literary Review*, September 29, 1911, 8.

"Reinterpretation." Review of *Evolution*, by Patrick Geddes and J. Arthur Thompson, and *The Biology of the Seasons*, by J. Arthur Thompson. *Friday Literary Review*, October 13, 1911, 1.

"Realistic Romance." Review of *The Song of Renny*, by Maurice Hewlett. *Friday Literary Review*, November 10, 1911, 1.

"Russia." Review of *Under Western Eyes*, by Joseph Conrad. *Friday Literary Review*, November 24, 1911, 1.

"On Retranslating Homer." Review of the *Iliad*, translated by Arthur Gardner Lewis. *Friday Literary Review*, December 1, 1911, 5.

"An Aesthetic 'Thriller.'" Review of *The Outcry*, by Henry James. *Friday Literary Review*, December 22, 1911, 1.

"The Frivolous Age." Review of *A Likely Story*, by William De Morgan. *Friday Literary Review*, December 29, 1911, 1.

"Degringolade." Review of *Jean Christophe in Paris*, by Romain Rolland. *Friday Literary Review*, January 12, 1912, 1.

"Dead Ladies." Review of *The Women of the Caesars*, by Guglielmo Ferrero. *Friday Literary Review*, January 19, 1912, 8.

"Recent Verse." Review of *In Vivid Gardens*, by Marguerite Wilkinson. *Friday Literary Review*, January 26, 1912, 5.

"Nietzsche's Autobiography." Review of *Ecce Homo*, by Friedrich Nietzsche. *Friday Literary Review*, February 2, 1912, 1.

"Self and Society." Review of *Democracy and Poetry*, by Francis B. Gummere. *Friday Literary Review*, February 9, 1912, 1.

"The World of Instinct." Review of *The Life and Love of the Insect*, by J. Henri Fabre. *Friday Literary Review*, February 23, 1912, 1.

"Max's First Novel." Review of *Zuleika Dobson*, by Max Beerbohm. *Friday Literary Review*, March 1, 1912, 1.

"The Undergraduate." Review of *Stover at Yale*, by Owen Johnson. *Friday Literary Review*, April 5, 1912, 1.

"Lady Gregory's Plays." Review of *Irish Folk History Plays*. *Friday Literary Review*, April 12, 1912, 1.

"John Masefield." Review of *The Everlasting Mercy and The Widow in the Bye Street* and *Multitude and Solitude*, by John Masefield. *Friday Literary Review*, April 19, 1912, 1.

"Montessori." Review of *The Montessori Method*, by Maria Montessori. *Friday Literary Review*, May 10, 1912, 1–2.

"Short Stories." Review of *If and Other Stories*, by Gouverneur Morris. *Friday Literary Review*, May 17, 1912, 1.

"The Beauty of Truth." Review of *Death*, by Maurice Maeterlinck. *Friday Literary Review*, June 14, 1912, 1.

"The Swarning." Review of *No Surrender*, by Constance Elizabeth Maud. *Friday Literary Review*, June 21, 1912, 1.

"Strindbergian Symbolism." Review of *There Are Crimes and Crimes*, by August Strindberg. *Friday Literary Review*, June 28, 1912, 1–2.

"His Sister's Nietzsche." Review of *The Life of Nietzsche*, by Frau Forester Nietzsche. *Friday Literary Review*, July 5, 1912, 1.

"Thackeray." Review of *The Harry Furniss Centenary Edition of Thackeray*. *Friday Literary Review*, August 9, 1912, 2.

"The Best of the New Fall Books." *Friday Literary Review*, September 20, 1912, 1–2.

"The Best of the New Fall Books." *Friday Literary Review*, September 27, 1912, 1.

"New Books—a Postscript." *Friday Literary Review*, October 4, 1912, 7.

"The New Spring Books." *Friday Literary Review*, March 7, 1913, 1–2.

"The New Spring Books." *Friday Literary Review*, March 14, 1913, 1–2.

"The New Spring Books." *CEP*, March 27, 1914, 9.

"The New Spring Books." *CEP*, April 3, 1914, 13.

Columns

Causerie. *Friday Literary Review*, August 11, 1911, through November 17, 1911; February 2, 16, and 23, 1912; March 1 and 29, 1912.

New York Letter. *Friday Literary Review*, October 18, 1912, through May 14, 1915.

Edited Books

The Provincetown Plays. Edited and selected by George Cram Cook and Frank Shay. Foreword by Hutchins Hapgood. Cincinnati: Stewart Kidd, 1921.

SUSAN GLASPELL

A Classified Primary Source Bibliography

Compiled by Tyler Preston

FICTION

Novels

The Glory of the Conquered. New York: Frederick A. Stokes, 1909.
The Visioning. New York: Frederick A. Stokes, 1911.
Fidelity. Boston: Small, Maynard, 1915.
Brook Evans. New York: A.L. Burt, 1928.
Fugitive's Return. New York: Frederick A. Stokes, 1929.
Ambrose Holt and Family. New York: Frederick A. Stokes, 1931.
The Morning Is Near Us. New York: Frederick A. Stokes, 1939.
Norma Ashe. Philadelphia: J. B. Lippincott, 1942.
Judd Rankin's Daughter. New York: J. B. Lippincott, 1945.

Short Story Collection

Lifted Masks: Stories by Susan Glaspell. New York: Frederick A. Stokes, 1912.

Short Stories

"Tom and Towser." *Weekly Outlook* 1 (December 26, 1896): 8.
"His Literary Training." *Delphic* 13 (January 1898): 83–85.
"The Tragedy of Mind." *Delphic* 14 (February 1898): 98–102.
"The Philosophy of War." *Delphic* 15 (October 1898): 24.
"The Unprofessional Crime." *Delphic* (February 1900): 109–12.
"On the Second Down." *Author's Magazine* 3 (November 1902): 3–11.
"The Girl from Downtown." *Youth's Companion* 77 (April 2, 1903): 160–61.
"In the Face of His Constituents." *Harper's Magazine* 107 (October 1903): 757–62.

"Contrary to Precedent." *Booklovers' Magazine* 3 (January–June 1904): 235–56.
"The Intrusion of the Personal." *Frank Leslie's Monthly Magazine* 57 (April 1904): 630–32.
"The Man of Flesh and Blood." *Harper's Magazine* 108 (May 1904): 957.
"Freckles M'Grath." *Munsey's Magazine* 31 (July 1904): 481.
"The Awakening of the Lieutenant Governor." *Munsey's Magazine*, August 1904, 630–32.
"The Work of Unloved Libby." *Black Cat*, August 1904.
"The Return of Rhoda." *Youth's Companion* 79 (January 26, 1905): 40.
"An Approximation." *Smart Set*, February 1905, 85–91.
"For Tomorrow: The Story of an Easter Sermon." *Appleton's Booklovers' Magazine* 5 (March 1905): 559–70.
"For Love of the Hills." *Black Cat* 11 (October 1905): 1–11.
"From the Pen of Failures." *Quax*, 1905, 215–18.
"The Boycott on Caroline." *Youth's Companion* 80, no. 12 (March 22, 1906): 137–38.
"How the Prince Saw America." *American Magazine* 62 (July 1906): 274.
"At the Turn of the Road." *Speaker* 2, no. 8 (1906): 359–61.
"The Lie God Forgave." *Black Cat*, July 1909, 14–23.
"From A-Z." *American Magazine*, October 1909, 543.
"With the American Consul." *Redbook Magazine* 14, no. 4 (February 1910): 682–88.
"The Rekindling." *Designer*, October 1910, 325, 384–85.
"Bound." *Smart Set* 33, no. 4 (April 1911): 107–13.
"According to His Lights." *American Magazine* 72 (June 1911): 153–62.
"At the Source." *Woman's Home Companion* 39 (May 1912): 5–6.
"A Boarder of Art." *Ladies' Home Journal* 29 (October 1912): 10–11, 92–93.
"The Anarchist: His Dog." In *Lifted Masks*, 215–39. New York: Frederick A. Stokes, 1912.
"At Twilight." In *Lifted Masks*, 149–72. New York: Frederick A. Stokes, 1912.
"His America." In *Lifted Masks*, 190–214. New York: Frederick A. Stokes, 1912.
"The Last Sixty Minutes." In *Lifted Masks*, 136–48. New York: Frederick A. Stokes, 1912.
"Out There." In *Lifted Masks*, 149–72. New York: Frederick A. Stokes, 1912.
"The Resurrection and the Life." *Smart Set*, September 1913, 65–68.
"Whom Mince Pie Hath Joined Together." *Ladies' Home Journal* 30 (November 1913): 10, 71–73.
"The Rules of the Institution." *Harper's Magazine* 128 (January 1914): 198–208.
"Looking After Clara." *Ladies' Home Journal* 31 (August 1914): 9, 35–37.
"The Manager of Crystal Sulphur Springs." *Harper's Magazine* 131 (July 1915): 176–84.
"Agnes of Cape's End." *American Magazine* 80, no. 3 (September 1915): 5–7, 67–72.
"Unveiling Brenda." *Harper's Magazine* 133 (June 1916): 14–26.

"'Finality' in Freeport." *Pictorial Review* 17 (July 1916): 14–15, 32.
"Her Heritage of Ideals." *Canadian Magazine* 48, no. 1 (November 1916): 63–68.
"Miss Jessie's Trip Abroad." *Woman's Home Companion* 43 (November 1916):
    9–10, 79.
"The Hearing Ear." *Harper's Magazine* 134 (January 1917): 234–41.
"A Jury of Her Peers." *Every Week* 5 (March 5, 1917): 488–502.
"Everything You Want to Plant." *Every Week* 5 (August 13, 1917): 5–7, 20–21.
"A Matter of Gesture." *McClure's* 49 (August 1917): 36–38, 65–67.
"Poor Ed." *Liberator* 1 (March 1918): 24–29.
"Beloved Husband." *Harper's Magazine* 136 (April 1918): 675–79.
"Good Luck." *Good Housekeeping*, September 1918, 44–46, 122–26.
"The Busy Duck." *Harper's Magazine* 137 (November 1918): 828–36.
"Pollen." *Harper's Magazine* 138 (March 1919): 446–51.
"Government Goat." *Pictorial Review*, April 1919, 18–29.
"The Escape." *Harper's Magazine* 140 (December 1919): 29–38.
"The Nervous Pig." *Harper's Magazine* 141 (February 1920): 309–20.
"His Smile." *Pictorial Review* 22 (January 1921): 15–16, 91.
"The Faithless Shepherd." *Cornhill Magazine* 60 (January 1926): 51–71.
"The Rose in the Sand." *Pall Mall Magazine*, May 1927, 45–51.

Undated Short Stories

"His Grandmother's Funeral." *Metropolitan Magazine*, 737–43.

Drama

Suppressed Desires. With George Cram Cook. *Metropolitan* 45, no. 1 (January
    1917): 19–20, 57–59.
Bernice. In *Plays*, 157–230. Boston: Small, Maynard, 1920.
Close the Book. In *Plays*, 61–95. Boston: Small, Maynard, 1920.
The Outside. In *Plays*, 97–118. Boston: Small, Maynard, 1920.
The People. In *Plays*, 33–59. Boston: Small, Maynard, 1920.
Tickless Time. In *Plays*, 273–314. Boston: Small, Maynard, 1920.
Trifles. In *Plays*, 1–30. Boston: Small, Maynard, 1920.
Woman's Honor. In *Plays*, 119–56. Boston: Small, Maynard, 1920.
Inheritors. Boston: Small, Maynard, 1921.
The Verge. Boston: Small, Maynard, 1922.
The Comic Artist. New York: Frederick A. Stokes, 1927.
Allison's House. New York: Samuel French, 1930.
Chains of Dew. In *Susan Glaspell: The Complete Plays*, edited by Linda Ben-Zvi
    and J. Ellen Gainor. Jefferson, NC: McFarland, 2010, 125–78.
Springs Eternal. In *Susan Glaspell: The Complete Plays*, edited by Linda Ben-Zvi
    and J. Ellen Gainor. Jefferson, NC: McFarland, 2010, 354–405.

Poetry

"Joe." *Masses*, January 8, 1916, 9.
"Stones That Once Were [a Temple]." Typescript of poem. Undated. Susan
    Glaspell Papers, Berg Collection, New York Public Library, New York, NY.

NONFICTION

Essays

"In Memoriam." *Delphic* 15, no. 5 (February 1899): 126–29.
"Bismarck and European Politics." *Delphic* 15, no. 6 (March 1899): 147.
"The Tragedy of My School Days." *High School Guard* (post-1899): 1–2.
"Dwellers on Parnassus." *New Republic* 33 (January 17, 1923): 198–200.
"Last Days in Greece." In *Greek Coin: Poems by George Cram Cook*, 31–49.
    New York: George H. Doran, 1925.
"John Noble." *New York Herald Tribune*, May 13, 1934, 7.

Journalism

Columns

Social Life. *Weekly Outlook*, July 1896–July 1897.
"News Girl Talks to the Girls from Mitchellville." *Des Moines Daily News*,
    November 17, 1899, 5.
"Dinner at Y. M. C. A. by a 'News' Girl." *Des Moines Daily News*, November 29,
    1899, 3.
"The News Girl Tells of Her Experiences in the Legislature This Winter . . .
    with Iowa Statesmen." *Des Moines Daily News*, April 4, 1900.
"'News Girl' on the Embryo Des Moines Lawyer." *Des Moines Daily News*, May
    19, 1900.
"'News' Girl on the Congress of Mothers." *Des Moines Daily News*, June 1,
    1900.
"'News' Girl on the State Field Meet." *Des Moines Daily News*, June 2, 1900.
"'News' Girl Discourses on Farm Life From the All-Wise City Girl's Point of
    View." *Des Moines Daily News*, June 16, 1900.
Two other News Girl columns: June 30, 1900, and July 3, 1900.

Stories on the Hassock Murder Case

"Prominent Farmer Robber and Killed." *Des Moines Daily News*, December 3,
    1900.
"Surrounded by Mystery." *Des Moines Daily News*, December 4, 1900.
"Sheriff After Mrs. Hossack." *Des Moines Daily News*, December 5, 1900.
"She Prepares to Fight." *Des Moines Daily News*, December 6, 1900.
"Goes to the Grand Jury." *Des Moines Daily News*, December 8, 1900.
"Preliminary Hearing in the Hossack Case." *Des Moines Daily News*, December
    8, 1900.
"It Is Still Unsettled." *Des Moines Daily News*, December 10, 1900.
"Now before Grand Jury." *Des Moines Daily News*, December 11, 1900.
"Mrs. Hossack May Yet Be Proven Innocent." *Des Moines Daily News*, Decem-
    ber 12, 1900.
"Mrs. Hossack May Come Here." *Des Moines Daily News*, January 14, 1901.
"Indicted Her for Murder." *Des Moines Daily News*, January 17, 1901.
"Trial Comes in March." *Des Moines Daily News*, February 27, 1901.

"Surprise Is Expected." *Des Moines Daily News*, March 23, 1901.
"Hossack Trial Begun." *Des Moines Daily News*, April 1, 1901.
"Hossack Trial on in Earnest." *Des Moines Daily News*, April 2, 1901.
"Hossack Begged Wife to Aid Him." *Des Moines Daily News*, April 3, 1901.
"Experts Say It Is Human Blood." *Des Moines Daily News*, April 4, 1901.
"Looks Bad for Mrs. Hossack." *Des Moines Daily News*, April 5, 1901.
"Testify for Mrs. Hossack." *Des Moines Daily News*, April 6, 1901.
"Arguing the Hossack Case." *Des Moines Daily News*, April 8, 1901.
"Allege Haines Was Murderer." *Des Moines Daily News*, April 9, 1901.
"Her Dreary Easter Day." *Des Moines Daily News*, April 9, 1901.
"Mrs. Hossack's Fearful Ordeal." *Des Moines Daily News*, April 10, 1901.
"Mrs. Hossack a Murderess." *Des Moines Daily News*, April 11, 1901.
"Mrs. Hossack's Parting Plea." *Des Moines Daily News*, April 19, 1901.

Biography

The Road to the Temple. New York: Frederick A. Stokes, 1927.

Children's Literature

Cherished and Shared of Old. New York: Julian Messner, 1940.

Miscellaneous Writings

"The Provincetown Players." *American Local History*. Provincetown Guide-
    book, Provincetown Mass. Art Association, 1928.
"Susan Glaspell Says We Need Books Today as Never Before." *Chicago Sunday
    Tribune*, December 6, 1942.
"The Right of Choice Is Freedom." *Chicago Sun*, December 2, 1945.
Letter to the editor, *Provincetown Advocate*, July 11, 1946, 5.

Unpublished Works

"Are We Birds, Are We Fishes." Unpublished typescript. Henry and Albert
    Berg Collection, New York Public Library, New York, NY.
"In a Factory Town." Story read March 1898 as the final proceeding of the
    Philomathian Society, Drake University, Des Moines, IA.
"Old College Friends." Story read June 14, 1899, at precommencement cer-
    emonies, Drake University, Des Moines, IA.
"Coming Years." Unpublished typescript (short story). Henry and Albert Berg
    Collection, New York Public Library, New York, NY.
"Faint Trails." Unpublished typescript (short story). Henry and Albert Berg
    Collection, New York Public Library, New York, NY.
"First Aid Teacher." Unpublished typescript (short story). Henry and Albert
    Berg Collection, New York Public Library, New York, NY.
"The Huntsmen Are up in America." Unpublished typescript (speech deliv-
    ered at the Boston Book Fair). Henry and Albert Berg Collection, New York
    Public Library, New York, NY.
"Linda." Unpublished typescript (short story). Henry and Albert Berg Collec-
    tion, New York Public Library, New York, NY.

FLOYD DELL

A Classified Primary Source Bibliography

Compiled by Tyler Preston

NOVELS

Moon-Calf. New York: Alfred A. Knopf, 1920.
The Briary Bush. New York: Alfred A. Knopf, 1921.
Janet March. New York: Alfred A. Knopf, 1923.
This Mad Ideal. New York: Alfred A. Knopf, 1925.
Runaway. New York: George H. Doran, 1925.
An Old Man's Folly. New York: George H. Doran, 1926.
An Unmarried Father. New York: George H. Doran, 1927.
Souvenir. Garden City, NY: Doubleday, 1929.
Love without Money. New York: Farrar and Rinehart, 1931.
Diana Stair. New York: Farrar and Rinehart, 1932.
The Golden Spike. New York: Farrar and Rinehart, 1934.

SHORT STORY/POETRY COLLECTION

Love in Greenwich Village. New York: George H. Doran, 1926.

ESSAY COLLECTION

Floyd Dell: Essays from the Friday Literary Review, 1909–1913. Edited by R. Craig Sautter. Highland Park, IL: December Press, 1995.

PLAYS

King Arthur's Socks and Other Village Plays. New York: Alfred A. Knopf, 1922. Includes *King Arthur's Socks, The Angel Intrudes, A Long Time Ago, Sweet and*

Twenty, Human Nature, The Chaste Adventures of Joseph, Legend, Enigma, Ibsen Revisited, The Rim of the World, and *Poor Harold.*
Little Accident. New York: Grosset and Dunlap, 1930.

BOOK-LENGTH NONFICTION

Women as World Builders. Chicago: Forbes and Company, 1913.
Were You Ever a Child? New York: Alfred A. Knopf, 1919.
Looking at Life. New York: Alfred A. Knopf, 1924.
Intellectual Vagabondage: An Apology for the Intelligentsia. New York: George H. Doran, 1926.
The Outline of Marriage. Pamphlets on Birth Control, no. 12. New York: The American Birth Control League, 1926.
Love in the Machine Age: A Psychological Study of the Transition from Patriarchal Society. New York: Farrar and Rinehart, 1930.

AUTOBIOGRAPHY

Homecoming: An Autobiography. New York: Farrar and Rinehart, 1933.

CRITICAL BIOGRAPHY

Upton Sinclair: A Study in Social Protest. New York: George H. Doran, 1927.

EDITED BOOKS

Poems [by Wilfred Scawen Blunt]. New York: Alfred A. Knopf, 1923.
Poems of Robert Herrick. Introduction by Floyd Dell. Little Blue Book, no. 701. Girard, KS: Haldeman-Julius Company, 1924.
Poems and Prose of William Blake. Little Blue Book, no. 677. Girard, KS: Haldeman-Julius, 1925.
The Anatomy of Melancholy. By Robert Burton (with Paul Jordan-Smith). New York: George H. Doran, 1927.
Daughter of the Revolution and Other Stories by John Reed. Introduction by Floyd Dell. New York: Vanguard Press, 1927.

UNCOLLECTED SHORT STORIES

"The Touchstone: A Political Misadventure." *Trident* 1, no. 13 (March 26, 1904): 7.
"Blood and Death: A Historical Nightmare." *Trident* 1, no. 16 (April 16, 1904): 5.
"A Saturday Sermon." *Trident* (May 28, 1904).
"Flower o' the Peach." *Trident* 1, no. 27 (July 2, 1904): 31–32.
"The Woman and the Poet." *Mother Earth* 4 (October 1909): 251–55.
"Mothers and Daughters." *International* 5 (January 1912): 26–28.
"Creators." *International* 5 (March 1912): 51–53.
"Jessica Screams." *Smart Set* 39 (April 1913): 113–20.
"A Perfectly Good Cat." *The Masses* 5 (January 1914): 14–15.
"Adventure." *The Masses* 5 (March 1914): 12–14.

"Why Mona Smiled." *The Masses* 5 (June 1914): 16.
"The Beating." *The Masses* 5 (August 1914): 12–14.
"The Dark Continent." *The Masses* 6 (December 1914): 17–18.
"The Ways of Life." *The Masses* 8 (December 1915): 16–17.
"Runaway." *Woman's Home Companion* 51 (October 1924): 15–16
"The Blanket." *Collier's* 78 (October 16, 1926): 18.

UNCOLLECTED POEMS

"The Quest." *Trident* (May 21, 1904).
"Your Hobby." *Trident* 1, no. 27 (July 2, 1904): 27.
"Memorial Day." *Davenport Times*, May 30, 1905.
"The Builders." *Tri-City Workers Magazine* 1 (November 1905): 24.
"The Founders." *Davenport Democrat and Leader* (1906).
"Waifs." *McClure's* 30, no. 5 (March 1908): 590.
"Actaeon." *Century* 76 (August 1908): 494.
"Tamburlaine." *Harper's* 118, no. 2 (January 1909): 299.
"The Seeker." *Harper's* 118 (February 1909): 440.
"My Rheumatic Neighbor." *Friday Literary Review*, April 30, 1909, 4.
"Joys." *Friday Literary Review*, November 17, 1911, 4.
"Poems of a Young Man." *Friday Literary Review*, March 8, 1912, 4.
    i. "The Dust whereof my Body came."
    ii. "O My Love is very fair!"
    iii. "I wonder if you understand."
"Poems of a Young Man." *Friday Literary Review*, March 15, 1910, 4.
    iv. "Dear Friend, we need each other, you and I."
    v. "To One Woman ("You do not know me, though we met")."
    vi. "Again the Thought comes back to me."
    vii. "When shall I cease to take Delight." (Feb. 1909).
    viii. "In Memoriam" ("I know not of one Creature else").
"Poems of a Young Man." *Friday Literary Review*, March 22, 1912, 4.
    ix. "The Quick and the Dead" ("Another Taunt flung in my face by Age").
    x. "How could you know."
    xi. "O, let my soul refuse one Gift."
    xii. "Out of old Idols' drifting Dust."
    xiii. "Outside" ("Now that the Night is wild outside").
    xiv. "You Shall Forget" ("These are the things you shall forget").
    xv. "Because my Star is lucky."
"Poems of a Young Man." *Friday Literary Review*, March 29, 1912, 7.
    xvi. "Prisoners" ("From out each narrow room").
    xvii. "A rose—it is so slight a thing!"
    xviii. "Midway of that enchanted Ground."
"Poems of a Young Man." *Friday Literary Review*, April 12, 1912, 4
    xix. "Tomorrow I shall look again."
    xx. "'Tis true she does not know the light."

    xxi. "Easter" ("Roses in the garden").
    xxii. "Tamburlaine." (Jan. 1909).
"Poems of a Young Man." *Friday Literary Review*, April 19, 1912, 4.
    xxiii. "Today, Dear Heart, to Lincoln Park."
    xxiv. "From the high Towers of the Spirit."
    xxv. "The May-Flies" ("Heaps I found in the Dust").
"Poems of a Young Man." *Friday Literary Review*, April 26, 1912, 4.
    xxvi. "Or what is right, or what is wrong."
    xxvii. "A perfect little ship I made."
    xxviii. "Tomorrow shall be ours, sweetheart."
"Poems of a Young Man." *Friday Literary Review*, May 10, 1912, 4.
    xxix. "Beckon me into the moon light."
    xxx. "Give me to know these swift, dim days."
    xxxi. "There are no Flowers like those that grow."
    xxxii. "May Day" ("The April rains are over").
"Delphi." *Friday Literary Review*, January 3, 1913, 4.
"On Seeing Isadora Duncan's School." *New York Tribune*, February 4, 1915, 8.
"Apologia." *Poetry* 6, no. 67 (May 1915).
"Where I Have Not Been for a Long Time." *New York Tribune*, May 6, 1916, 11
"Summer." *The Masses* 4 (February 1917): 23.
"Mabel's Song." *Vanity Fair* 8, no. 56 (May 1917).
"On Reading the Poems of Edna St. Vincent Millay." *Liberator* 1, no. 41 (May 1918).
"Two Sonnets." *Liberator* 1, no. 34 (October 1918).
"Sonnet." *Pearson's Magazine* 40, no. 78 (December 1918).
"Pigeons." *Liberator* 1, no. 18 (March 1919).
"Song." *Poetry* 15, no. 22 (October 1919).
"A Birthday Sonnet." *Liberator* 3, no. 25 (May 1920).
"Natural History." *new numbers* (October 1920): 11–12.
"To Certain Readers." *New York Evening Post Literary Review* 2, no. 500 (March 11, 1922).
"Cupid's Holiday." *Bookman* 61, no. 518 (July 1925).
"Song of Travel." *New York World*, October 28, 1925, 15.
"Ode on the Imitations of Immorality." *New York World*, December 22, 1925, 13.
"Education." *Saturday Evening Post* 198, no. 70 (March 20, 1926).
"The Ballad of a Fool." *New York World*, June 16, 1930. Signed "Peter Piper."
"On the Washington Monument." *Washington Post*, February 24, 1943, 1.
"Ships." *St. Nicholas* 70, no. 15 (April 1943).
"Birthday in War-Time." *Commonweal* 38, nos. 114–115 (May 21, 1943).
"Mimi and Captain." *St. Nicholas* 70, no. 19 (June 1943).
"Bridal Song in War-Time." *Commonweal* 38, no. 218 (June 18, 1943).
"To Each His King." *Freeman* 4, no. 169 (November 30, 1953).
"To a Poet Once Resident in Washington, D.C." *Walt Whitman Newsletter* 3, no. 39 (September 1957).

"Wedding Anniversary." *Socialist Call* 26, no. 13 (September 1958).

UNCOLLECTED ESSAYS

"Diphtheria in Davenport." *Tri-City Workers Magazine* 1, no. 2 (December
   1905): 5–6. Signed "Thersites."
"Socialists and Their Critics." *Tri-City Workers Magazine* 1, no. 2 (December
   1905): 11–13. Signed "Thersites."
"A Candy Factory from the Inside." *Tri-City Workers Magazine* 1, no. 3 (January
   1906): 17–20. Signed "Sally Thompson."
"The Davenport Public Schools." *Tri-City Workers Magazine* 1, no. 3 (January
   1906): 11–14. Signed "John Smith, Sr."
"The Only Original Socialist." *Tri-City Workers Magazine* 1, no. 3 (January
   1906): 10–11. Signed "Thersites."
"The Children vs. the Library Board." *Tri-City Workers Magazine* 1, no. 4
   (February 1906): 16–17. Signed "Thersites."
"Socialist and Kindergarten." *Tri-City Workers Magazine* 1, no. 4 (February
   1906): 7–11.
"Our Autocratic School Board." *Tri-City Workers Magazine* 1, no. 7 (May 1906):
   13–14. Signed "Vesuvius."
"The Salvation of the Working Class." *Tri-City Workers Magazine* 1, no. 9 (July
   1906): 8–10.
"A Municipal Crime! Moline's Antiquated Garbage Dump." *Tri-City Workers
   Magazine* 1, no. 10 (August 1906): 1–5.
"Socialism and Backbone." *Tri-City Workers Magazine* 1, no. 11 (September
   1906): 10–12.
"Why People Go to Brick Munro's." *Tri-City Workers Magazine* 1, no. 11
   (September 1906): 1–4.
"On Taking Out One's Key Ring." *Chicago Evening Post*, February 11, 1909, 4.
   Signed "Billaire Helloc."
"Taming the Young Revolutionist." *Chicago Evening Post*, February 12, 1909, 4.
"Chicago's Libraries." *Friday Literary Review*, June 11, 1909, 5.
"Chicago's Libraries—II. The Newberry Library." *Friday Literary Review*, June
   18, 1909, 7.
"Walt Whitman." *Friday Literary Review*, June 11, 1909, 6. Signed "Rose L."
"Chicago's Libraries—III. The John Crerar Library." *Friday Literary Review*,
   June 25, 1909, 7.
[Chicago's Libraries—]"IV. At the Universities." *Friday Literary Review*, July 9,
   1909, 3.
"Steinheil Case and Another." *Chicago Evening Post*, November 9, 1909, 6.
"Causerie." *Friday Literary Review*, December 22, 1911, 4.
"This Time of Year." *Chicago Evening Post*, May 25, 1912, 6.
"Browning and the Theater." *Friday Literary Review*, May 31, 1912, 1.
"The White Man's Burden." *Chicago Evening Post*, June 8, 1912, 8.
"The Editor's Diary." *Friday Literary Review*, December 13, 1912, 4.

"Stringberg Plays at Local Little Theater." *Chicago Evening Post*, February 7,
    1913, 11.
"Recipe for Dramatic Criticism." *Play-book* (Wisconsin Dramatic Society)
    (July 1913): 17–19.
"The Littlest Theater." *Harper's Weekly* 58 (November 29, 1913): 22–24.
"Chicago in Fiction." *Bookman* 38 (November–December 1913): 270–77, 375–79.
"Homer and the Soap-Box." *The Masses* 5, no. 4 (January 1914): 11.
"Indicted for Criminal Libel." *The Masses* 5, no. 4 (January 1914): 3.
"Confession of a Feminist Man." *The Masses* 5 (March 1914): 8.
"The Libel Case." *The Masses* 5, no. 6 (March 1914): 14.
"Socialism and Feminism: A Reply to Belfort Bax." *New Review* 2 (June 1914):
    349–53.
"The Drama of Dynamite." *New Review* 2, no. 7 (July 1914): 404–10.
"Obituary of a Poet." *Little Review* 1, no. 6 (September 1914): 37.
"War-Time Reflections." *New Review* 2, no. 10 (October 1914): 592–96.
"The Nag-itator." *The Masses* 6 (November 1914): 19.
"Socialism and the Sword." *The Masses* 6, no. 4 (January 1915): 9.
"The First Few Books." *The Masses* 6, no. 5 (February 1915): 17.
"Our Village School Board." *The Masses* 6, no. 6 (March 1915): 11.
"Change in American Life and Fiction." *New Review* 3, no. 5 (May 15, 1915):
    13–15.
"A Correction." *New Review* 3 (May 15, 1915): 46.
"Walt Whitman, Anti-Socialist." *New Review* 3, no. 8 (June 15, 1915): 85–86.
"Love Among the Theorists." *New Review* 3, no. 10 (July 15, 1915): 134–35.
"Obituary [of Elbert Hubbard]." *The Masses* 6 (July 1915): 13.
"Morality and the Movies." *New Review* 3, no. 12 (August 15, 1915): 190–91.
"'The Six Best Novels.'" *New Review* 3, no. 14 (September 15, 1915): 240–41.
"Lampito on Socrates." *New Review* 3, no. 15 (October 1, 1915): 261–62.
"Adventures in Anti-Land." *The Masses* 7 (October–November 1915): 5–6.
"Criminals All." *The Masses* 7 (October–November 1915): 21.
"A Discontented Woman." *The Masses* 7 (October–November 1915): 11.
"The Mind of a Censor." *New Review* 3, no. 18 (December 1, 1915): 325–26.
"Speaking of Psycho-Analysis: The New Boon for Dinner Table Conversation-
    alists." *Vanity Fair* 5 (December 1915): 53.
"The Weavers." *New Review* 4 (January 1, 1916): 16–17.
"The Meeting of Pericles and Aspasia. By Our Own Theodore Dreiser. Chapter
    CCCCCCCCLXVIII." *New York Tribune*, January 27, 1916, 9.
"Physical Culture as a Religion: A Growing Faith, Beautiful and Stern." *Vanity
    Fair* 5 (February 1916): 47.
"The Passing Glories of Greenwich Village: An Oasis in the Great Metropoli-
    tan Desert." *Vanity Fair* 6 (March 1916): 49, 126.
"The Russian Ballet." *New Review* 4 (March 1916): 81–2.
"Horizontal Talking." *The Masses* 8 (April 1916): 18.
"Twenty Books Recommended by Floyd Dell." *The Masses* 8 (April 1916): 3, 27–8.
"What Does It Mean?" *The Masses* 8 (April 1916): 23.

"Alcoholiday." *The Masses* 8 (June 1916): 30.
"Shaw and Religion." *Seven Arts* (November 1916): 82–88.
"Chick Lorimer." *The Masses* 9 (December 1916): 39.
"Lord Roberts on War." *The Masses* 9 (December 1916): 14.
"The Soul of a Bell-Boy." *The Masses* 9 (December 1916): 38.
"Anatole France." *The Masses* 9 (January 1917): 29.
"Back to the Dark Ages?" *The Masses* 9 (January 1917): 24.
"The Sacred Sisterhood." *Slate: A Magazine for Teachers Who Are Not Dead; And for Their Friends* (January 1917): 8–9.
"On Trial for Blasphemy." *The Masses* 9 (March 1917): 27.
"Fatten the Calf!" *The Masses* 9 (May 1917): 13.
"Film-Flamming." *The Masses* 9 (June 1917): 23.
"My Country, 'Tis of Thee." *The Masses* 9 (June 1917): 41.
"Siberian Exiles' Relief Fund." *The Masses* 9 (June 1917): 26.
"On Not Going to War." *The Masses* 9 (July 1917): 21–22.
"We Wonder." *The Masses* 9 (July 1917): 29–30.
"The Chance of Peace." *The Masses* 9 (August 1917): 25, 28.
"Conscientious Objectors." *The Masses* 9 (August 1917): 29–30.
"Book Notes." *The Liberator* 1 (March 1918): 39.
"Liberator Book Shop." *The Liberator* (March 1918): 38–39.
"Rodin." *The Liberator* (April 1918): 46.
"Books." *The Liberator* (June 1918): 35.
"The Story of the Trials." *The Liberator* (June 1918): 7–18.
"Russia in America." *The Liberator* (December 1918): 16–19.
"Randolph Bourne." *New Republic* 17 (January 4, 1919): 276.
"Two American Poets." *Pearson's Magazine* 40 (January 1919): 107–9.
"What Are You Doing Out There?" *The Liberator* 1, no. 2 (January 1919): 14–15.
"Apologies." *The Liberator* 1, no. 2 (March 1919): 50.
"The Truth About Breshkovsky." *The Liberator* 1, no. 2 (March 1919): 36–37. Signed "X."
"Walt Whitman and the American Temperament." *World Tomorrow* 2 (March 1919): 70–71.
"Beating Prohibition to It." *The Liberator* 2 (April 1919): 15–18.
"Ten Days that Shook the League of Nations." *The Liberator* 2 (April 1919): 29–31.
"The Death Train of Siberia." *The Liberator* 2 (May 1919): 14–16.
"The Invincible I.W.W." *The Liberator* 2 (May 1919): 9–11.
"Art Under the Bolsheviks: —From Documentary Reports, Decrees and Plans of the Soviet State." *The Liberator* 2 (June 1919): 11–12, 14–18.
"His Majesty's Government Writes History." *The Liberator* 2 (June 1919): 33–44. Signed "X."
"Religion Under the Bolsheviks." *The Liberator* 2 (July 1919): 21–24. Signed "X."
"Whittier, Prophet and Poet." *World Tomorrow* 2 (October 1919): 271–74.
"Pittsburgh or Petrograd?" *The Liberator* 2 (December 1919): 5–8, 10.
"Aphrodite Without Any Nightie." *The Liberator* 3 (January 1920): 34–36.
"A Psycho-Analytic Confession." *The Liberator* 3 (April 1920): 15–19.

"Dear Old Tirps." *The Liberator* 3 (May 1920): 48.

"Guilty by Inference." *The Liberator* 3 (May 1920): 17–19.

"Fellow Criminals!" *The Liberator* 3 (July 1920): 35–41.

"Psychanalysis [*sic*] and Recent Fiction." *Psyche and Eros* (July 1920): 39–49.

"Communism But." *The Liberator* 3 (September 1920): 27–29.

"New Soviets for Old." *The Liberator* 3 (October 1920): 25–27.

"Now That You've Got the Vote—." *The Liberator* 3 (October 1920): 14–16.

"What Is a Moon-Calf? Floyd Dell Defines the Title of His Much Discussed Book." *New York Tribune*, February 27, 1921.

"The Menace of the Idealist: The Recent Emergence into Public Life of the Imaginative Young Man." *Vanity Fair* 15 (February 1921): 41, 90.

"A Confession: In Which the Author of Moon-Calf Admits Himself an Unsocial Socialist." *Brentano's Book Chat*, April 1921, 23–24.

"Knut Hamsun the Seeker: Several Reasons Why America Has Just Discovered One of the Greatest Living Continental Novelists." *Vanity Fair* 16 (May 1921): 30, 78, 94.

"Marriage and Freedom." *The Liberator* 4 (July 1921): 16–17, 20–21.

"Marriage and Freedom: II. Board and Bed." *The Liberator* 4 (August 1921): 16–17, 20–21.

"Marriage and Freedom: III." *The Liberator* 4 (October 1921): 22–26.

"Would You Like to Be a Child?" *The Liberator* 4 (Nov. 1921): 22–24.

"The Difference between Life and Fiction." *New Republic* 30 (April 12 1922): 7–8.

"Explanations and Apologies." *The Liberator* 5 (June 1922): 25–26.

"Edna St. Vincent Millay (The Literary Spotlight: XIV)." *Bookman* 56 (November 1922): 272–78.

"The Poems of the Month." *Bookman* 56 (January 1923): 614–16.

"Private Classics." *The Liberator* 6 (January 1923): 14–17.

"Criticism and Bad Manners." *Bookman* 57 (May 1923): 257–62.

"The Ethiopian Art Theatre." *The Liberator* 6 (June 1923): 29–30.

"The Freedom of Art." *The Liberator* 6 (July 1923): 15.

"Hamlet (The Parody Outline of Literature, No. 11)." *Bookman* 58 (October 1923): 125–30.

"Literature and the Machine Age: Part I—A Preface on Life and Literature." *The Liberator* 6 (October 1923): 12–15.

"Literature and the Machine Age: II." *The Liberator* 6 (November 1923): 23–25.

"Literature and the Machine Age: III." *The Liberator* 6 (December 1923): 27–29.

"Literature and the Machine Age: IV." *The Liberator* 7 (January 1924): 27–29.

"Literature in the Machine Age: V." *The Liberator* 7 (February 1924): 29–31.

"Literature in the Machine Age Part II—We Ourselves: VI." *The Liberator* 7 (March 1924): 27–29.

"Two American Poets: A Study of Possibilities." *Nation* 118 (16 April 1924): 439–40.

"Literature in the Machine Age: VII." *The Liberator* 7 (April 1924): 26–29.

"Noted Writers of World Plan Its Reconstruction." *New York Tribune*, May 17, 1924, 9.

"Can Men and Women Be Friends?" *Nation* 118 (May 28, 1924): 605–6.
"Emerson's Essays, A Gospel of Revolt." *Bookman* 59 (May 1924): 278–80.
"Literature in the Machine Age: IX [VIII]." *The Liberator* 7 (May 1924): 27–28.
"Literature in the Machine Age: X [IX]." *The Liberator* 7 (June 1924): 25–28.
"Literature in the Machine Age: XII [X]." *The Liberator* 7 (July 1924): 27–29.
"Literature in the Machine Age: XIII [XI]." *The Liberator* 7 (Aug. 1924): 30–32.
"Do You Believe in Marriage or in Free Love? I Have Tried It Both Ways."
    Hearst's International 46 (September 1924): 50–51, 134–35.
"Literature in the Machine Age: XIV [XII]." *The Liberator* 7 (September 1924):
    28–30.
"Literature in the Machine Age: XV [XIII]." *The Liberator* 7 (October 1924):
    28–29.
"I'd Rob a Bank—for Her." *Cosmopolitan* 77 (November 1924): 30–31, 130–31.
"Stephen Crane and the Genius Myth." *Nation* 119 (December 10, 1924):
    637–38.
"Alcohol as the Servant of Art and Friendship." *World Tomorrow* 8 (February
    1925): 45–46.
"St. Thomas Chatterton." *Bookman* 61 (July 1925): 513–14.
"My Favorite Character in Fiction." *Bookman* 62 (January 1926): 548–50.
"They Wanted to Tell." *Nation* 122 (February 10, 1926): 146–47.
"American Penmen to Recommend List for Translation." *Chicago Tribune*,
    April 17, 1926, 14.
"Shell-Shock and the Poetry of Robinson Jeffers." *Modern Quarterly* 3
    (September–December 1926): 268–73.
"Critic's Magic." *Bookman* 64 (December 1926): 446–50.
"In Defense of the New School." *Current History* 26 (April 1927): 26–30.
"The Artist in Revolt." *Bookman* 65 (May 1927): 316–22.
"A Literary Self-Analysis." *Modern Quarterly* 4 (June–September 1927): 148–52.
"Keats's Debt to Robert Burton." *Bookman* 67 (March 1928): 13–17.
"The Anti-Birth Control Neuroses." *Birth Control Review* 12 (September 1928):
    252–54.
"Crystal Eastman." *New Masses* 4 (September 1928): 14.
"How to Write Plays." *New York Times*, October 28, 1928, 2.
"Upton Sinclair in America." *New Masses* 4 (November 1928): 6.
"Mental Hygiene Poetry." *New York World*, June 30, 1930, 11.
"Do Men Want Children?" *Parents' Magazine* 5 (November 1930): 14–15, 67.
"Edna St. Vincent Millay." *New York Herald Tribune Magazine*, May 3, 1931, 3,
    12, 25.
"Sex in Adolescence." *Child Study* 8 (May 1931): 256–61.
"Why They Pet." *Parents' Magazine* 6 (October 1931): 18–19, 60–63.
"Reading as Emotional Experience." *Child Study* 9 (November 1931): 73–74.
"An Autobiographical Critique." *Psychoanalytic Quarterly* 1 (1932): 715–30.
"Phantasy and Fiction." *Child Study* 9 (March 1932): 187–90.
"Adolescent Education: A Parental and Psychological View." *Progressive Educa-
    tion* 9 (November 1932): 473–81.

"Edna Millay Finds a Cook." *New York Herald Tribune Magazine*, March 19, 1933, 4–5, 16.
"Peace—That Is Yuletide Wish of Floyd Dell; Recalls Events of Years Gone By." *Chicago Tribune*, December 9, 1933, 20.
"The Melodrama of Childhood." *Child Study* 11 (January 1934): 101–3.
"A Father Speaks His Mind." *Delineator* 125 (November 1934): 34, 57.
"Can They Afford to Marry?" *This Week (New York Herald Tribune)*, April 21, 1935, 21, 23.
"Marriage without Money." *Delineator* 127 (August 1935): 9, 44–45.
"The Editors' Page." *Child Study* 13 (October 1935): 1.
"From Moon-Calf." *Child Study* 13 (May 1936): 240–41.
"If They Want to Get Married." *Parents' Magazine* 11 (December 1936): 14–15, 77–81.
"Bernard De Voto and Kitty Smith." *Nation* 144 (January 23, 1937): 98–99.
"The Adolescent Steps Out—and How!" *Child Study* 14 (April 1937): 201–2.
"Preparing Them for Hard Realities." *Parents' Magazine* 12 (October 1937): 36, 90–93.
"Tipica." *Educational Music Magazine* 19 (November–December 1939): 39, 59–60.
"Youth Faces 1940." *Parents' Magazine* 15 (January 1940): 16–17, 30, 33.
"Ceiling Price." *Interdepartmental War Savings Bond Committee Monthly Bulletin*, January 1945, 11.
"Rents Were Low in Greenwich Village." *American Mercury* 65 (December 1947): 662–68.
"Sex in American Fiction." *American Mercury* 66 (January 1948): 84–90.
"How about Junior College?" *Parents' Magazine* 23 (May 1948): 26–27, 60, 62, 64, 66.
"Memories of the Old *Masses*." *American Mercury* 68 (April 1949): 481–87.
"My Friend, Edna St. Vincent Millay." *Mark Twain Journal* 12 (Spring 1964): 1–2.

INDEX

Page numbers in italics refer to photographs. All businesses, organizations and geographic places are located in Davenport, Iowa, unless otherwise specified.

trade unions. *See* Davenport, Iowa:
  trade union activities in
Treadwell, Sophie: *Machinal*, 82
Tri-City Social Service Club, 69
Tri-City Workers Magazine, 13, 20, 39,
  40, 44, 158, 167–68n13
Trident (magazine), 20, 25, 26, 158
Trimberger, Ellen Kay, 7
True Woman, 6, 108
Tuesday Club, 19, 21, 98, 100, 157;
  Glaspell's attendance at, 99, 101
Turner Hall, 18, 22, 37–38, 43,
  50, 157
Turngemeinde (Turners), 33, 36–37,
  38
Turnverein, 23, 36–37, 39

unions. *See* Davenport, Iowa: trade
  union activities in
Unitarian Church, 47, 158. *See also*
  Judy, Arthur Markley; Lilliefors,
  Manfred

Van Doren, Carl, 12–13, 155
Van Doren, Mark, 12–13
Veblen, Thorstein, 49
Vilhauer, William Warren, 135–36,
  137, 187n44
Vollmer, Henry, 31, 69, 169n48

Ward, Theodore: *Big White Fog*, 156
Waterman, Arthur, 91, 180–81n27
Waterman, C. M., 96
Webb, Beatrice: Floyd Dell's praise
  of, 54
Wells, Ida B., 6

white supremacy, 113. *See also*
  nativism; Negro suffrage
  movement; race/racism
Wilson, Edmund: plays for the
  Provincetown Players, 139
Withers, Sarah, 109
Wittenmyer, Sarah Ann (Annie)
  Turner, 25
women's suffrage movement: in
  Davenport, 23–32; Floyd Dell's
  support for, 48, 54–55; Glaspell's
  promotion of, 7; socialists'
  support for, 4, 26, 44. *See also*
  feminism/feminists; New Woman
Wood, Sharon E., 23, 30–31, 169n48,
  172n8
Woollcott, Alexander, 88, 125–26
Wordsworth, William: quote from, 3
World War I: effects on
  Provincetown Players, 130–31;
  protests against US involvement
  in, 10, 14, 62, 85–86, 109; US entry
  into, 84–85, 104
World War II, 117, 155
Wundrum, Bill, 28

Young, Art: on trial for violating the
  Espionage Act of 1917, 10, 63, 104
Young, Stark, 116; plays for the
  Provincetown Players, 139

Zenger, John Peter: libel trial of
  1734, 103
Zorach, Marguerite, 8, 121; set
  designs, 90, 124
Zorach, William, 8, 121, 139

Marcia Noe, Professor of English and Director of Women, Gender, and Sexuality Studies at The University of Tennessee at Chattanooga, is author of *Susan Glaspell: Voice from the Heartland* and over twenty other publications on this Pulitzer Prize–winning playwright. She edits the academic journal *MidAmerica* for The Society for the Study of Midwestern Literature.